Broadcasting and Society 1918-1939

MARK PEGG

CROOM HELM
London & Canberra

© 1983 Mark Pegg
Croom Helm Ltd, Provident House, Burrell Row,
Beckenham, Kent BR3 1AT

British Library Cataloguing in Publication Data

Pegg, Mark
   Broadcasting and society 1918-1939
   1. Broadcasting — Great Britain — Social aspects
   2. Broadcasting — Great Britain — History
   I. Title
   302.2'344'0941   ~~HE8689.9~~

   ISBN 0-7099-2039-3

Printed and bound in Great Britain by
Biddles Ltd, Guildford and King's Lynn

CONTENTS

Contents

TABLES

FIGURES

PREFACE

I would like to thank those who have helped me with the preparation of my book. Many individuals and institutions have provided assistance and facilities in the course of my work and I owe them my gratitude. My greatest debt is to Brian Harrison. He set me on course at the very beginning and has tirelessly provided helpful criticism and encouragement at every stage of writing and research. I must also make special mention of Asa Briggs who made many valuable suggestions and corrected errors of fact.

My colleagues John Kanefsky and Nick Tiratsoo freely gave their comments and ideas. Joan Ratcliffe typed the text patiently and carefully. Finally, I must express my appreciation for the considerable support of my parents and of Jane Sutton, with whom I discussed most of the problems which arose in writing the book.

I have been granted permission to reproduce several photographs and tables. I would like to acknowledge the kind consent of the following bodies: the BBC for Tables 1.1, 1.2 and 5.1-9; the British Library for Figures 2.3, 3.1, 7.1 and 7.2; the Victoria and Albert Museum for Figure 2.5; the Low Trustees and the Evening Standard for Figure 4.1 and the Derbyshire Times for Figure 7.2. I apologise if I have inadvertently infringed any other copyrights.

Mark Pegg

Twickenham
October 1982

INTRODUCTION

The relationship between technological development and social change is a fundamental theme in human development, a theme which has spread wider and continually intensified since the dawn of the Industrial Revolution. In the case of radio, the development and utilisation of the invention proceeded very rapidly. As the basis for a regular broadcasting system, established in 1922, radio soon consolidated its position in British society, so that by 1935, 98% of the British population could hear broadcast programmes if they possessed a receiver and the audience consisted of some thirty million people. [1] The power of radio as a medium of instant communication and entertainment brought almost everyone within its reach. Such a persuasive and persistent influence generated considerable social changes and the manner and extent of these changes in the crucial and formative stages between 1918 and 1939 demands detailed and critical investigation.

Broadcasting came into contact with so many social activities that the range of subjects which can be examined is enormous. It will be fascinating to learn whether broadcasting was successful in keeping people better informed, in introducing wider interests and creating a new sense of national identity. Furthermore, it will be important to examine the influence of radio on social behaviour - the pattern of family life and the enjoyment of leisure.

There are many difficulties in answering these questions. Before 1939, the medium always attracted a great deal of interest and comment. From the beginning of the BBC service in 1922, there was a great willingness to attribute social changes to broadcasting - indeed it would be surprising if such a powerful and potentially influential phenomenon had been ignored. Unfortunately, very few socially

1

conscious writers, novelists or researchers attempted to substantiate their rather circumstantial observations with detailed evidence or sustained analysis. [2] They were probably discouraged by a lack of perspective to assess the changes in British society and the way in which the evidence on the relationship between broadcasters and the audience was diffused into almost every aspect of life. The influence of radio was not readily separable from the influences of other mass media and it required some resourcefulness and dedication to identify its contribution. [3]

Since 1945, more research has been undertaken to study the social influence of mass media in general. The role of radio was radically changed by wartime conditions and the post-war rise of television, but some of the methods used to analyse the contribution of broadcasting to social change are valuable. [4] The most popular approach used can be neatly summarised by the phrase, 'who says what, in which channel, to whom, with what effect'. [5] This usefully emphasised the importance of looking carefully at the broadcasters and their programmes when searching for social effects in the audience. More recent research has preferred to stress the way in which the audience uses the media to satisfy its needs. [6] This approach shows the importance of moving away from approaches which concentrate on broadcasting institutions at work and recommends, instead, studying the audience in its social and economic context, using radio to meet its demands for information and entertainment.

Before proceeding further a few definitions are required. Radio, wireless, and broadcasting were all used in a fairly random way. Radio tended to be the more formal term for the process of sending signals without physical connections between transmitter and receiver. Derived from the Latin for rays, it was preferred because radio was considered to be the most accurate, scientific term and it was hoped to use it as the basis for a common international vocabulary. In practice, wireless was usually adopted in everyday conversation. Marconi preferred wireless telegraphy to describe his first successful experiments in 1896. The first legislation prepared to help the Post Office handle the new medium was styled the Wireless Telegraphy Act in 1904. [7] When speech was transmitted, the term was naturally enough, wireless telephony and the abridged form wireless was confusingly applied to both methods of communication. The choice of wireless was only superficially obvious since even the most primitive crystal set needed an extensive aerial wire and a tuning coil using considerable quantities of wire. This, and the rather negative form of the definition, contributed to the rejection of the term by formal circles. Broadcasting was used equally casually to describe almost any form of signal transmission and reception. Only gradually was it limited to mean the more specific transmission of programmes by telephony for large audiences as opposed to private messages from, for example, ship to shore. The arrival of television complicated the definition still further and the BBC attempted, without success, to amend broadcasting to sound broadcasting for the sake of clarity. In both lay and official usage, the terms wireless and radio were interchangeable with radio gradually gaining the upperhand before 1939.

The first task in this enquiry must be to establish a demographic profile of the growing radio audience as a basis for understanding the social changes wrought by broadcasting. The licence returns are the main raw material and they must be used carefully in relation to census information to show the composition and location of the audience. [8]

Technical and economic factors constantly impinged on radio transmissions and determined the conditions in which listening took place. They require detailed attention. It must not be assumed, for instance, that transmissions were consistent in quality. Radio was not invented in a magnificent and spontaneous combination of scientific knowledge and technical skill, rather it evolved and improved as new inventions and improvements were applied. There was never a uniform provision of the broadcasting service before 1939. Conditions varied according to the wavelengths used, the provision of BBC transmitters and physical geography which blocked the signals. The social consequences of these technical changes and the economic circumstances in which they were applied must be considered, otherwise many reasons for the pattern of listening would remain obscure.

On the listening side of the microphone, the growth of the audience was heavily influenced by the technical development of radio sets and by the financial circumstances of the population. Early sets were often cheap but rather crude, inefficient and temperamental. Later sets were more expensive but possessed greatly improved performance and reliability. By 1939, the typical set had been improved out of all recognition from the sets available at the beginning of public service broadcasting in November 1922. The changing costs

of radio sets and the ten shilling (50p.) annual broadcast
licence were important factors for potential listeners to consider. Nevertheless, radio was always a very economical
means of supplying entertainment and information. It was
very good value for money and eventually came within reach
of all but the poorest.

The diversity in the audience can be overwhelming -
the almost infinite shades of opinion and preference. One
way of getting some focus is to gather the views of organised
pressure groups which articulated many of the audience's
views towards radio. Pressure groups were especially important in the early days of broadcasting between 1918 and
1922 because they then formed the largest part of the
audience and had a crucial role to play in the formation of
the British Broadcasting Company.

An investigation of the social influence of broadcasting
inevitably involves consideration of the relationship between
the broadcasters and the audience. Broadcasters determined the programme content. Furthermore, through observation and correspondence with listeners, the BBC was in a
unique position to gather information about the tastes and
habits of listeners. However, it was really only after systematic listener research began in 1936 that the BBC acquired
a detailed knowledge of audience behaviour. Between 1936
and 1939, the BBC's Listener Research Committee worked
quickly to produce a considerable body of evidence, revealing
a great deal about the location, age, sex and social class of
listeners, as well as something about the times when they
listened and the programmes they preferred.

One of the most obvious places to see the influence of
broadcasting is in the local community where the social
changes actually occurred. Using the slender resources of
inter-war social surveys and press comment, supported by
a detailed scrutiny of local records, it is possible to compare the responses of listeners living in towns with those
residing in the countryside. The local community is the
ideal place to judge the extent to which broadcasting informed
and educated the public. It also provides an opportunity to
study the influence on the enormous variety of dialects
spoken in Britain - did broadcasting introduce a tendency towards a standardised form of English?

Another aspect of listening concerns the role of radio
in the national community. Listening was normally a home-
centred, individual or family experience but, at the same
time, it was also in total a mass audience occasion. The

relationship between the nation and the individual was transformed by radio. National occasions could now be heard as they happened, creating an obvious sense of involvement. Two features stand out and need analysis. The political life of the country was changed by radio's ability to relay the views of political leaders directly to the electorate. Similarly, the relationship with the monarchy now assumed a quite different, more intimate form.

Broadcasting must also be seen in the context of leisure and recreation in inter-war Britain. Most listeners were able to experience more leisure time in the period, particularly working class listeners, either voluntarily, through the advent of a shorter working week or, more tragically and involuntarily, through the high level of unemployment which persisted throughout these years. This context will guard against the danger of seeing broadcasting as a solitary influence and ensure that the interaction with other media or social influences is understood.

The outbreak of war in 1939 brought an abrupt end to the formative era of broadcasting because the peculiar conditions of wartime placed new demands on radio and introduced a completely different phase in its use and influence. By 1945, radio was substantially changed in form and soon fell into a new role in the shadow of television. Television was developed in the twenties and transmissions began in November 1936, but the audience never rose above 10,000 and was confined entirely to the Alexandra Palace transmitter reception area before it was closed down in 1939.[9] Consequently, television was not a serious force for social change at this time and radio reigned supreme as the pre-eminent form of mass communication.

Chapter One

LISTENING PATTERNS

Demography

Initially, the fascination of radio was its magical quality: its
marvellous ability to generate sound from an apparently life-
less box; its capacity to allow even the most isolated soul to
listen to the very best music or the finest orator, without
moving from the comfort of the fireside. Almost everyone
seemed to have at least some enthusiasm for such a simple
way of being informed or entertained. Although, inevitably,
some professed to dislike the broadcast cacophony, the
possession of a wireless set soon passed from being a
novelty to that of a necessity. Fortunately, the growth and
distribution of set ownership and, hence, the audience can be
judged from wireless licence returns. An analysis of this
raw material is of primary importance. Broadcast licences
were issued at Post Offices and it was the responsibility of
the GPO to collate the returns and supply revenue to the
BBC. The annual returns provided a broad idea of the
growth of licence holding between 1922 and 1939 (see Table
1.1). The tremendous rate of growth was immediately
apparent and the figures were seized upon by the BBC as
proof of its success. Each year the BBC Handbook featured
the latest increase as prominently as possible.
        Interestingly, the BBC did not originally attempt to
relate these licence statistics to the rapidly growing number
of listeners. [1] Since only one licence per household was required - regardless of the number of people in that household or the number of wireless sets which they possessed -
the number of listeners was very different from the number
of licences. Using statistics for the number of persons per
private family as defined by the Census and estimates prepared by the Registrar General, it is quite possible to gain

Table 1.1: Total Licences issued 1922-1939²

Year Ending on 31st Dec.	UK Population (Estimated)	Total of all Licences issued (including Licences for the Blind)	% increase over previous year	Estimated total of people able to listen	Estimated number of households in the UK	Approximate number of licences per 100 households
1922	44,325,000	36,000	-	149,000	10,706,500	1
1923	44,550,000	595,496	-	2,465,000	10,761,000	5.5
1924	44,866,000	1,129,578	89.7	4,676,500	10,837,000	10
1925	45,014,000	1,645,207	45.6	6,811,000	10,872,000	15
1926	45,185,000	2,178,259	32.4	8,713,000	11,296,000	19
1927	45,394,000	2,395,183	10	9,581,000	11,348,500	21
1928	45,580,000	2,628,392	9.7	10,513,500	11,395,000	23
1929	45,685,000	2,956,736	12.5	11,827,000	11,421,000	26
1930	45,878,000	3,411,910	15.4	13,648,000	11,469,500	30
1931	46,038,000	4,330,735	26.9	16,327,000	12,250,000	35
1932	46,335,000	5,263,017	21.5	19,841,500	12,290,500	43
1933	46,520,000	5,973,758	13.5	22,521,000	12,339,500	48
1934	46,666,000	6,780,569	13.5	25,563,000	12,378,000	55
1935	46,869,000	7,403,109	9.2	27,910,000	12,432,000	60
1936	47,081,000	7,960,573	7.5	30,409,500	12,325,000	65
1937	47,289,000	8,479,600	6.5	32,392,000	12,350,000	68.5
1938	47,494,000	8,856,494	4.4	33,832,000	12,470,000	71
1939	47,762,000	8,893,582	0.4	33,973,500	12,503,000	71

a good impression of the number of households in Britain
between 1922 and 1939 and, by relating them to the licence
statistics, prepare a more relevant guide to the national
radio audience. As Table 1.1 shows, the result is a considerably more
illuminating impression of the growing audience. By 1939,
for instance, the rate of growth in licence holding had considerably diminished but 13. 5 million people (or 3. 6 million
households) appeared to have no direct means of listening to
a radio set in the home. Of course, this figure can be reduced by licence evasion but it does suggest that a considerable minority of the population did not have regular access
to a radio set. Some may have abstained from listening
voluntarily but evidently other causes prevented maximum
set ownership. More positively, it is clear that, from 1934
onwards, more than half the population, or 25. 5 million
people, had the capacity at their fingertips to hear a single
speaker - a feat which 25 years previously would have
seemed quite incredible. The scale of listening and thus the
achievement of radio broadcasting has to be seen in this
context.

To support this broad analysis it is possible to provide
a regional comparison of the licence statistics for the years
1931 and 1938. GPO statistics for years before 1930 are no
longer available. After 1930, they were summarised and
included in the BBC Handbooks and they are the main source.[3]
Unfortunately, the GPO regions used in licence returns do
not always conform precisely to the counties used as the
basis in the tables and, in many cases, the coverage for a
large county such as Yorkshire may disguise wide variations
in licence holding within each area. On the other hand, it is
possible to show the regional distribution of households for
1931 and 1938 so that it becomes easier to gain a more
accurate impression of the regional variations in the audience. This aspect is expressed in Table 1. 2 and cartograph-
ically for easier comparison in Figures 1. 1 and 1. 2.

It is worth emphasising that licence figures are not
definitive guides to radio listening and certainly to radio
influence. All these statistics can do is indicate ownership.
They cannot give any clue to the number of members in a
family who listened regularly or the extent of their listening.
For instance, it was not necessary to actually own a set to
listen to radio. Indirect distribution of radio information
took place even if it is difficult to quantify or verify. When
sets were scarce, verbal exchanges of knowledge derived

from radio sources were likely to be more frequent - even if precise information about the extent of this practice is impossible to gather. Furthermore, many listeners would have visited the homes of relatives or neighbours to hear programmes in the early stages when sets were relatively scarce. This would have considerably swelled the numbers listening regularly. Radio soon became the aural centre of the community, but it was only when set ownership had expanded substantially that it became possible to argue that this aural centre had, by and large, passed into the household. Hence the size of the audience was probably larger than it appeared, particularly if licence evasion is taken into account. However, the exact dimension must remain elusive.

With these words of caution, a further analysis of the statistics can proceed. A study of the maps reveals some of the trends. Since these maps show proportions, not absolute figures, they do underline the under-representation of certain areas. In both 1931 and 1938, the greatest proportions of households with licences were concentrated in the South-East and the Midland Counties, with reasonable levels in the West of England, North Wales, the northern English Counties and East Anglia. Counties with conurbations retained the lead in licence holding. Lower levels of licence holding can be seen in the North East and North West of England and South Wales.

The far North of Scotland and Northern Ireland were particularly under-represented. Physical barriers and interference may have had a part to play in this but the areas concerned do tend to have a predominantly rural character. The solace of radio for isolated communities was not apparently sufficiently attractive. [4]

Despite the uneven distribution, the statistics and maps make it transparently clear that the overall picture was one of growth. In many cases the percentage of households with licences doubled or trebled between 1931 and 1938, the increased number of households being easily surpassed by the increase in the number of licences issued. Notable increases were in the North Region - where the number of households with sets in Cumberland, Westmorland, Durham and Northumberland trebled. Many other counties saw the same effect to a slightly lesser degree. Some of the outer reaches of Scotland and Northern Ireland showed similar increases even though absolute levels were normally lower. Elsewhere the normal increase was a doubling of the 1931 level, with proportions of 84% in South Oxfordshire and Northamptonshire. The uneven growth and distribution of

Figure 1.1: Licence Distribution According to Counties 1931

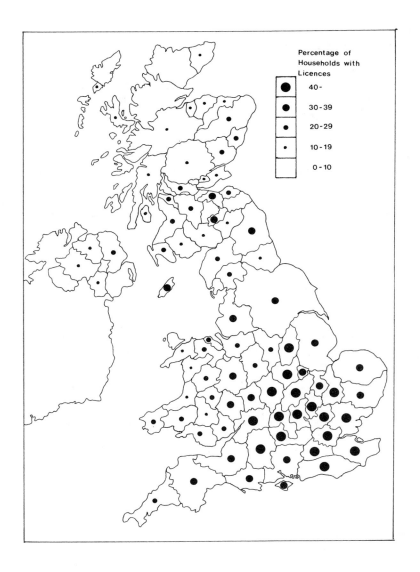

Figure 1.2: Licence Distribution According to Counties 1938

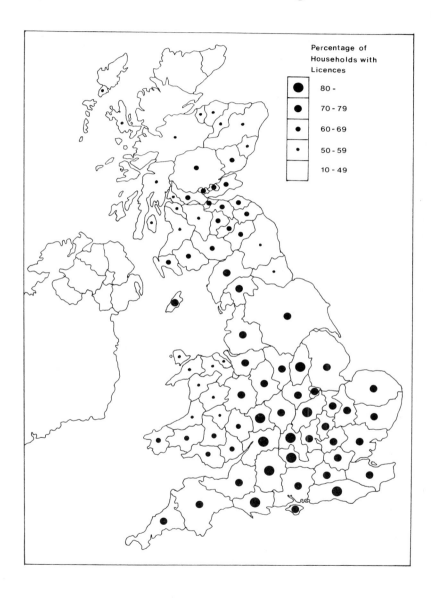

Table 1.2: Regional Comparison of Licence Holding 1931 and 1938[5]

Area	1931 Licences	% Households with Licences	1938 Licences	% Households with Licences
London Region				
Bedford	29,109	47	53,300	76
Berkshire & S. Oxford	59,535	50	103,400	84
Buckingham	31,739	42	60,400	73
Cambridge & Huntingdon	35,926	46	60,900	77
Channel Islands	8,318	32	19,700	76
Hampshire	95,689	39	226,800	79
London & Home Counties: Essex, Hertford, Kent, Middlesex & Surrey	1,352,788	46	2,271,800	74
Norfolk	47,823	34	107,400	77
Suffolk	35,170	32	80,900	74
Sussex	87,610	40	177,100	80
Total	1,783,707	44	3,161,700	75

Northern Region

Cheshire, Lancashire & Isle of Man	543,258	33	1,138,200	70
Cumberland & Westmorland	20,050	24	57,800	71
Durham & Northumberland	121,600	22	281,700	69
Lincolnshire	62,889	38	130,200	79
Yorkshire & N. Derby	426,945	33	946,000	73
Total	1,174,742	31	2,553,900	69

West Region

Cornwall & Devon	100,866	34	228,300	79
Dorset & Wiltshire	58,545	39	132,800	84
Somerset & S. Gloucester	99,912	36	212,300	77
Total	259,323	36	573,400	79

Table 1.2 (cont'd)

Area	1931 Licences	% Households with Licences	1938 Licences	% Households with Licences
Midland Region				
Hereford	10,090	34	19,700	69
Leicester & Rutland	59,997	40	119,300	75
Northampton	47,768	47	87,600	84
N. Gloucester & N. Oxford	41,907	43	79,700	80
Salop	23,731	37	48,300	78
S. Derby & Nottingham	96,541	36	233,100	83
Stafford & Warwick	277,542	37	619,700	79
Worcester	43,766	39	95,800	82
Total	601,342	38	1,303,200	80
Wales				
Mid-Wales: Cardigan, Merioneth, Montgomery, & Radnor	9,105	20	20,800	50

North Wales: Anglesey, Caernarvon, Denbigh & Flint	30,490	26	68,700	59
South Wales: Brecon, Carmarthen, Glamorgan, Monmouth & Pembroke	126,286	25	306,000	64
Total	165,881	25	395,500	63
Northern Ireland Total	96,140	34	119,800	41
Scotland				
Aberdeen & Kincardine	21,148	25	52,600	59
Argyll & Bute	3,617	17	11,200	55
Ayr, Dumbarton, Lanark & Renfrew	117,288	21	336,700	58
Banff, Inverness, Moray & Nairn	5,738	13	25,500	56
East Central Scotland: Clackmannan, E. Lothian, Fife, Kinross, Midlothian, West Lothian & Stirling	71,052	25	204,400	68

15

Table 1. 2 (cont'd)

Area	1931 Licences	% Households with Licences	1938 Licences	% Households with Licences
Scotland (cont'd)				
Angus & Perth	23,598	22	70,600	65
North Scotland: Caithness, Orkney, Ross & Cromarty, Shetland & Sutherland	3,096	8	14,400	37
Border: Berwick, Dumfries, Kirkcudbright, Peebles, Roxburgh, Selkirk & Wigtown	12,694	19	42,000	63
Total	258,231	22	757,400	61
United Kingdom				
Total	3,391,042	27	8,864,900	71

licence holding does require further explanation. Obviously the influences which led to the inexorable advance of radio in some parts of the country were absent from others.

Technical Policy and Development

One factor which emerges from an analysis of demographic trends in the radio audience is that the ideal world of perfect reception, perfect choice of stations, and free access to the means of receiving programmes did not exist before 1939 - nor has it existed since. The basic desire to listen was easily obstructed by inadequate transmitters or receiver facilities. Listeners wanted the immediacy of news reception, excitement from sporting commentaries, and entertainment from music or drama. All of these motives for listening were important but none could be entirely separated from the technological or economic constraints on listening: they were inexorably shaped by them and deeply interwoven with them. Even an ideal broadcasting system which could pander to all tastes would founder on the rock of dissatisfaction and frustration caused by the weakness of the radio signal or the poverty of potential listeners. Consequently these technological and economic limitations, and the BBC policies which controlled them must be considered as a substantial influence on the attitudes of the radio audience.

In 1967, the British Broadcasting Corporation introduced the first of its local radio stations.[6] This form of radio was introduced to satisfy what was felt to be a need for closer contact between the medium and the local community. In fact, these new stations completed a circle in public broadcasting policy because the first form of radio was local radio. In both cases, technical considerations were very influential - even if the policy processes which created them had quite different intentions in mind. [7]

In 1922, the inability to produce a high-power, low frequency transmitter meant that it was technically impossible to broadcast programmes to audiences more than twenty-five miles away using crystal receivers or approximately a hundred miles away for efficient two valve sets. [8] In 1967, very high frequency (VHF), frequency modulated (FM) transmitters were used deliberately to reduce the propagation distance; VHF signals having the advantage in localising signals and reducing interference, whilst, simultaneously extending the available wavebands for domestic broadcasts in the United Kingdom. [9]

In the early twenties, the restricted propagation distances meant that transmitters were built in the centre of urban concentrations. Consequently, reception was very good for those within range of a station such as the BBC's 2LO, broadcasting from Marconi House and later from the roof of Selfridges Store in Oxford Street, but almost impossible for those living in rural Hampshire or Wiltshire. These technical restrictions meant that localities fortunate enough to receive BBC programmes heard broadcasts produced by each station with its own production staff. Simultaneous broadcasting (SB) of the same programme from all transmitters was only occasionally possible on an experimental basis.

Local broadcasting was a technical limitation which actually ran counter to the avowed BBC policy to provide a full national service, based upon the terms of the monopoly granted to it by the Post Office.[10] The aim was simple; to provide everyone with at least one programme on a relatively cheap receiver.[11] However, this period was brief and the BBC, ever anxious to fulfil its obligations, continued to develop new and improved transmitter facilities: through the research work of its own engineering department and that of the component companies. Originally, firms such as Marconi, Western Electric and Metropolitan Vickers had built the first BBC transmitters for their own research purposes and after handing them over to the Company they continued their work intensively. Once the technical complications were overcome, simultaneous broadcasting became far more frequent, partly prompted by the financial savings which could be made. The first tests were made in 1923 after which SB was common practice - the savings in providing one programme instead of nine different ones were obvious.[12] (See Figure 1.3)

The next course was to expand the service area to reach listeners using crystal sets outside the main urban areas. With the development of the high power, long-wave transmitter, it proved possible to provide crystal strength reception for 85% of the population - compared with the 60 to 70% who could receive the existing local stations.[13] The new station at Daventry in Northamptonshire, call sign 5XX, opened on the 27 July 1925, using 25 kW compared with the 1. 5 kW of the local stations. This made national broadcasting plausible for the first time.[14]

The construction of 5XX did not mean that every listener now had perfect conditions for listening. Interference with transmitter signals was still a serious problem. The broadcasting of speech and music required the use of thermionic valves and continuous wave transmission but in the early days of public broadcasting this co-existed with morse code signalling using 'spark' transmitters. This system was widely used by shipping as it was fairly economical and relatively reliable. The only disadvantage was that the 'spark' spread interference over a wide band of the broadcasting spectrum, thus damaging reception severely in coastal areas - especially in Kent and on the South and East coasts.[15]

Other areas inland suffered from interference too, either through weak signals due to physical barriers or from being on the edge of service areas. For instance, Sheffield suffered particularly badly on both counts.

The other problem concerned the radio waves themselves. Medium-wave transmissions vary in their propagation distance according to the wave-length of the signal, the amount of solar activity and the ambient atmospheric temperature. When the signal is transmitted there are, crudely speaking, two components: the ground wave and the sky wave - the one carrying directly to the receiver, the other bouncing back off the ionosphere.[16] When the two meet on the ground the result is interference: the so-called 'mush area'.

For local stations, the best reception was had in the daylight, declining quickly after nightfall, with the signal travelling along the ground now foreshortened and losing strength. Paradoxically, the clear reception area for the sky wave was well beyond the horizon after dusk, so that at night time, listeners at the limits of the service area could receive the signal better than those at an intermediate distance from the transmitter. The sky wave travels further at night because of changes in the ionosphere caused by the loss of direct solar energy. Thus, long-wave listening was better at night-time during long cold winter nights and autumn saw the launching of the new season for listening, not only because of restricted out-door activities, but also because of the better quality of the signals. Unfortunately, this effect made listening irritating for those in the 'mush area' or those at the extreme edge of a service area and even for those close to a transmitter where any other signals might be swamped by the nearby station. But it did increase listening to continental stations by listeners in Britain and vice versa. This tendency was particularly marked throughout this era, since it was the only way of avoiding the BBC monopoly. Radio had

possessed this international character from the first Marconi
tests at Poldhu. [17] Early commercial stations such as PCCG
in the Hague attracted large audiences for its English speaking broadcasts even before the BBC was created. [18] In the
thirties, the commercial giants of Luxembourg and Normandie
were particularly popular and at the end of the period, there
was the significant, if eccentric, listening to the broadcasts
of Lord Haw-Haw emanating from Radio Hamburg. [19]

This long-distance exchange of signals using the medium wave had other more unfortunate side-effects. Very
quickly, the concept of 'the crowding of the airways' - one of
the fears which led to the BBC monopoly - became a reality.
Interference reached serious proportions and some form of
international co-operation and control became essential.
Prompted by the BBC, the Union International de Radiophone
(UIR) was formed in April 1925. The UIR soon agreed on an
international system of control - the Geneva Plan. [20] This
confined the BBC to eight exclusive wavelengths, two shared
wavelengths and one common wavelength for relay stations,
all on the medium wave, plus one long wavelength at 1600
metres. The implementation of this scheme began in the
winter of 1926. [21] This new arrangement meant that the BBC
relay stations (relaying from the local stations) had to be
synchronised properly. Although the relay stations only had
a crystal reception range of five to ten miles, interference
with each other would cause serious signal distortion or
fading. [22] The work of the UIR continued throughout the
period up to 1939 - international co-operation was crucial to
the development of radio in Europe. The BBC had to observe
the recommendations of a further agreement - the Prague
plan of 1929 - which hastened the need for another phase of
transmitter changes. [23]

Changes under the Geneva plan were implemented fairly
easily as they did not require anything more than a few adjustments to existing receivers. The introduction of the next
stage of wavelength changes had a much greater impact upon
the domestic audience. The entire pattern of transmission
and reception was transformed. Yet, despite the dislocation
that this caused, the process was fully in accord with the
BBC's previously announced aims: to provide service areas
for those previously excluded, to reduce interference and,
ultimately, to provide a choice of programme for as many
listeners as possible in Britain. The Chief Engineer, Peter
Eckersley, had proposed the provision of a choice as early as
1924, [24] and it had been accepted as policy by the BBC's

Control Board in 1926. [25] As on previous occasions, the
uppermost considerations were those of technical potential
and financial efficiency.

The technical problems revolved around the fact that
the BBC had still not been offered by the manufacturers, or
developed itself, a sufficiently powerful medium wave transmitter. The BBC had also encountered strong resistance
from the GPO, which strenuously objected to the proliferation
of the projected high powered stations, operating on wavelengths which might interfere with its own, military or
governmental transmissions. [26] There was also the threat to
aircraft from the taller masts which would be needed. [27] The
BBC only managed to remove the restrictions on the development of the necessary transmitters, after an independent
committee - the Eccles Committee created to arbitrate in the
dispute - ruled in the BBC's favour and the scheme rapidly
went ahead. [28] The only other resistance came from the
wireless trade which thought that it had a vested interest in
preserving the status quo. However, by giving plenty of
warning, the BBC was able to convince the traders that they
had time to convert production lines and actually take advantage of the increased sales which the change would bring. [29]

The BBC Engineering Section had, in the meantime,
been attempting to turn the policy of listener choice into a
practical proposition. [30] This led eventually to the development and construction of an experimental 50 kW medium
wave station at Daventry. The new station, call sign 5GB,
began transmissions on 21 August 1927, and the first practical step on the road to what was soon called 'the Regional
Scheme' had been made. [31]

There were excellent economic motives, too, for
putting the scheme into practice. Once the licence fee had
been fixed at ten shillings per annum for all types of
listeners, on 1 July 1924, [32] the main struggle for income
came from increasing the number of licence holders and
from a less successful struggle to increase the share of this
licence revenue vis-à-vis the GPO. [33] Allegedly to cover
collecting costs, the GPO originally retained $12\frac{1}{2}\%$ of the
revenue and this was only reduced to 10% in 1932. In
addition, the BBC could only collect 90% of the revenue on
the first million licences, 80% on the second million, 70% on
the third million and 60% on the remainder; the rest being
retained by the Postmaster-General. [34] Furthermore, in
1931, the BBC also agreed to make a 'voluntary' contribution
of £200,000 to the Exchequer during the national economic

crisis, for payment in 1932-1933. [35]

Clearly the expansion in listeners did not necessarily produce a commensurate increase in the BBC's financial standing. Consequently, any extension of the service would have to draw in proportionately more listeners before it could be cost effective. It was hoped that the Regional Scheme would satisfy this requirement, the new transmitters would expand the service area and yet be cheaper to build and maintain than the existing local transmitter and relay station system. [36] Obviously a fairly large licence base would be needed before the BBC could approve the initial capital expenditure necessary to build a series of high power transmitters, only then could the long term savings be enjoyed. Once the audience in urban areas was sufficiently large to sustain expansion, it would be possible to provide a nationally available service and use the resources liberated from local stations to provide alternative programmes. The public would get its choice but, in the process of providing this service, the BBC placed any local listening requirements well down the list of priorities. [37]

The Regional Scheme

The BBC's Regional Scheme subordinated the local cultural and social needs of listeners to national, economic, technical and even bureaucratic considerations. This was hardly unexpected: the process conformed with the BBC model of monopoly control. The BBC gazed out of its metropolitan base at Savoy Hill (and later Portland Place) on to an audience which it regarded vaguely or sometimes with indifference. The justification for the Regional Scheme was that listeners throughout the country could be brought into contact with national figures, national events and hear a higher quality of programme. Better programmes, it was argued, would result from the concentration of resources which the Regional Scheme would permit. As Reith remarked with great clarity:

> Even on the most ordinary occasions we find the amenities of metropolitan culture made available in large measure to those who live in circumstances of the greatest physical isolation equally with those who inhabit the great centres of population. They are present equally at functions and ceremonials upon which national sentiment is concentrated; they are in touch equally with the movements of thought and the processes of

action which determine national destiny, and there are set before them equally the problems which are vexing the statesman of their day. [38]

This attempt to create a sense of national identity may have been valuable but it was pursued to the exclusion of important parochial interests. The key-word used by the BBC to describe this policy was 'centralization' - a natural policy extension from the technical progress made in simultaneous broadcasting. To break this monolithic concept into manageable administrative and transmission areas, it was employed hand in hand with 'regionalisation.'[39]

Regionalisation was a reflection of somewhat casual thinking about the distinction between 'local' and 'regional' - inside the BBC the two were often considered to be virtually synonymous. In reality this vagueness rode roughshod over many important distinctions. The BBC thought it knew something about its audience but in reality it possessed little precise knowledge at this time. Most of the BBC production staff were wholly convinced of metropolitan superiority and preferred to set their own standards for programmes rather than be seen to pander to regional variations in taste which, in any case, they considered to be merely capricious. [40]

Certainly, a locality or region is not easy to define for cultural rather than administrative purposes. A locality generally revolves around a small part of a county, or a single urban area. A region can spread across several counties. The exact size varies: local perceptions of size may vary and there are no firm rules. Hence, there is a problem in respecting any distinct qualities which an area may have. The common denominator may be only geographical rather than a cultural factor such as dialect. However, the BBC Regions were so large and all-embracing that it is difficult to see any rationale for them beyond that of administrative, economic or technical convenience. The North and West Regions were particularly large, covering many hundreds of communities.

For the sake of perspective, it must be stressed that regionalisation was not a BBC invention. [41] Census and Poor Law Commissioners had evaluated such areas in the nineteenth century. Political and administrative convenience took precedence in their organisation at that time. [42] Furthermore, the BBC had a great deal in common with the move towards industrial regionalisation in the twentieth century, particularly because of the concern for economic and technical convenience. For instance, the grouping of the Railway Companies in 1921 had many similarities, as did the creation of the regions for the national electricity grid in 1926. [43] Certainly, the BBC shared the bureaucratic public image of these organisations, particularly in the thirties, but its special form of daily contact with the audience gave the BBC a decidedly different character. The BBC possessed a much more identifiable and vivid connection with its consumers. The output provided a constant reminder - perhaps because of the jarring accent of the announcers, the style of the programmes or even the apparent irrelevance of the news bulletins. The addition of this cultural effect made the influence of the BBC unique and, in consequence, any clumsiness in handling social and regional differences of taste or interest were likely to be much harder for the consumer to bear. Broadcasting might eventually produce an erosion of local distinctions but, in the short run, the audience reaction to the implementation of the Regional Scheme might be expected to be fairly hostile. In fact the audience response was one of qualified approval.

BBC opinion on the validity of the scheme may have confused local and regional interests but at least some of the staff began to consider some non-metropolitan variations in taste and interest. From the early planning stage, Peter Eckersley, the Chief Engineer, recognised, as others such as his brother, Roger, and the Drama Director, Val Gielgud, did not, [44] that variations in regional taste did exist and that they merited some consideration. [45] In this sense there was some audience satisfaction with the Regional Programme as a limited contrast to the National Programme. In fact, there were few complaints from the listening public in the cases where old local stations or relay stations were replaced by a good quality service - offering better reception standards and a choice of programme.

Complaints were often aimed simply at the change in itself rather than at the quality of the replacement service or the enforced obsolescence of equipment. In fact the quality of reception was extremely influential in deciding the audience response. Much as the BBC hoped, [46] the loss of local content was accepted, provided the quality of the new National and Regional Programmes equalled or exceeded the standard of the old service in terms of modulation, purity or volume.

The BBC recognised that change in itself would be a cause for complaint and therefore gave prominence to the detailed preparation of the audience for the changeover to the

Regional Scheme. The lesson had been learnt the hard way at the very beginning of the scheme with the introduction of the new Birmingham station. Here inadequate prior publicity caused a storm of protest when the 5IT Station, sited in Birmingham, was fully replaced by the Daventry Experimental Station, 5GB, on 21 August 1927. Curiously, Peter Eckersley had expected the storm and had prepared to ride it out - indeed the riding of the storm was the 'make or break' test for the whole Regional policy. As Eckersley remarked:

> We knew, from measurements, that the new station would give perfectly adequate signals in Birmingham, albeit weaker than those the Birmingham people were accustomed to receive, and so we knew that while there would be plenty of complaint it would not be justified. But unjustified or not the volume might be embarrassing. Indeed, it might be so great as to prejudice the whole scheme. So 'changing over' was a crucial test of the problem of 'dislocation'. Would listeners willingly adapt their receivers to the new conditions or would they just howl to get back the super signal they were accustomed to receive?

The prediction was correct but it was a 'damned close run thing', and some palliatives were needed to reduce the strain on the nerves. [47] This lesson produced a much greater public relations effort. For the next stage of the scheme at Brookmans Park, a pamphlet was widely distributed to explain the change, anticipate its effects and help prepare the listener for any practical changes to his or her receiver. [48] In this pamphlet the BBC recommended changes to aerials according to proximity and in a further pamphlet, The Reception of Alternative Programmes, suggested the fitting of a wave-trap to crystal sets, so that the choice of programme could be clearly separated by such unselective sets. At that time, a wave-trap would cost between 1s. 6d, and 2s. 6d. [49] In private, Peter Eckersley was more contemptuous of such adjustments: 'If we had to wait until everybody gave up using old junk and expensive toys before we could institute any new schemes we might just as well never make any changes at all.'[50] Nevertheless, the BBC used similar public relations techniques as the scheme was applied over the next ten years.

One of the greatest problems during the course of this implementation was not the level of resistance to the scheme but the envy aroused in areas outside it. Some areas on the

Table 1.3: Transmitters

(a) <u>Main and Relay Stations 1922-4</u>

Station	Call Sign	Opening Date	Closing Date
Main Stations:			
London (Marconi House)	2LO	11 May 1922	5 Apr 1925
London (Selfridges)	2LO	6 Apr 1925	4 Oct 1929
Manchester	2ZY	16 May 1922	17 May 1931
Birmingham	5IT	15 Nov 1922	21 Aug 1927
Newcastle	5NO	24 Dec 1922	19 Oct 1937
Cardiff	5WA	13 Feb 1923	28 May 1933
Glasgow	5SC	6 Mar 1923	12 June 1932
Aberdeen	2BD	10 Oct 1923	9 Sept 1938
Bournemouth	6BM	17 Oct 1923	14 June 1939
Belfast	2BE	24 Oct 1924	20 Mar 1936
Relay Stations:			
Sheffield	6FL	16 Nov 1923	16 May 1931
Plymouth	5PY	28 Mar 1924	13 June 1939
Edinburgh	2EH	1 May 1924	12 June 1932
Liverpool	6LV	11 June 1924	16 May 1931
Leeds	2LS	8 July 1924	16 May 1931
Bradford	2LS	8 July 1924	16 May 1931
Hull	6KH	15 Aug 1924	16 May 1931

Nottingham	5NG	16 Sept 1924	1 Nov 1928
Dundee	2DE	12 Nov 1924	12 June 1932
Stoke-on-Trent	6ST	21 Oct 1924	16 May 1931
Swansea	5SX	12 Dec 1924	28 May 1933

(b) National and Regional Stations to 1 September 1939

Station	Opening Date
Droitwich (National)	Oct 1934
Brookmans Park (National)	Mar 1930
Moorside Edge (National)	July 1931
Westerglen (National)	June 1932
Moorside Edge (North Regional)	May 1931
Stagshaw	Oct 1937
Westerglen (Scottish Regional)	June 1932
Burghead	Oct 1936
Redmoss	Sept 1938
Washford (Welsh Regional)	May 1933*
Penmon	Feb 1937
Brookmans Park (London Regional)	Oct 1929
Lisnagarvey (N. Ireland Regional)	Mar 1936
Droitwich (Midland Regional)	Feb 1935
Start Point (West of England Regional)	June 1939
Clevedon	June 1939

* As West Regional Station

Figure 1.3: Transmitter Map 1922-1939

periphery had a genuine grievance because of the weakness of the new signal - in some cases a great deal weaker than the old local transmitter signal. These included Hull, Sheffield, North Wales, the Highlands, Newcastle and some rural parts of the southern English Counties. All were eventually provided with a better service before 1939. [51] In the interim, protests forced the perpetuation of some of the old local stations - either independently or in relay for Regional Programme broadcasts. These included the Newcastle, Bournemouth, Plymouth and Aberdeen stations. Another amelioration of grievances was the introduction of a more powerful National Programme, from the new Droitwich transmitter which replaced the station at Daventry on 6 October 1934. [52] The shadow areas could now receive at least one programme properly. (See Table 1.3 and Figure 1.3)

The London Region was the first to see a full service from the Regional Scheme, with the introduction of the full alternative programme service in March 1930. [53] This was deliberately delayed to allow the public to make preparations following the introduction of the National Programme, broadcast from the Brookmans Park transmitter on 21 October 1929. The audience was favourably disposed towards the innovation and definitely appreciated the introduction of a choice. [54] Complaints were expected and even predicted in the newspapers, although most hoped that the BBC would weather the storm without concession. Advice was given by national newspapers on how to take advantage of the service by aerial alterations and the fitting of wave-traps. [55] The delay certainly helped to diminish the extremes of public response. In some cases, crystal sets may have been jammed by the two signals but great stress was laid on the fact that even these crude receivers could be saved by simple alteration. With the wide dissemination of this advice the crisis soon passed. [56]

Potentially, the North Regional Scheme presented a more difficult task - largely because the area to be covered was so vast. The local press met the plans with some trepidation. [57] Special fears were devoted to the uneven quality of reception which was expected - either through 'swamping', as in Huddersfield, or through the weakness of the signal, as at Hull. [58] Generally, however, the new station at Moorside Edge, near Slaithwaite, was met with sympathetic anticipation. The building of the mast and station was closely monitored and the first tests met with adulation. [59] The 'giant' transmitter was capable of a much superior quality and choice of

broadcasting when compared with the old fashioned local
stations and their loss was mourned barely at all. The
swamping effect was considerably less than expected. [60] In
the Yorkshire and Lancashire areas the main dispute centred
on the more trivial issue of the name of the new station.
'Slowit' was generally agreed to be the most correct pronunciation of Slaithwaite. [61] There were more serious problems
elsewhere, mainly for listeners in Northumberland and
Durham. The Newcastle Station, 5NO, was to be synchronised with Moorside Edge to relay the North Regional Programme and give an improved signal strength. At first, the
plan was welcomed - as the Newcastle Evening Chronicle
remarked:

> A large amount of this programme will come from the
> Newcastle, Manchester and Leeds studios and from
> other sources in the North of England, and Mr. Liveing
> /North Regional Director/ indicated the other night,
> some of the extremely interesting plans the BBC has
> for entertaining features in this North Country Pro-
> gramme. It is distinctly promising to find Mr. Liveing
> and his staff so keen to make this programme a source
> of real satisfaction to Northern listeners, and I do be-
> lieve that Northern officials have a better idea of the
> tastes and sympathies of the ordinary working class
> and middle class wireless listeners than have some of
> the staff at London Headquarters who live in an atmos-
> phere remote from that of the man in the street. [62]

This favourable attitude, demonstrating no sign of
regret at the loss of local programmes, soon evaporated. The
reason was technical. The relay synchronisation system
failed and effectively jammed all BBC programmes during a
trial held during August 1931. The Durham area, already an
area of low licence holding levels, was cut off in a 'mush
zone' of high signal interference. 5NO became 'Five No
Good'. An outcry led to the dropping of the scheme. [63] 5NO
continued on its own wavelength until the opening of the Stag-
shaw transmitter in 1937 when the relay of the North Regional
Programme was carried out successfully and the audience
growth rate stimulated.

The West was the last of the English Regions to be provided with a service. This was not greeted as a mark of
favour, rather of neglect. [64] When the station was finally
built, the Region was subject to the most serious of the disputes over local interests. The main conflict rounded on the

Welsh language programme service, which was shared with
the rest of the West programmes. The Cornish listeners
were especially annoyed by this, as they had an inferior
reception quality to that of South Wales listeners. [65] Listeners in North Wales were also aggrieved. A few could receive
the North Regional Programme but not the West Regional
Welsh language programmes. This rather obvious clash of
local interests was only resolved by the separation of the two
regions and the provision of extra transmitters at Penmon
and Start Point. Before they could be built, the relay
stations at Plymouth and Bournemouth provided some support
for the service - a rather unsatisfactory compromise.

In Scotland, the existing service had been so poor that
the construction of the Burghead transmitter in 1936 belatedly
opened up whole new areas for radio reception. The Aberdeen
station had been maintained as an interim measure but the
new transmitter gave many areas of the Highlands a service
for the first time. The Scottish character of their regional
programme seems to have been at least adequate and was
certainly infinitely better than no programme at all. [66]

After the initial gratitude for the new service, some
problems did begin to emerge, even in areas which had a
very good regional and national service on the medium wave,
plus the Droitwich National Programme and in some cases,
the regional programme of a neighbouring region. The BBC
aware of this dissatisfaction sent the Director of Regional
Relations on a tour of the Regions. He produced his report
in January 1936. The Director, C.A. Siepmann, severely
criticised the overall policy of centralization as one of the
main reasons for the grievances:

> The danger inherent in the power and range of broad-
> casting of achieving a uniform pattern of thought, of
> standardising taste and values according to the author-
> itarian few and 'expert' are too obvious to need
> elaboration.

Related to his criticisms of metropolitan supremacy were his
fears about the consequences of this type of development at
regional level. 'Regional centralization' was caused by a
shortage of regional resources - both in financial and
personnel terms:

> This leads to a tendency to draw material and artists
> for the purpose of convenience from the area in which
> the officers happen to be. This is much resented by
> towns and districts further afield within the Region.

Another criticism was the lack of a full regional programme choice on the alternative programme. Standards
were set which contained an implicit metropolitan bias. As
Siepmann stated:

> It is appropriate that national services should achieve
> as high a standard of excellence as possible, but the
> purist's concern for artistic integrity can be carried
> too far, and the case for Regional broadcasting cannot
> be measured by this single yardstick of artistic achieve-
> ment. There are subordinate considerations which are
> bound to qualify the mere concern for high standards of
> achievement. The patronage of all the arts, the repre-
> sentation of local life and of local interests are limiting
> factors from a Head Office point of view, but need to be
> carefully weighed in the balance of advantage in consid-
> ering the purpose on which our Regional programme
> policy depends. Concessions are necessary, though I
> should be the last to defend a lapse of standards beyond
> a certain point. [67]

One enemy was particularly detested - that was 'diagon-
alization' - where a programme was broadcast on all
frequencies at once; normally because it was considered too
important for any other programme to challenge for an
audience. After leaving the BBC, Peter Eckersley attacked
this practice:

> The extra wavelength is an administrative convenience,
> not an extra facility to expand the scope of the service.
> It might have been thought that the two programmes
> would always be different, both in items and inspiration.
> Not only have they, in today's practice, the same
> inspiration but often the two wavelengths both carry
> the same item. [68]

Admittedly Eckersley had an axe to grind and wanted the
alternative programme to be handed over to private enterprise for the necessary contrast, but his view was shared by
others who advocated different solutions.

Siepmann feared the effect this policy might have on regional talent. Whilst observing that: 'Despite broadcasting
and other influences, the vigour and conservation of local life
and local interests persist,' he also saw the dangers should
this extraordinary resilience be broken down:

> The provinces are the seed-ground of talent and the
> ultimate source of our supply for London programmes.

> The existence and development of our Regional work
> provides an effective insurance policy against the
> drying up of sources of supply for our programmes. [69]

The BBC Control Board accepted some of these comments
but they did so grudgingly, with reservations about the extent
of any concession:

> As a matter of policy the general tendency outside
> broadcasting towards centralisation on the metropolis
> is regarded as bad, and broadcasting can counter this
> by representing the local point of view and encouraging
> local talent, but not at the expense of replacing metro-
> politan by regional centralisation. [70]

The Board also took up another of Siepmann's suggestions.
He had advocated a 'Charter of Rights' to try and strengthen
the position of the Regional Station Directors in their discussions with Portland Place over programming. The
Control Board agreed to this, but left only a small gap for
more regional programmes to enter. The 'Charter' stated:
'A regional broadcast must either (1) have a local justification, or (2) if it is general programme material, be better,
or at least as well performed in the Regions as elsewhere. '
These changes in emphasis were communicated to the BBC
Departments but the public were more likely to benefit from
the continued expansion of the Regional transmitter system
in the late thirties than from the almost imperceptible move
towards more regionally generated programmes.

The main benefit of Siepmann's action was a contribution to the internal BBC debate about the collection of information concerning the audience. Siepmann frequently alluded
to the ignorance about the needs and character of the audience
in the regions. He pressed for the greater use of the Public
Relations Officers, recently attached to each station, and for
a campaign of audience research:

> Regional correspondence is small and, great as is the
> collective knowledge of the staff of Regional character-
> istics and sentiment, I could not fail to be perplexed in
> my survey by the total lack of evidence as to the atti-
> tude of listeners to our Regional services. Our work
> here remains an act of faith and I found a general
> concern on the part of Regional Programme Assistants
> for more guidance as to listener's needs and for the
> setting up of the machinery to secure reliable data for
> the determination of future policy. Regional offices are

to my mind the proper centres for the establishment of some such information service as is universally demanded. [71]

Eventually, the Control Board did approve the use of listener research to end the information starvation and put the Public Relations Officers to work gathering listener responses. [72] The policy makers finally had to admit that the imposition of the Regional Scheme had created some problems and that closer contact with the public would verify whether the scheme needed improvement to reduce the dependence upon personal estimations of the public taste.

Nonetheless, the absence of a really adverse audience reaction was the most noticeable response to the Regional Scheme. Only where language, or some other distinctive cultural variation existed was there likely to be major frustration at the imposition of an alien culture to replace the old locally created programme. With the creation of a separate Welsh Region and the reallocation of some areas of North Staffordshire and North Nottinghamshire even this problem was greatly eased. [73]

The lack of any great opposition to the loss of local stations can be explained in several ways. First, the audience greatly appreciated the arrival of a truly national service and some recognition should be given to the achievement of Sir John Reith's main ambition. Secondly, the Regional Scheme had many positive features - particularly the greatly expanded strength and quality of the signals which reached more potential listeners than ever before and gave them a choice of programme. Parts of the country which had been on the periphery of, or even completely outside, a reception area obviously preferred the Regional Scheme as a more equitable way of sharing out the opportunities for local expression. Those who had lost a local station were normally prepared to accept the change, provided that the alternative programme was a genuine one and that the available time on the new regional programme was shared out fairly amongst the constituent localities. In addition, the provision of a full national service and alternative programme was some compensation, satisfying the strong demand in all localities for a broader cultural diet and national information. Most of the complaints arose when it was realised that the BBC could not always live up to this promise.

The Regional Scheme could not eliminate local needs and interests. After its introduction, the interest in appearances by local artists and the coverage of local events was undiminished, arousing as much, if not more, pleasure than before. [74] Indeed, when it became technically feasible to provide a local service alongside national programmes in the nineteen sixties, these unrequited local needs and interests re-emerged to lobby for their expression in broadcasting, eventually culminating with the introduction of the BBC Local Radio Service.

The introduction of the Regional Scheme did change the relationship between the BBC and its audience. Its introduction drew more listeners within reception distance of a transmitter for the first time and provided the majority of listeners with a choice of programme, before 1939. For most of the audience the new scheme was an improvement and the service was accepted as a change towards better programmes, better reception and a closer relationship between the needs of listeners and the output of the broadcasters. The BBC, for its part, accepted the need for better public relations and positive efforts to research the tastes, habits and problems of the audience. Nonetheless, the reins of control for the regional programmes were still held tightly in London. Regional broadcasting stations were restricted in the range of the programmes they could produce and in the size of their budgets for new initiatives. By 1939, few inside the BBC would have argued that a regional service was not an essential adjunct to the main National Programme although, as the Report on the Regions showed, a great deal of potential was left untapped by the restrictive nature of BBC central control.

Chapter Two

THE MEANS OF LISTENING

Wireless Equipment

Early radio receivers suffered from serious technical limitations and made good reception very difficult to obtain. The
crystal set was the most popular of the early receivers
because it was the cheapest, easiest to operate and crudest
form of listening. No power supply was needed and the only
components were an aerial, an induction coil, a crystal
detector and a pair of headphones, as Figure 2.1 shows. The
signal transmitted reached the aerial and set off a sympathetic oscillatory current, the wavelength of the aerial being
adjusted to match that of the incoming signal by altering the
length of wire in the circuit at the point where it is wrapped
around the coil. The resultant current was then detected by
the quartzite or carborundum crystal, which was set in
motion. The minute currents were then transmitted by a
spiral of copper wire or 'cat's whisker' to the headphones.
    The crystal set was clearly very easy to build and home
set construction quickly became common. Many simple
explanations of the method of construction and operation were
made available by specialist wireless periodicals and local or
national newspapers in the period between 1923 and 1925.[1]
The circulations of the specialist periodicals proved that, for
a short time at least, this method of obtaining a set was very
popular.[2] It can be guessed that the set builders of the time
were willing to overcome some simple technical barriers in
order to satisfy the eager desire to 'listen-in' using the most
economical way possible. The disadvantages were numerous.
Because the sets relied upon the power of the transmitter,
they were extremely insensitive. For the $1\frac{1}{2}$ kW stations,
sets had to be within a fifteen mile radius for any kind of reasonable reception and a hundred miles was the maximum for

Figure 2.1: Circuit Diagram of a Crystal Detector [3]

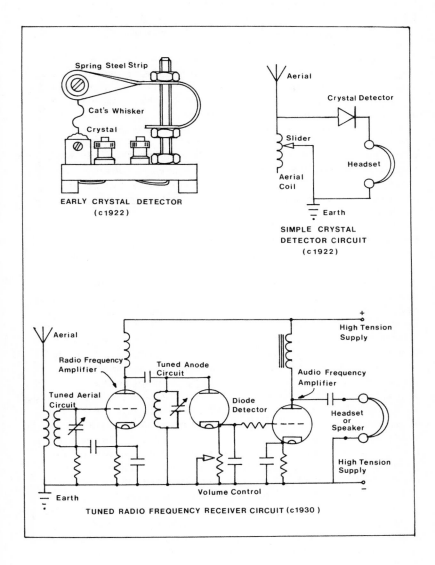

Figure 2.2: Circuit Diagram of a Valve Set [4]

the Daventry long wave transmitter. They were also incapable of separating signals of equivalent strength, unless these were widely separated on the waveband. The GPO normally laid down restrictions on the length of aerial which could be used - a hundred feet being specified among the restrictions listed on the back of each licence.

The crystal set was soon obsolete - a fragile and unreliable instrument at the best of times - the crowding of the airways increasingly interfered with reception, particularly with the introduction of the Regional Scheme. Dwellers in urban areas frequently found that they could not receive sufficient signal strength and the alternative programmes could not be separated by the insensitive detectors. A wavetrap could be fitted to filter the signal but this presented more complex technical problems for the average listener and was, in any case, not always successful in cutting out unwanted signals. [5] The crystal set was then very quickly laid to rest, lingering on only in the hands of the very poor, of those in areas not yet reached by the Regional Scheme or, more often, in the hands of the enterprising schoolboy. One or two even found a resting place in the local museum. [6] The valve set quickly replaced the crystal set for 'listeners-in' as the first listeners called themselves. It amplified the incoming signals and was much more sensitive. Such sets were more complicated to build especially as technical improvements were made. Nonetheless, most of the articles about home construction were devoted to this type of set throughout the twenties, in the heyday of the wireless magazine. [7]

The valve set needed a power supply to provide the thermionic valve with enough energy to amplify the incoming signal. The valve, invented by Fleming in 1904 and developed as the triode by de Forest in 1906, was essential for good quality transmissions of speech and music. [8] At first, the valve set was only essential for reception at distances outside the normal crystal range - where amplification and selectivity were required to provide audible sound without interference. Eventually, the sheer volume of transmissions and the resultant interference, along with the addictive search for better reception, led to a rapid conquest by valve sets. It became the minimum equipment necessary to benefit fully from the BBC service. In some areas modified crystal sets were quite successful but generally they were declared redundant as the Regional Scheme was progressively applied. [9] Precise figures do not exist but it seems safe to say that few crystal sets remained in the early thirties and loudspeaker sets were virtually universal. [10]

Improvements of valve sets over crystal sets were numerous and more were added continuously throughout the period before 1939. The use of multi-valve sets increased, with anything from six to nine valves being used. By 1930, valve technology was sufficiently advanced to make two or three valve sets the normal arrangement for satisfactory amplification. Portables and electric mains sets appeared for the first time in 1924. By 1932 mains sets were sold in greater numbers than battery sets and thereafter formed a majority of new sales before 1939. [11] Radiograms first appeared in 1927 and they, too, soon acquired a sizeable share of the market.

Many other inventions also considerably improved performance, the quality of sound, the selectivity and sensitivity of the receiver. The moving coil loudspeaker first appeared in 1927 and soon replaced the moving magnet loudspeaker in all but the cheapest sets. [12] The most significant of the inventions was the exotically named supersonic heterodyne. The 'superhet', as it was known, used an oscillator within the set to heterodyne the incoming signal - in other words to convert it to a lower frequency for improved amplification and tuning. [13]

These improvements made sets smaller, more compact and more portable - all advantages to encourage more listeners. Early portable sets sold well during the first boom for portables in the summer of 1925. [14] Other technological changes outside the purely radio sector also had beneficial effects. The first sets relied on batteries or accumulators but the rapid expansion of mains electricity permitted the use of mains converters to transform the mains current into a suitable power supply. The introduction of standardized voltages permitted the transformers and rectifiers to be fitted as integral parts of the sets, [15] but these were more expensive and accumulator sets were only gradually displaced during the late thirties. [16] The main disadvantage was that the accumulator normally needed recharging at the local radio or bicycle shop at least once a week and this became an established part of British life.

The growth of mains electricity also increased the amount of interference from other household appliances and most electrical goods had to be fitted with suppressors. [17] The motor vehicle also became more widespread and its ignition system needed suppressors. An older and more established form of public transport also caused serious problems: in 1932, urban tramways accounted for 60% of the complaints to the BBC about electrical interference. [18]

However, the main source of interference was that induced by the incorrect use of the receiver. This type of interference or 'oscillation' was caused by the method of positive feedback or 'reaction' applied to the tuning coil of the receiver. The valve began to oscillate and this oscillation was transmitted by the aerial, producing a localised but extremely annoying, high pitched whistle which often cut out a station altogether. Oscillation soon became the bane of listening. The 'super-het' made things worse since it used feedback oscillation in the amplification of the signal, and a badly adjusted 'super-het' was a very efficient method of jamming signals over a local area. It was only in the thirties with the introduction of a radio frequency (RF) amplification stage, placed between the detector valve and the aerial, that the problem was satisfactorily resolved. [19]

Oscillation is an important part of the social history of radio. It was a great distraction at a time when the technical problems of listening were of paramount importance, whilst programme policy or content were secondary considerations. 75% of the correspondence to the BBC complained about oscillation and related problems during the twenties[20] - 15,000 letters in all. [21] The BBC wrote pamphlets advising listeners on how to prevent the problem. The issue was discussed in the national press and in specialist periodicals. It also filled many of the wireless columns of local newspapers. [22] 'Oscillators', as the offenders were called, were also subject to vigorous lampooning as Figure 2.3 shows.

The Cost of Listening

The expense of the annual licence fee was a considerable influence on the growth of listening. The original receiving licence used by experimenters with no transmitter capacity was introduced in July 1922, and cost ten shillings. From the 1 November 1922, a new licence was introduced for general listeners: the Broadcast Licence, also costing ten shillings. The ordinary listener now had three choices. He or she could buy a set with the BBC stamp on it (see Figure 2.4), indicating that a royalty on the set had been paid to the BBC, and obtain the Broadcast Licence; or, buy an Experimenters' Licence and build a set from separate components, thus avoiding the royalty legitimately; or, simply evade the licence altogether. [23]

Figure 2.3: Oscillation Cartoon 1929[24]

DETECTIVES LOCATING AN OSCILLATOR

Reproduced by permission of the British Library

In January 1923, the flood of listeners taking out the old style Experimenters' Licence led the GPO, under pressure from the BBC,[25] to refuse their issue, unless the applicant could prove an interest by technical qualification or knowledge. Membership of an amateur wireless society was not, in itself, regarded as proof of experimental ability. For applicants failing to meet its technical criteria, the GPO suggested a special 'Constructors' Licence, at ten shillings but the BBC refused to accept this since it allowed avoidance of the royalty payment on a finished set and encouraged the use of

Figure 2.4: BBC Royalty Stamp, 1922-24

components which had also evaded the royalty. The BBC
pointed out that small manufacturers could fulfil the conditions of the BBC stamp and royalty by becoming a member
of the Company, after payment of a £1 share. Inevitably
however, smaller firms saw no advantage in joining a
company dominated by the 'Big Six' - manufacturers who had
founded the BBC: Marconi's, Radio Communication, Metropolitan Vickers, Western Electric, British Thomson Houston
and the General Electric Company. Only four hundred firms
joined, many stayed out and the main offenders - the imported set and component manufacturers - remained unaffected
by any BBC restrictions. [26]

With the solution of this impasse in mind, the Postmaster-General recommended the formation of a committee
of inquiry and this was established under the chairmanship of
Major-General Sir Frederick Sykes on 24 April 1923: the
first departmental committee of inquiry on broadcasting. The
terms of reference were very wide-ranging but the main aim
was to solve the problem of those building their own sets.
The committee had to work quickly, since approximately
33,000 applications for the Experimenters' Licence were
held under embargo. The committee reported in August
1923, [27] and recommended an end to the system of royalty
payments with the introduction of a universal ten shilling
licence. However, the findings were suppressed until the
GPO and the BBC could apply these recommendations in a
formal agreement.

This was reached on 1 October 1923. It possessed all
the characteristics of the classic British compromise.

Until 31 December 1924 there were to be three licences: royalties on sets would also continue. There would be the ten shilling Broadcast Licence as before, with the conditions concerning the BBC stamp. There would also be a fifteen shilling Constructors' Licence: the licencee giving an undertaking that in constructing apparatus, equipment manufactured outside Great Britain would not be used. The third licence was intended to cover evaders, caught in the previous bureaucratic trap. It would also cost fifteen shillings but no questions would be asked about the nature of the equipment.[28]

The period of confusion thus came to an end. In fact, the fears of the 'Big Six' about trading prospects were quite unfounded. Trade moved ahead at such a pace that on 1 July 1924, the BBC terminated the alternative licences and introduced a universal ten shilling licence.[29] The royalty payments came to an end on the 31 December 1924 as previously agreed.

This struggle over the licence was very significant: the collective power of six large industrial firms, with their legalised monopoly and powers of royalty and licence revenue collection, came to naught against the irresistible pressure of wireless set constructors, led by the press and the wireless experimenters. The strength of determination to listen also gave some indication of the pleasure that radio reception aroused. The success in beating the royalty system must have helped to induce many more listeners to take out licences. Evasion, where it did take place, was partly due to the bureaucratic barriers which deterred licence holding during the course of the dispute in 1923-1924. It was also due in part to ignorance. Some thought that crystal sets did not need licences, and others that only one licence was needed for each building whereas the household definition was applied by the GPO.[30]

The story of the Broadcast Licence is an excellent example of a voluntary response to a specific form of taxation. Consent through parliamentary representation was only indirect - because, formally, the GPO collected it on behalf of the BBC. Before the creation of the Corporation, it could be argued that it was unethical for a government department to collect money on behalf of a private company. Some other constitutional considerations were also raised, since the licence was arguably raised for a specific purpose, yet considerable parts of the revenue were withheld for purposes other than GPO collection costs.

The voluntary aspect was important in the case of the

Broadcast Licence. The powers of detection and coercion were more limited than for other forms of taxation. There was no check at the point of purchase and there were, in any case, too many home constructors. Until the GPO made detector vans available and began prosecuting evaders, the payment of the licence depended entirely on a spirit of altruism. [31] Certainly the BBC felt that the lack of coercive action led to large scale evasion. Reith advocated instalment payments to help poorer listeners but this was rejected by the GPO. [32] He also demanded much tougher action against evaders. One black spot was Northern Ireland. As the BBC complained,

> The local traders assume that there are 120,000 sets in use and licences are approximately 25,000 ....
> I very much hope that you will be able to do something about the matter - it is really appalling. [33]

Sheffield was another area, and one resident, Mr. R. M. Ford, caused a minor furore in November 1924 by openly challenging the GPO to prosecute him for evasion. The case attracted some publicity and Reith was concerned that this form of open civil disobedience would spread. He pressed the GPO to act quickly and firmly. [34] However, the emphasis in BBC appeals against evasion was placed upon moral obligation rather than the threat of legal action. For instance, Savoy Hill advised Station Directors to transmit an appeal along the following lines:

> We are aware from licence figures that many people are not taking out licences, and that the so-called pirate or the man who lets other people pay for his pleasure is on the increase.
> We need hardly remind our British audience that it is unsporting and unfair to let other people pay for a service which is, for what is given, the cheapest possible form of entertainment.
> If you know of people who are listening without a licence, your best action would be to indicate to them that it is not in any sense of the word honourable for them to receive our entertainment at other people's expense. [35]

Wireless set prices had some influence on the level of set ownership. Throughout the period, there was usually a wireless set on sale to suit almost any pocket but not all sets gave value for money. At the beginning, with the very expensive sets available, the purchaser was paying for a slight improvement in the efficiency of reception and a very large increase in the finish, quality and size of the cabinet which held the set. The crystal set in urban areas was not necessarily inferior in the quality of reception. It was only with the introduction of the Regional Scheme that a high efficiency set became essential in many parts of the country. Then valve sets were required, the cheapest crystal set became obsolete and price became a considerable determinant of set ownership.

In the period 1922 to 1929, a casual glance through the local press advertising reveals the enormous price differentials at the very beginning of public broadcasting. In Oxford, valve sets cost as much as 49 guineas (£51. 45) for a large valve set called the 'Wootophone' produced by F. W. Wootten Limited, of High Street, Oxford, [36] and £73 for a similar set made by the rival Oxford Wireless Telephony Company. [37] Crystal sets ranged from £2. 10s. to £7. [38] A nationally available set, the 'Gecophone' made by General Electric, was advertised at £2. 10s and this seems to have been a good average price for 1923. [39] Small local firms in Oxford had already moved into this market and were selling their own sets as early as 1922. [40] This increased competition and completed crystal sets were normally about £1 although a set as cheap as 7s. 6d. , was on sale. [41]

Even at this price it was still possible to make savings. A key factor in reducing the prices of finished sets was the competition from wireless component traders supplying the home constructor. The crystal set was simplicity itself to construct and, if this was done at home, the labour cost and retailer's profits were partially avoided. The number of home constructors is quantifiable for 1923-1924. In 1924 there were 284, 500 constructor's licences and 224, 500 interim licences. [42] If allowance is made for evaders and the result multiplied by the average size of family then there must have been approximately 2. 2 million listeners to such sets in the spring of 1924. [43]

Another indicator of the home construction boom was the rise of the wireless magazine. Almost all of these, including the respectable Wireless World, included articles providing a step by step guide to the construction of a crystal or valve set. [44] A certain amount of technical skill was required and some special tools needed, but if the constructor was within strong crystal range and had some determination, then even the most ham-fisted individual could build at least a crystal set. Valves presented more problems but detailed plans, photographs of the processes and step by step guides took some of the pain out of construction for those without technical skills. [45]

The circulations of the specialist wireless magazines were considerable in the mid-twenties, giving some indication of radio's wide appeal. The readership would have been somewhat in excess of the circulation, assuming quite fairly that many magazines were read by more than one person. Of the weekly magazines, Modern Wireless, price one shilling, and Popular Wireless, price three pence, were amongst the largest with circulations of 125,000 each in the autumn of 1924. Amateur Wireless, price two pence, sold 100,000 copies per week. [46] Radio Press was the market leader amongst the publishers. In November 1925, its monthly magazine, Wireless Constructor, price sixpence, [47] had a peak circulation of 253,000 whilst Wireless, its weekly stable companion at two pence, produced 450,000 copies for its first issue and averaged 150,000 copies per week. [48]

For a brief period in the twenties, the expansion of the wireless industry and wireless audience was reflected in these periodicals by enormous excitement and interest. At the peak, from 1924 to 1926, an average of thirty monthly or weekly specialist magazines were on sale. Some were enduring but the majority were rather ephemeral. [49] The enthusiasm of the editors and their staff was tremendous. Radio Press described this atmosphere in the Wireless Constructor:

> This magazine has brought thousands of new readers into contact with Radio Press Limited. From now on you will be our friends and we do not want you to think that the Radio Press is a cold-blooded publishing company. It is not. It is a collection of the keenest wireless enthusiasts - names known throughout the world - the authors of articles translated, because of their merit into a dozen different languages.
>
> If you knew us you would realise the feeling of responsibility we have. What we say goes out to 450,000 readers every month in our three papers. We realise our influence, and we never intend to let you down. [50]

The proprietor, John Scott-Taggart had already sold 500,000 books on wireless in his own right by 1925. [51] He even turned his hand to manufacturing valves. [52] Both the Wireless Constructor and its rival the Wireless World, were so saturated with correspondence from curious readers that limits had to be placed on handling the letters. [53]

An example of the work of these magazines shows the appeal of wireless to good effect. The <u>Wireless Constructor</u> showed how to construct the 'Crusoe Crystal and Valve Set'.[54] Economy and simplicity were the essentials. The only expense was the wire, costing 2s., the crystal at 6d., and, the most expensive item, the headphones at around ten shillings. The valve conversion of the set would cost anything from 10s., to £1 for the valve and £1 to £2 for the accumulator. Three pennies were also needed to help form the grid condenser - wrapped in waxed paper and held with a paper clip. [55]

The introduction of the Regional Scheme was a tragedy for many crystal set owners and there is no doubt that the need to employ a valve set in urban areas, which had hitherto enjoyed good reception on primitive equipment, affected low income listeners most severely. Newspaper advertisements provide some clues to the kind of prices a potential listener could expect to pay for an efficient radio set. In 1931, for instance, Curry's offered some typical examples in their annual sale. Two-valve sets were priced at 29s. 6d., (£1. 47½) and three-valve sets at 59s. 6d., (£1. 97½), or if hire purchase was preferred 1s. 6d., (7½p) weekly. Elsewhere accumulators cost 6d., per week for hiring and charging, whilst a typical mains set cost twelve guineas (£12. 60) or 4s., per week. [56] In 1935 Curry's offered several sets ranging from £5. 15s. to twelve guineas or 1s. 6d., per week. Sets were generally more expensive than in 1931 and the range was somewhat more limited. [57]

However, a full explanation of cost constraints is only possible in relation to incomes and the cost of living. Unfortunately, patterns of wireless set sales by quantity, value and price between 1918 and 1939 are not fully available. [58] Consequently another, less precise, approach must be used to provide an outline of wireless set sales. If the average price of the cheaper sets for the twenties is taken as a crystal set at between £1 and £2 and, for the thirties, a valve set at £5 to £6, some idea of the target is established. To match this against disposable income available for such consumer durables is more problematic. Between the wars, two of the largest occupational groups were agricultural workers and miners. Incomes for these groups of manual workers normally fell into the band £1. 10s., to £2 per week during the period between 1918 and 1939. [59] These figures are only relevant if they are related to the cost of living and

hence deflation by a weighted index of retail prices is
necessary to give the real earnings. Broadly speaking, real
earnings rose gradually from 1923 to 1935 and declined
slightly between 1935 and 1937. [60]

Needless to say the period 1930 to 1933 was the period
of the greatest numerical increase in wireless licence holding.

To calculate how much of £1.10s., was actually available for expenditure on consumer durables is difficult to
assess. Obviously, it had a lower priority than food, clothing
and rents. The desire to purchase a set and spend 10s., on
the annual licence would also have been blunted by short time
working or unemployment. Anything which would eat into the
surplus income set aside for luxuries and entertainments
would affect the ability to buy a set. Since unemployment
never fell below one million in the period and rose as high as
2.7 million in 1932, this has to be considered as a restriction
on set ownership for a sizeable body of people. [61]

There was a brighter side. Households with more than
one income earner were more likely to have a surplus for
expenditure on sets. [62] Overtime working was possible in
some industries to add to basic earnings and provide a surplus for such luxuries. Methods of purchase could be changed.
Rather than save for one cash payment, long term payment
by instalments could be arranged. Hire purchase deals
began in the twenties and were widespread in the thirties,
although some purchasers would be lured in this way to buy
sets that they could ill-afford - simply because the price was
so deceptively attractive. [63]

A wireless set could also be seen as a long term invest-
ment, which would save expenditure on rival forms of information or entertainment: on newspapers or on visits to the
pub or cinema. Radio was not necessarily a direct competitor for other entertainments, indeed it frequently stimulated
interest in them, but radio could provide one of the cheapest
retreats for a long winter evening - in terms of cost per
hour of entertainment.

In 1939 the working class was still under-represented
in the audience and the residuum was not fully absorbed until
the introduction of the 'utility set' in 1944. With this reservation, radio had made tremendous advances and was very
close to becoming a universal medium of communication. As
the BBC observed in its Handbook for 1940, out of nine million
licences, 4.2 million had been taken out by those on incomes
between £2.10s., and £4 per week: two million licences were

held by those earning less than £2.10s. [64]

The Radio Industry

The radio manufacturing industry had an important part to
play in the expansion of listening. The listener had many
sets to choose from, while competition and technological improvement eventually permitted reductions in the price of
some sets. However, in 1935 the Ullswater Committee on
Broadcasting criticised the radio manufacturing industry for [65]
its failure to produce a really cheap set for the mass market.
The reasons for this failure seem to lie in the structure of
the industry. Most of the market was controlled by monopoly
interests which sought to maintain high profit margins
through price fixing. The remaining demand was soaked up
by a plethora of small firms, able to sustain higher prices
provided the market continued to expand.

By founding the British Broadcasting Company, the six
largest manufacturers had a clear advantage in the radio
market. Marconi's, in particular, had great influence
because of the company's control of a large number of vital
wireless patents. Even the largest rivals were obliged to
take out expensive licences for their use. This gave
Marconi's a great financial as well as technological advantage. [66] In theory, the Broadcasting Company was not
restricted to the 'Big Six'; other companies were entitled to
join, provided they made the commitment to pay royalties
to the BBC on sets and components - the royalties being
intended to underwrite the expansion of the transmission side
since none of the larger firms expected the licence revenue
to be adequate. [67] In practice, few firms would accept these
terms and tolerate the domination of the large manufacturers.

Royalty payments could be expensive. From the formation of the BBC in October 1922 until 1 October 1923, royalties ranged from 7s.6d., for a crystal set to as much as
£3.5s., for a three valve set, whilst loudspeakers were
charged at 3s. [68] From 1 October 1923 to the abolition of the
royalty on 31 December 1924, a revised tariff applied:
crystal sets were now charged at 1s.0d., two valve sets at
17s.6d., and three valve sets at £1.2s.6d. [69] The BBC
stamp was affixed to sets and components on which the royalty had been paid:[70] its main purpose, apart from raising
revenue, was to preserve the market exclusively for British
firms. With an example of blatant protectionism in an era of
supposedly free trade, the GPO refused to issue a licence
for sets manufactured outside Britain. The restriction

continued with the constructor's licence and only ended with
the termination of the royalty payments. The main enemy
was the well established industry in the USA which could
easily undercut any British rivals. In fact, overseas supplies
reached home constructors, thus undermining the royalty
system and contributing to its downfall. The GPO initially
encouraged protectionism to ensure that the transmitting side
of broadcasting was adequately funded, without GPO support.
In return for this monopoly, dividends were held down at $7\frac{1}{2}\%$.
Otherwise there was no real attempt to prevent the monopoly
keeping prices at high levels.

The restriction on profits did, however, lead to a distinct loss of interest in maintaining the Company: compound-
ed as it was by the level of foreign competition in the home
construction market. However, the real death blow was
dealt by the public response to the introduction of a national
broadcasting system. The pessimistic forecasts of 1922
were shattered and the sales boom exceeded all expectations.
The Crawford Committee's report in favour of formal public
control of broadcasting was received by the manufacturers
without any serious animosity. [71]

The formation of the Corporation marked the end of
direct influence by the manufacturers on the transmitting
side of broadcasting, and confined them essentially to activities on the commercial side. The effects of lobbying were
limited. The big manufacturers were now only one of many
voices and a united front was necessary to staunch the decline.
The large firms were already joined together in the National
Association of Radio Manufacturers, formed in 1923. The
smaller firms outside the Broadcasting Company were
members of the British Radio Manufacturers and Traders
Association. On 6 September 1926 they joined together as
the Radio Manufacturers' Association (RMA). [72] The organisation fulfilled the usual trading functions and represented
the manufacturers in meetings with the BBC. It also submitted evidence to the Ullswater Committee. [73] The RMA
consistently pressed for brighter programmes from the BBC,
hoping that this would increase sales amongst the relatively
untapped working class audience. It also turned a blind eye
to the support which many of its members gave to commercial
stations, such as Luxembourg and Normandie, in the hope
that this, too would stimulate trade. [74]

Once the market for radio sets was established,
smaller firms proliferated and helped to soak up demand.
Despite the impact of the newly permitted imports, the

twenties saw the growth of all manner of makeshift radio set and component manufacturers. [75] This small-scale operation led to instability in supply and a wide variation in technical standards - all exceedingly inconvenient for the potential consumer. Many finished sets were inferior to the best of those constructed at home. [76] There was a considerable turnover in the numbers of firms. As early as 1923, a minor slump in trade, caused by the uncertainty during the dispute over the licence fee, was enough to lead to a small flurry of bankruptcies. [77] Because of the localised nature of many small firms and their sales, some areas suffered more than others but the effect is impossible to measure. Perhaps the lack of standardisation and the financial insecurity of the industry affected consumer confidence. Generally, however, it seems to have been of temporary concern since licence holding continued to increase at a greater rate.

The reign of the larger manufacturer was only restored properly in the thirties, as the valve set came into its own to meet the new conditions created by the Regional Scheme. The larger manufacturers had the capital to weather any temporary slumps in demand and possessed the reserves to invest in the production of more complex sets. In fact, the demand from consumers continued to exceed all expectations and considerable profits were still to be made. The industry shared the good fortune of the whole electrical sector and remained buoyant throughout the depression of 1929-1933. Early fears about the level of import penetration of the wireless market were clearly unfounded. The success was noticeable enough for the Labour Research Department to turn its eye to the radio industry - with allegations of vast profiteering. The condemnation was sweeping:

> Although a large proportion of the total trade is held by a comparatively small number of firms, the wireless industry is a stronghold of the small employer who rigs up any old shanty in which to house his cheap boy and girl labour. The retailer's profit in the trade is exceedingly high and the heavy demand stimulates the growth of the small mushroom employer. [78]

Trimming labour costs was one way of keeping price competitiveness but generally more savings could be made from the economies of scale in mass production; exploiting technical developments and new materials, such as Bakelite, to keep profits up and reduce costs. The larger manufacturers did best and continued to try and remove opponents in

51

Table 2.1: The Wireless Trade in Figures[79]

(a) Sales of Sets by Price in 1932

Battery Sets	Sales	Mains Sets	Sales
£6.10. & under	262,412	£12 & under	142,864
£6.10. - £13	301,954	£12 - £17	352,901
£13 +	88,442	£17 - £23	142,476
		£23 - £30	104,254
		£30 - £50	35,071
		£50 +	6,475

(b) Wireless Set Sales 1930-1933

Date	1930	1931	1932	1933
Battery Sets	450,100	738,000	652,808	376,440
(of which portables)	(163,700)	(217,000)	(99,424)	(?)
Mains Sets	199,000	519,660	784,041	591,360
Total	649,100	1,257,660	1,436,849	967,800

(c) Types of Receivers Produced in 1931:

Details	Production Figures	
	Mains	Batteries
Two Valve Set	107,000	164,750
Three Valves	230,000	52,650
Four Valves	84,050	168,850
Multi-Valve	36,250	53,850
Home Constructor's Kits	- - - -	298,450
Radiograms	61,400	- - - -
Totals	519,600	738,550
Grand Total	1,258,150	

order to restore the monopoly, so that price levels could be held up and profits maximized. Even some of the original six companies were absorbed, although a few of the smaller concerns survived surprisingly well before 1939.

Production and retail statistics give some idea of the rapid growth of listening from a different angle. Despite their scarcity these useful statistics create a clearer impression of listeners as consumers. They demonstrate the changing pattern of sales from the domination of home construction, to battery sets and finally to mains sets. They also show the distribution of sales by price giving a very broad guide to the likely social composition of purchasers. Such statistics must be used with care - their collection may not always have been reliable and they lack correlation with the actual use of sets. Licence holding and audience research provide a much more precise guide to listening behaviour.

Some other areas of industrial activity had considerable social influence. These included advertising, the design of sets, radio exhibitions and retail distribution. Advertising can yield useful information about pricing, sales and technical developments in the radio industry but it is also of interest in its own right. At first, advertising in newspapers assumed a purely informational role. References were made, quite bluntly, to prices, the choice of sets and where they might be demonstrated or purchased. [80] Soon the style changed. Price competition was one influence and often the hire purchase arrangements received more publicity than the actual price - with the down-payment printed in the largest type. [81] At the same time special events were seized upon as sources of good advertising copy. The start of the first formal broadcasting season in January 1923 was an obvious choice. From then onwards it became quite normal to prepare potential customers for the autumn season and the long, tiresome winter nights ahead when radio came into its own. [82] Later, the replacement set market had to seize on special events in order to encourage people to change sets when there seemed no other sensible reason for doing so. The favourite events in the period included such obvious commercial occasions as Christmas but also General Elections, the 1926 General Strike and particularly the 1937 Coronation.[83]

Another method used to persuade the customer to replace his or her set, or to coax the suspicious individual into purchasing a set for the first time, was to emphasise the technical advances in new models. New types of valves,

Figure 2.5: Wireless Set Design, the Ecko AD65 of 1934[84]

Victoria and Albert Museum, Crown Copyright.

mains adaptors, portables, direct mains sets, super-heter-odynes and radio gramophones were all displayed prominently as attractive advances, combinations or variations which would make the set more useful to the customer.

Some advertisements for sets were 'works of art' in their own right. Radio advertising did not reach the creative heights of some other industrial products or alcohol and tobacco but there were some interesting artistic and photographic achievements. Manufacturers soon realised that visually appealing advertisements drew the consumer's attention and could be influential in establishing a strong sales image for the company. They were also increasingly aware of the importance of set design. Crystal set design was normally entirely functional and the exceptions were, therefore, all the more remarkable. One set of 1922 was a classic: a Grafton China Figure in the shape of a gentleman wearing a top hat, the bow-tie served as the crystal, the watch chain was the cat's whisker, the base was fitted with the headphone connections and the top hat served as the coil. Another crystal set appeared as a book called appropriately the 'Listener' by 'E. R. Fone'. [85]

It was with the valve sets that fiercer competition encouraged manufacturers to employ designers to improve the aesthetic appearance of the set. With the very early valve sets the main intention was to disguise the equipment as a piece of furniture. With the introduction of more manageable sets, particularly those without the cumbersome accumulators, it was sensible to treat the design of the set as a way of asserting radio's individual quality. In the competition for markets, particularly in the late thirties when the rate of growth in licence holding declined, the aesthetically pleasing as well as the practical set would win over the consumer. At first, design was limited to the improvement of control facilities, such as clearer tuning dials with illuminated panels listing the main stations and their wave-lengths. From then on firms decided to give designers their head. Using traditional materials or, more often, exploiting the flexibility of new materials like Bakelite, a whole new vista was revealed. Murphy employed a furniture designer, Gordon Russell, whilst E. K. Cole (Ecko) employed architects, Serge Chermayeff, Wells Coates and Misha Black. [86] The aesthetically pleasing set sold well particularly in the replacement market and radio firms continued to search for new designs to use on their latest models. Inevitably this stimulated the design industry - a process helped by similar moves through-

out the electrical appliance industry. Lacking the attraction
of any of the really major technical advances which had
characterised the earlier days of radio, sets simply had to
sell by appearance as much as by performance. Pevsner
reflected on this important consideration when he analysed
Serge Chermayeff's design for Ecko in 1933 as an example
of industrial art:

> The shape of it was something completely new, nothing
> comparable existed, either in England or abroad. It
> was the result of a careful study of function and a gen-
> uinely artistic imagination. The firm is thus breaking
> away from all traditions, took a great risk, and some
> opposition within the firm had to be met. If sales did
> not exceed 10,000 sets in the first year, it would be a
> serious failure. What happened remains as an im-
> mense credit to the English public. The new cabinet,
> so uncompromisingly functional in appearance became
> exceedingly popular almost from the first month.
> About 100 per cent more sets were sold in the 1933-34
> season than in the previous season. [87]

A contributory factor in this success was radio's increasing acceptance as an aural centre-piece in the home.
It fulfilled a human psychological need for this sound to
emerge from what was also a satisfactory focal point: something which had a pleasing character of its own. [88] Set design
began as a commercial operation but its success and perpetuation pointed to some important changes in social attitudes.
The wireless set was no longer a magical box owned by some
technically-minded fanatic. Now it was an essential household commodity, separated from other consumer durables
by the cultural contribution which it could make. The public
demand for attractive sets thus emphasised the prominence
which wireless had gained in domestic life and leisure.

'Radiolympia' was another important method of boosting
sales. Olympia was first chosen to hold a radio exhibition
in 1926. [89] It attracted an enormous amount of publicity and
very quickly it became essential for manufacturers to produce a new model in time for the annual show, held to coincide with the autumn broadcasting season. At its peak,
between the mid-twenties and the late thirties, 'Radiolympia'
was a major social occasion. [90] It attracted large crowds
from the public as well as from the retail trade and generated
a good deal of free publicity for radio in the press. The BBC

not only had a stand but also put on a special performance at the show for the benefit of the visitors. [91]

This kind of publicity certainly contributed to the eventual saturation of the market. Some bought sets because of the novelty value of listening, some were probably seduced by the advertising and persuaded to buy sets beyond their means but, increasingly, the market was composed of listeners looking for better sets, with a diminishing minority without sets who were constantly reminded of the presence of radio and felt more and more excluded from a necessity of everyday life.

Relay Exchanges

An alternative method of listening to radio was by relay. The relay exchange was similar to a large radio set to which loudspeakers in the homes of subscribers were linked by cable. By this means a very efficient high quality set could be installed at a central point and the running cost shared amongst as many as could be conveniently connected to its loudspeaker terminals. [92]

This had important social implications. The normal method of payment for such a service was by weekly rental. This was an incentive for working class individuals who wanted to listen. They could rent a relay service rather than buy a set - even with the increasing availability of hire purchase. There was no need to have a domestic electricity supply or to run a battery power pack to be able to listen to a relay loudspeaker and this could be an advantage at a time when mains electricity supply was by no means universal. [93] Aerial wires were also unnecessary, and in urban areas a relay set was a useful defence against local interference from trams or domestic electrical appliances. The relay system offered solace to the technically backward. As the then former Chief Engineer of the BBC, Peter Eckersley, remarked:

> The listener has no bother either in operating and maintaining a complicated wireless set which, to women especially, is often frightening and mysterious. It is the reliability, simplicity and cheapness of rediffusion which makes it so popular. [94]

The system had other advantages over normal radio listening. In many areas the poor quality of reception from the transmitter facilities provided by the BBC due to a weak signal or shipping interference, could be considerably enhanced by relay.

There were some disadvantages. The subscriber was
obliged to listen to the programmes which the relay exchange
chose to broadcast and in some cases only a single channel
was provided, although the average was a choice of two
channels and in a few cases there were three. Normally the
channels would be made up of BBC programmes but it was,
of course, possible to make up the service with the best programmes broadcast by foreign stations, including the commercial stations. Apart from this limitation on freedom of
choice, there was also the physical confinement of relay
exchanges to densely populated areas. The cable connections
were not a practical proposition for rural areas, given the
distance to be covered and the resultant cost. Moreover, for
all subscribers there was the denial of portability - the loudspeaker had to be kept at home. Poorer subscribers still
had to consider the compulsory annual payment of ten
shillings for the broadcast licence.

Relay exchanges were introduced commercially in
Southampton during 1924. A. W. Maton charged 1s. 6d. per
week but had only extended the service to twenty subscribers
by August 1926. From these small beginnings the number of
exchanges and subscribers grew at a steady but limited rate
before 1939 - with only minor fluctuations. Considering the
advantages of relay exchanges this rate of growth was not
very impressive. By 1931, for instance, there were 132
exchanges with 43, 889 subscribers, but this meant that only
1. 01% of licence holders used this method for listening. By
1935, the number of exchanges had risen to 343, with
233, 554 subscribers, but this was only 3. 15% of licence
holders. Of course, it is important to relate subscribing to
the likely level of listening. Between 1935 and 1939 the
number of listeners rose from 0. 95 million to over a million,
assuming the normal multiplier of persons per private family.
This gives a more accurate picture of listening but even this
was, nonetheless, disappointing for the relay companies.

The pattern of relay exchange distribution was very
uneven and some areas did take up relay exchanges to a much
greater extent. In the case of the eighteen exchanges with
more than two thousand subscribers, there is a clear concentration in areas such as the South West, the South coast, the
North East coast, Humberside and the North West. All of
these areas had a poor provision of conventional radio facilities - such as the North East - or were subject to very high
levels of coastal interference such as Plymouth, Brighton

Table 2.2: The Growth of Relay Exchanges, 1927-1939[95]

Date	Exchanges	Relay Subscribers	Subscribers Multiplied by Persons per Private Family*	% Subscribers to Licence Holders
Sept 1927	10	446	1,784	0.02
Dec 1928	23	2,430	9,720	0.09
Dec 1929	34	8,592	34,368	0.29
Dec 1930	86	21,677	86,708	0.64
Dec 1931	132	43,889	165,462	1.01
Dec 1932	194	82,690	311,741	1.57
Dec 1933	265	130,998	493,862	2.19
Dec 1934	318	192,707	726,505	2.84
Dec 1935	343	233,554	955,899	3.15
Dec 1936	333	250,978	958,736	3.15
Dec 1937	331	255,236	975,002	3.01
Dec 1938	325	256,294	979,043	2.89
Dec 1939	284	270,596	1,033,677	3.04

* For assumptions used in this calculation see Table 1.1:

and Hull. Most relays were found in urban areas - London having twenty-two exchanges, four of them with over a thousand subscribers. Within these urban areas concentrations of subscribers could be found particularly in blocks of flats - where local interference was a problem - and new council estates - where a relay exchange could be fitted very conveniently during construction to offer an economical service for the residents. [96]

A BBC investigation of relays revealed many of the obvious advantages to subscribers - such as ease of operation and better reception - and also quantified the economics of relay subscription. The investigation showed that the average payment was £4 per annum or 1s. 6d. per week. This was a marginal improvement on the terms offered by a typical hire purchase agreement. Of course, the subscriber would be spared extra costs such as the outlay on an aerial or battery and maintenance costs would probably be less. There were, inevitably, some cheaper relays and those operating at 30s., per annum or 7d., per week were clearly good value. [97] But the subscriber to a relay exchange would need to pay continuously rather than for a limited period. Thus the flexibility of radio would probably be preferred to the relay set where costs were equivalent and no special listening conditions applied.

Relays denied freedom of choice for the consumer because the selection of programmes was made at the exchange usually on the basis of known operating loads acquired from power consumption meters fitted to the exchanges. Thus, there was normally a bias towards programmes of majority interest; any other choice would have been commercial nonsense. [98] In poor reception areas there would be an advantage, since choice would already be effectively denied, but in many areas the real gain would be in listening to overseas broadcasts. Relays gave the chance to listen to foreign programmes in poor reception areas and also in good reception areas where conventional sets could not compare with the quality of reception for long distance broadcasts achieved by the relay exchange. Considerable listening to foreign stations was revealed by Rowntree's study of listening to the relay exchange in York. [99] The radio critic, Garry Allighan, used the electrical meter readings of the seven leading relay exchanges to show that the percentage of listening to the BBC on Sundays varied from 10% to 35% compared with 40% to 80% for continental stations. [100] Research at the Mansfield relay exchange showed some interesting loadings on weekdays: in the morning peak, 50% of the listening was to foreign broadcasts of light music, with only 25% listening to the BBC. At 7.30 p.m., 30% of listening went to foreign stations with 50% listening to the National Programme. It was only after 8.00 p.m. that the BBC succeeded in picking up 95% of listeners by broadcasting a variety show on the Regional Programme.[101]

The growth of relay exchanges was often obstructed by official intervention. If a relay company wished to establish an exchange in an area it had to seek local authority permission. Sometimes companies vied with each other to offer the best payment to the authority in return for permission to erect the necessary cables. However, permission was often refused, usually because of the unsightliness of the cables. This argument had a slightly feeble ring to it since urban areas were increasingly acquiring trolley bus, electric and telephone cables. The real reason probably lay in the resistance of local interests in radio and electrical retailing which would have been adversely affected by the intrusion of relay exchanges.

The most serious barriers were, however, presented by the GPO and the BBC.[102] The BBC wanted to control the relay companies because it felt that the companies, by allowing foreign programmes to be broadcast, disrupted the Corporation's programme balance.[103] This was broadly the case presented by the BBC to the Ullswater Committee. On the other hand, the GPO retained licensing control over the relay exchanges and opposed the BBC wholeheartedly. For instance, in October 1931 the BBC reached agreement with two large relay companies to rediffuse only BBC programmes but the Postmaster-General refused to countenance the deal on the grounds that this would be an unfair extension of the monopoly to listeners who would be denied the right, held by conventional licence holders, to listen to other, non-BBC, programmes.[104] Unfortunately for the relay companies, the GPO was not willing to allow exchanges to relay their own programmes - such as the broadcasting of local civic events - nor would it permit programme sponsorship.[105]

The Ullswater Committee on broadcasting gave the relay companies an opportunity to make their case against such restrictions through their representative body, the Relay Services Association of Great Britain (RSAGB).[106] The RSAGB was ably assisted by the former Chief Engineer of the BBC, Peter Eckersley, representing British Insulated Cables Limited, (BICL).[107]

These efforts were unrewarded. The BBC assisted by the Radio Manufacturers' Association opposed the RSAGB and the Ullswater Committee did not suggest any relaxation of controls. Instead, the committee recommended that the GPO should take over the ownership and operation of the relay exchanges. [108] The Government prevaricated, however, and its response to the Ullswater recommendations on relay exchanges, the White Paper of June 1936, delayed the final decision. The threat of compulsory purchase continued but the GPO licences were extended for three years whilst the GPO undertook experiments to improve the quality of rediffusion. The exchanges were allowed to continue their relays of commercial and other foreign broadcasts, but where a choice of channels was provided, one channel had to be confined to BBC programmes. [109] This was important for the listener because it placed the relay subscriber or potential subscriber in a state of almost complete uncertainty. Before Ullswater, the exchanges had been continuously at the mercy of short term GPO licences. With the capital commitment of an exchange, greater security was essential if an efficient service was to be provided. The original novelty of the relay exchange had meant that the first formal licence was only conceded hurriedly in 1926. Thereafter the licence terms were restricted first in 1930, again in 1932 and finally, with the publication of the White Paper, still further restrictions were proposed. [110] Each change or brief extension of the licence, left the exchanges and their subscribers in a state of further bewilderment. An expensive commitment could be lost over-night and any potential subscribers lost confidence in the service. After Ullswater the trade stagnated and equipment was not renewed. Some exchanges closed down and the service deteriorated.

GPO experiments to improve the relay systems were attempted in the Southampton area but these were severely hampered by a combination of technical difficulties and the resistance of the local council to the extensive excavations needed for the underground cables. [111] These experiments were a further example of the way in which public interest in relays was checked. The most effective use of the system was never allowed and its technological potential greatly restricted. [112] GPO experiments were also devoted to a suggestion, supported by the Ullswater Committee, that telephone or electricity wires should be used to carry signals from relay exchanges. This would have saved the enormous expense of a separate cable network and would have reduced the unsightly proliferation of overhead wires. The resultant saving in cost would have made relays more competitive and simultaneously reduced the number of local authorities which resisted the provision of a relay service. Peter Eckersley had first suggested this in the mid-twenties and his book, The Power Behind the Microphone, was virtually a crusade for this cause. Unfortunately the Electric Lighting Act of 1882 and the Telegraph Act of 1869 effectively combined to prohibit the use of such cables for this purpose. The electricity companies were prevented by the GPO from supplying electricity to the relay exchanges if electric or telephonic cables were employed for relaying broadcasts. Although the two Acts pre-dated the invention of radio and could not, therefore, have intended its restriction, attempts to reform this Victorian legislative quirk were defeated in Parliament.[113]

The reluctance to reach a firm decision on the application of the technological developments in relays reduced Eckersley to sheer frustration. After Ullswater, BICL cancelled its research and there was no further progress before the outbreak of war. Eckersley's vision of an audible spectrum, free of interference, at first supplementing the existing system and then superseding it completely, was totally unfulfilled.[114]

Relay exchanges rarely fulfilled their promise of cheap and efficient reception of radio programmes. With only 3% of licence holders using rediffusion, their service was clearly a minority concern. Although some technical problems were encountered, in most cases their development was discouraged by the indifference or active hostility of national and local authorities. Furthermore, the BBC ran an effective campaign to diminish the reputation of relay exchanges and their controllers. The opprobrium poured upon the relay exchanges by the various authorities is nowhere summarised more effectively than by a Times leader printed during the debate on the White Paper of 1936:

> What is certain about the relay system is that, under present conditions, it will spread both widely and rapidly among the poorer classes of the population; and this country will not for long be able to congratulate itself on a broadcasting system under which, while broadcasting is controlled with enlightenment and impartiality by a responsible public corporation, the listening is controlled by Tom, Dick and Harry.[115]

Chapter Three

WIRELESS ORGANISATIONS

Origins

As broadcasting developed, organisations were created to
further its cause and press for a regular public service.
Several of these organisations emerged to represent the
specific needs of wireless users and listeners. Whereas
other groups with an interest in broadcasting had some other
specialist field as a common basis for action, such as music,
drama or journalism, specialist wireless organisations
usually had no point of contact or common interest other than
broadcasting itself. These wireless organisations provide
useful information about the audience response towards
broadcasting, both before and after the foundation of the
British Broadcasting Company. Because their primary
purpose was to influence wireless telephony and broadcasting
activities, they were often the most important critics of the
new company. As effective opinion leaders, they provided a
clear indication of many of the wider public attitudes towards
broadcasting. They initiated well organised campaigns, representing widely shared grievances, and contributed to
public knowledge about the possibilities of broadcasting by
their practical example and by the effective way they publi-
cised their technical achievements. If the development,
structure, methods and policies of these organisations are
examined, the important social consequences of their actions
for the emergent radio audience can be recognised.
    Wireless organisations fell into two main categories:
there were those which catered for individuals interested in
the technical aspects of radio, such as the building of sets
or the participation in transmission techniques, and normally
some level of technical proficiency or certainly some aptitude
would be required; for the non-scientific, wireless united an

extremely disparate group of people into general listener organisations, and normally their aim was to formulate
critiques of programme policy and present them collectively
to the BBC and the public. Often these societies provided
some form of protection for the non-technically minded
through the provision of technical advice services which
arranged for visits to the member's home and the offer of
wireless set insurance schemes. Otherwise, the two types
of society had many similarities of aims and interests. Each
society developed some theory of control for the broadcasting
system, and usually this meant more representation for
audience interests in the programme planning stage. This
aim was not purely selfish in origin - the societies wanted
the representation of many interests, not simply their own.
Nor did they seek to break the autocracy, which they saw in
the existing British Broadcasting Company, merely to replace
the fetters with anarchy. There was a general appreciation
of the technical complexities and a realisation, derived from
the example of conditions in the United States, that a chaos
of interference and jamming would result if some restrictions on civil liberty were not accepted. [1] The concept of a
public service monopoly was grudgingly conceded, albeit
never fully accepted, by all of the societies. [2]

On a more practical level the societies were active in
publicising radio: to educate the public in the correct use of
wireless sets and encourage a more informed appreciation of
the full potential of broadcasting. Societies also took voluntary action to allay public fears of exploitation, by the
registration of retailers in wireless equipment. Shops were
given plaques to indicate that they were approved dealers.

There were conflicts between the societies. The introduction of a full broadcasting programme each day meant
that there was a clash of interest between those members of
non-specialist societies who wanted BBC programmes continuously, and those specialists who wanted silent periods to
permit reception of their transmissions. Conflict arose
from the distaste which the non-specialist felt for the alleged
snobbery of the technically minded cognoscenti and for the
caricature image of manic enthusiasm which, it was popularly
assumed, all amateurs possessed. [3] In fact, the non-specialist societies owed their separate creation in part to the
belief that the technical societies were too committed to their
work to deal with other questions and because it was thought
that they would be condescending in their relations with the
uninitiated listener. [4]

Specialist Organisations

The London Wireless Club was founded on the 5 July 1913.[5]
Essentially, there were two motives for founding such a society: to encourage the interchange of technical information
amongst wireless enthusiasts[6] and, secondly to provide a
basis for political lobbying to free wireless transmitters and
receivers from government licencing controls and other
similar restrictions on broadcasting. Other societies had
been founded as early as 1911 but they had too few members
and were too scattered geographically to be able to apply any
serious political pressure.[7] The London Wireless Club was
closer to the reins of power - geographically if not otherwise - and had the potential to provide a proper nucleus for
the co-ordination of an efficient lobby with a consequently
greater chance of success.

In 1914 the outbreak of war and the introduction of the
Defence of the Realm Act brought the activities of these societies to an abrupt end. Equipment was impounded and transmissions were forbidden.[8] When hostilities ended most
societies had to begin again completely from scratch. There
had, however, been considerable pre-war gains. A line of
communication with the authorities at the GPO had been
opened, there had been some realisation of the need for coordinated action by the societies and each society had managed to contribute something to publicise the cause of wireless and broadcasting. What was lacking was a sufficient
level of broad public contact. The societies were very much
confined to the specialist and the technician. There was no
trace of pressure for a national public broadcasting system
and the lobbying had concerned itself wholly with the grievances of a small band of enthusiasts. In August 1914, for
instance, only 2, 150 wireless licences were current.[9]

The war changed this basic deficiency in numbers and
expanded the potential influence of the societies. At the outbreak of war and increasingly as the conflict proceeded,
amateurs were in great demand as the backbone of the
developing military use of wireless telegraphy.[10] This use
of wireless produced many more skilled technicians who, on
leaving the armed services, sought to continue their professional experience as amateur experimenters or even broadcasters.

This potential was to be realised only slowly. Because
of this massive expansion in wireless use by the military and
the perpetuation of the full provisions of DORA after the

67

cessation of hostilities, the Government was extremely re-
luctant to lift its specific restrictions on any non-military
uses of wireless. [11] Wireless amateurs were trapped in a
vicious circle. Well-organised wireless societies operating
in unison were needed to press for a relaxation of the legal
constraints but the suppression of wireless activity had a
debilitating effect on membership. The London Wireless
Club, now renamed the Wireless Society of London (WSL),
did not revive until October 1919 and by December 1921 the
society had only added another 118 members to the pre-war
level.

Nonetheless many interested non-members did not for-
get their war-time experience so easily. Quantification is
difficult, but there were many thousands who had worked in
wireless communications during the war and some of them
continued to show interest. Individuals operating alone could
still have an influence even where it was confined to ad hoc
guidance in the immediate locality. If societies lacked
members, they could still organise themselves more effectively to make their views felt more strongly in government
circles. One method of coalescing the disparate, localised
energies of the re-emerging societies was an affiliation
scheme. The WSL was the foundation stone and in January
1920 the society successfully approached several other
societies. The first annual conference of wireless societies
took place on 27 February 1920. Just fifteen affiliated
societies attended but the conference achieved immediate
success when Commander Loring of the GPO spoke to the
assembly, and promised a rapid relaxation of some restrictions on wireless transmitting licences. [12]

The attendance of a GPO official was typical of the
closer relationship which the societies began to enjoy with
government bodies, the press, armed services and manufacturers at this time. Amateur enthusiasts were drawn from
the ranks of MPs, GPO employees, journalists, naval personnel and manufacturers. [13] Common interests permitted
an understanding of the technical questions involved and
provided a means of applying more effective political
pressure to resolve the grievances of wireless amateurs.

After the First World War the essential grievances of
the amateurs concerned the restrictions on transmission and
reception licences, the refusal of the GPO to permit the sale
of thermionic valves and the limits placed on the use of
simple equipment such as telephones and spark coils. [14] Only
when some concessions on these practical problems had been

made could the enthusiasts turn towards the provision of a public broadcasting service. The GPO objections were a function of fears held by the government communications service and the armed services. Both the GPO and the amateurs accepted that the proliferation of wireless meant some controls would still be needed, but the myths derived from wartime experience were not broken easily. Immensely tortuous bureaucratic barriers were raised against criticisms by the amateurs - the services feared for the secrecy of their transmissions, they worried about the jamming of important signals and considered that overcrowding of the aether would hamper the government should any new emergency arise. [15]

At first, the GPO was prepared to lift the pettiest restrictions. Some equipment used in telegraphy was permitted to be sold freely - although the widespread commercial use of such equipment had already made the regulations difficult to enforce. Receiving licences charged at ten shillings per annum were issued to those using receiving sets, but aerials were limited to one hundred feet and valves could only be employed with special permission from the Postmaster-General. [16]

More consequential concessions came in April 1920 when, as promised, the GPO permitted the use of transmitters with various limitations on aerial length, wavelengths, hours worked and total power emission limited to ten watts. Candidates had to be British citizens and be able to demonstrate their capacity for genuine scientific research. The WSL received such a licence on 7 April 1920. Other individuals, pressing their claims as bona fide scientific researchers received rather more tardy attention. By March 1921, there were only 150 transmitting licences and 4,000 receiving licences. [17]

In the winter of 1920-21, therefore, the amateurs were able to begin serious experiment with telephony. They could now make proper tests by communicating with each other at the times allowed and on their own wavelengths - around 180 metres - to avoid interference with official signals. There were some grounds for self-congratulation. Largely through their own efforts, the societies had freed wireless from many restrictions. They had broken down the pernicious control of DORA and successfully challenged the myths propounded by the military concerning jamming and interference. Once amateur transmissions had begun it proved to be possible for the two sides to coexist. At that time there was only the faintest suspicion that an increase in the number of experimenters might also increase the amount of interference. By August 1921, for example, it had already become necessary to arrange a meeting of amateurs transmitting in the London area to prepare voluntary constraints on transmitting times to reduce interference. [18]

Amateur activity showed that there was a market for wireless equipment. In lieu of adequate commercial supplies, amateurs were snapping up all kinds of surplus wartime equipment: the favourite being the short wave Mark III set, sold at between £4 and £5. A typical commercial set at the time, such as the Burndept or the BTH two valve, could cost anything up to £35. Price was therefore a considerable disincentive to anyone thinking of taking up the hobby without the ability to build equipment. [19] Eventually, manufacturers were stimulated to increase production and reduce prices through the economies of large scale production needed to meet the growing market. Many amateurs became employees of such firms: others founded their own manufacturing companies, or moved into the growing specialist wireless periodical market.

Another part of the amateur success came from their growing contact with the national press. At first, the press maintained its interest in a rather casual way: marking the main concessions from the GPO with ad hoc articles. Progress in wireless technology was described with considerable technical ignorance, sensationalising new steps as part of the conquest of the 'magical' medium. [20] For the specialist reader, the wireless societies succeeded in gaining access to column space in the English Mechanic, the Electrical Review and the authoritative wireless magazine, the Wireless World. The paper directly encouraged the formation of more societies and attempted to attract new members by publicising the activities of existing societies. [21] There was also the useful provision of technical advice and lists of amateur transmitters and their wavelengths. [22]

The wider implications of the work of the societies at this time were only slowly appreciated. The societies speeded the arrival of public broadcasting by their experiment and development in telephony. Further, they contributed to the future success of broadcasting by demonstrating to the public that broadcasting was a practical proposition. Even if their sole achievement had been to keep up the pressure on the authorities and maintain interest in the science, then the contribution of the societies would still have been considerable.

In fact they were able to contribute more than this, but it would be wrong to see the societies setting out purely as agitators for the introduction of a public service broadcasting system. This pressure took some time to develop because in the beginning it took a strong imagination to foresee the full potential of radio. It was only after post-war research in Britain and the United States had developed new equipment that these prospects emerged.

Efficient organisation contributed to the success of the societies as a political lobby although their limited size and specialised membership made them distinctly élitist in appearance. Paradoxically, this élitist image was matched by a heterogeneous social composition. The WSL and all the other societies drew their membership from the widest possible spectrum of society. In London, admirals rubbed shoulders with factory workers but even the average society united solicitors and businessmen in a common cause with labourers and shop assistants: the strength of their technical interests cut through class barriers.

In the spring of 1921, the amateurs resumed their political campaign. At the second Annual Conference of Wireless Societies held on 1 March 1921, the amateurs prepared a formal request for a regular telephonic transmission service. [23] In this instance the amateurs worked more closely with the manufacturers. The Marconi Company held a general licence to experiment in wireless telephony and during 1920 had successfully managed several tests, including a regular series between 23 February and 6 March 1920, when a half hour programme was broadcast daily. [24] However, the undoubted highlight of the test series was the concert by Dame Nellie Melba broadcast on the 15 June 1920 from Chelmsford. The use of a famous operatic singer attracted more attention to wireless than ever before. [25] It was important because it demonstrated the prospects for wireless as a public broadcasting system which could entertain as well as inform, and did much to break down the prevailing view of the uninitiated that wireless was a telegraphic medium of relevance only to armies, navies and shipping companies.

The amateurs had their part to play because only they could receive the test transmissions and pass on the news of their success to the rest of the public, through the local and national press. [26] Indeed one of the functions of the tests was to prove to the GPO that a potential audience existed for such broadcasts. Despite the proof that one did, the GPO was

more influenced by complaints about interference. As each
broadcast required special permission, the number of these
broadcasts was gradually reduced until, under pressure from
the armed forces, the Postmaster-General banned them altogether. [27] The amateurs had to fall back on the growing
number of broadcasts from European stations such as Radio
Paris, Radio Eifel Tower or PCCG of the Hague, or muse
wistfully about the more privileged position of listeners in the
United States. [28]

Marconi's were reduced to making telegraphic calibra-
tion signals and this increased the pressure from the amateurs for more telephonic broadcasts. They duly began to
lobby the GPO. The response was icy. The Postmaster-
General pointed to the example of the USA as a case of widespread interference caused by a lack of planning and control
which, if repeated in Britain, could cause chaos. The amateurs understood his fears but did not regard them as an
argument for preventing regular broadcasting altogether. [29]

At the Second Annual Conference, the Post Office representative, Commander Loring, had spoken in reply to the
demands of the participants:

> As to the possibility of regular telephony transmission,
> that will be favourably considered by the Post Office
> when it is put forward, but we do not altogether like it
> coming from the Marconi Company, as it puts us in
> rather an awkward position. It would come very much
> better from the Wireless Society. The Marconi Com-
> pany's representatives will, I am sure, understand
> what I mean. The application will be much easier for
> us to deal with if it comes from an organisation like
> the Wireless Society than from a firm. We cannot
> give the Marconi Company preferential treatment over
> any other firm, so that if they asked for permission to
> send out for half an hour every week, half a dozen
> other companies could come along, and we should have
> to give them similar permission, whereas if the Wire-
> less Society of London were to apply it would make it
> much easier for us. [30]

The wireless societies were therefore presented with
an opportunity to force the pace simply because they were the
only serious amateur representatives of the radio audience
at that time. Unfortunately, the informal pressures suggested by Loring did not coax the GPO into concession particularly
quickly, and a stronger, more public course of action was

chosen. The societies reached the zenith of their influence with their petition to the Postmaster-General, F. G. Kellaway MP, presented on 29 December 1921. The signatories to the document included sixty-five affiliated societies, representing 3,300 members out of an estimated 4,000 licence holders. [31]

Concession was now more rapid and at the Third Annual Conference of Affiliated Societies on 25 January 1922 it was announced that the Marconi Company had been authorised by the GPO to begin telephony programmes for half an hour each week. The radio station, call sign 2MT, at Writtle began operating on 14 February 1922. Writtle was a victory for the amateurs but it also proved to be the final verification for the manufacturers that a regular broadcasting service would attract a commercially viable audience. Within weeks any residual fears were swept away and 'Two Emma Toc' became an institution for the rapidly growing amateur fraternity. [32]

The Writtle experiment was dominated by Captain P. P. Eckersley. His programmes captured the imagination of all who listened and satisfied the demand for entertainment which had been so sadly missing from the airways (see Figure 3.1). He and Noel Ashbridge had been amateur enthusiasts and both went on to become Chief Engineers at the BBC - an example of the assistance provided by the amateurs in supplying a pool of skilled technicians. Eckersley was, however, able to make a further contribution as an entertainer, establishing what might be possible if the system was adopted on a larger scale.

The net effect of the Writtle tests was to accelerate the arrival of public broadcasting. The prospect of the tests had been enough to boost receiving licence holding up to 6,986 at the beginning of February 1922. The membership of radio societies also grew quickly: from a total of 3,300 members in 65 societies in 1921, numbers rose rapidly to an estimated 30,000 members in 180 societies in December 1923. [33]

The amateurs had broken through an inertia barrier. Although the American experience was reasonably well known through coverage in the press, the general awareness about the real prospects for broadcasting needed to be increased by the experience of wireless in Britain itself. The wireless amateurs were able to show through their reception of Writtle that public broadcasting was a practical possibility and not a scientific miracle of the future conjured from the pages of a novel by H. G. Wells. [34] Without the practical demonstrations

Figure 3.1: 2MT Writtle in 1922

APRIL 1, 1922   THE WIRELESS WORLD AND RADIO REVIEW   xi

CQ de 2MT!

The ENGLISH CONCERTS

 **TUESDAY EVENINGS - $\frac{1}{4}$ kW**

THE MARCONI SCIENTIFIC INSTRUMENT COMPANY, LIMITED, cordially welcomes the co-operation of amateurs in making these Concerts, and the telegraphic transmissions following them, of real interest and usefulness to all.

Information regarding reception will be appreciated, and communications will receive individual acknowledgment. Where desired, the Company will be glad to advise upon points presenting difficulty.

The Programme, as arranged at present, is indicated below :—

STATION CALL-   -   -   2 MT
„   LOCATION   -   WRITTLE, near Chelmsford

TIME (G.M.T.)	TYPE of TRANSMISSION	λ (metres)	POWER
1900—1925	Telephony	700	$\frac{1}{4}$ kW.
Including 5 intervals each of 2 minutes	C.W. Calibration Signals	1000	1 kW.
Followed by	,, ,, ,,	,,	$\frac{1}{2}$ kW.
	,, ,, ,,	,,	$\frac{1}{4}$ kW.

LISTEN IN!

The MARCONI SCIENTIFIC INSTRUMENT Co., Ltd.
OFFICES & WORKS: **21-25, ST. ANNE'S COURT, DEAN ST.,** } **LONDON, W. 1**
SALES & ENQUIRIES: **40, DEAN ST.**
Telegrams THEMASINCO. WESTCENT   Telephone : GERRARD 7745 (Pvte. Bch. Ex.)

provided by the amateurs, many people would not have had
the vaguest idea of the capacity of broadcasting: they could
not know fully what they wanted from it until they had heard
it for themselves.

The amateurs were barred from the negotiations on the
creation of the public broadcasting system between the
Postmaster-General and the six large manufacturers which
began on 18 May 1922. There was a definite feeling of exclusion - suspicions about the motives of the negotiators were
aroused. The only contact with the progress of the negotiations was derived from the public statements made by the
negotiators. [35]

During the protracted course of the negotiations, the
amateurs kept broadcasting alive - indeed they attracted
many more members to their societies - and found plenty to
interest both themselves and the general public. They organised public lectures and exhibitions throughout Britain. At
the Third Annual Conference of Affiliated Wireless Societies
held in London in 1922, the Sheffield Society put the case for
public lectures:

> We have felt that if, say, once at least during the
> session, we could get some very prominent man to
> come down either from London or elsewhere and give
> us a paper with practical demonstrations, it would be
> very much to the benefit of the Society. We have cer-
> tainly proved that at Sheffield during this last session.
> We had one Marconi Company man down, and he gave
> us an excellent lecture with demonstrations, and when
> I say that we filled a hall with 400 people and we could
> have filled it twice over as we made it a semi-popular
> lecture, I think that indicates the general enthusiasm
> which would be shown in almost any town with a society,
> if such a scheme as the one proposed were carried out
> properly so that it would come on the ordinary pro-
> gramme. [36]

A new publicity opportunity was created with the opening of
the All British Wireless Exhibition and Convention held under
the auspices of the WSL at the Horticultural Hall, Westminster
from 30 September - 7 October 1922. [37] However, the amateurs had to come to terms with their ambivalence towards
public broadcasting now that it was an imminent reality.
Many amateurs realised that a serious conflict of interest was
in prospect - between the demands of amateur experimenters
and the demands of the ordinary listener, content to listen

passively to the public broadcasts. This new listener would have no interest in transmitting and, indeed, was likely to be positively hostile to any interruptions in his service necessary to permit experimental work.

Interference was already a serious problem. Amateur frequencies were changed from 1,000 metres, which interfered with government installations, to 150-200 metres and 400 metres in May 1922. Unfortunately this was only a temporary respite. It soon became clear that the public broadcasting system would jam the 440 metre band for many amateurs and confine them to wavelengths below the 200 metre band which were then considered to be useless for serious broadcasting.

Further it was clear as early as May 1922 that some distinction in the licensing arrangements would have to be made between the two types of listener. As Wireless World observed:

> No doubt full consideration has been given by the authorities to the possibility of serious interference if the wireless telephone receiving sets supplied to the general public are of such a nature as to permit radiation. This point is still more important when we consider that the vast majority of those who will be installing wireless telephone receivers in the near future will be ignorant of the most elementary points of wireless theory, and will operate their sets entirely by rule of thumb. It would seem desirable that in issuing permits for the reception of telephony, that the Postmaster-General should make a very marked distinction between permits for experimental wireless and permits for the installation of a set where the user merely desires to avail himself of the broadcasting service. [38]

The GPO realised that the conflict of interest could not be resolved in favour of the experimenter, simply because of the disproportionate weight of numbers. The first action came with the creation of two distinct licences: an experimenter's licence and a broadcast receiving licence, by which means the GPO was able to reduce the opportunities for new listeners to take out experimental licences. Before November 1922, this had been a virtual formality. Now strict criteria of technical knowledge and controls on set construction were to be introduced by the GPO. If the amateurs could not prevent interference from their sets when listening to Writtle, then the technically ignorant listener would cause chaos if allowed similar freedom. [39]

Amateurs were very surprised at the rapidity of the changes brought about by the introduction of a full broadcasting service in November 1922. Many amateurs could not come to terms with the loss of their leadership of the wireless audience. The most obvious and irritating effect of broadcasting for the amateur was that experiments on the 440 metre band were effectively banned between the hours of 5.00 p.m. to 11.00 p.m. when the BBC was operating. However, some amateurs, including Hugh Pocock, the editor of Wireless World, accepted reality and prepared to seek some form of compromise which would allow experiments to continue in the shadow of the public service. [40]

All was not lost for the amateur cause. The seeds of a new conflict for the amateurs to fight were sown in the structure of the new licensing system. [41]. Those who built their own sets and avoided the BBC royalty, but could not demonstrate satisfactorily to the GPO that they had any experimental interests, fell into a twilight zone outside the licensing system. The amateurs now had a battle to fight as the leaders of this considerable body of less technically-minded listeners and backed the GPO in its proposal for the introduction of a third type of licence to cover these home constructors.

During the spring of 1923, the WSL began to change its structure to meet the new demands. A change in nomenclature helped to reform the image of the society: the WSL became the Radio Society of Great Britain (RSGB). The Society hoped to gain more strength by the use of a more precise description of its interest and by appearing to possess a proper national character. Status was acquired by adopting the Prince of Wales as patron and a more democratic system adopted, incorporating members of affiliated societies on central committies for the first time. [42]

When the Sykes Committee was established to look into the licence problem on 24 April 1923, the RSGB was strongly represented. [43] D.H. Eccles, President of the Society, and Sir Henry Norman MP, a member of the Society, were selected to serve. The RSGB's evidence was presented on 7 June 1923 by A.A. Campbell Swinton. He advocated a relaxation of the restrictions on the experimenter's licence, a thirty minute silent period each evening to facilitate tests and the introduction of a scheme to educate listeners on the uses and abuses of wireless listening. The royalty system was condemned as 'exploitation of the public', although the

RSGB did not object to some restriction on imported components for their own proposed licensing scheme. This plan involved the use of four licences - a simple broadcast licence and an experimental licence, both charged at 10s. , together with a constructor's licence at £1 and a special licence for broadcasting in public places charged at £5 to £10. [44] The RSGB recommendations did not have the imagination of some proposals to the committee - Herbert Morrison and the London Labour Party, for instance, advocated full public control and greater audience participation in the broadcasting system to replace the manufacturers' monopoly[45] - but in the end, the solution to the licence problem followed the lines of the RSGB suggestions more closely than could have been expected. The Sykes Committee recommended a uniform licence fee of ten shillings but further pressure from the members of the Broadcasting Company persuaded the Postmaster-General to use a three-tier licensing system as an interim measure before the adoption of the Sykes recommendations in full. [46] If anything, the GPO was firmer in resisting the manufacturers than the RSGB and the suggested constructor's licence was eventually introduced at fifteen shillings. Superficially, the eventual solution to the licence question appeared to be a victory for the RSGB. However, the Postmaster-General was already pre-disposed to favour an end to the royalty payments and confine listening to the experimental licence and a broadcast licence, both charged at a uniform rate. As the Postmaster-General, Joynson-Hicks, remarked to the BBC Board:

> The home constructor will represent the less wealthy portion of the population, and it would be, in my view, ridiculous to charge the ten shilling licence to the man who may purchase from your Company a £100 receiving set, and the twenty shilling licence to the lad who desires to make at the lowest possible price a Crystal Set for his own use and experiment. [47]

During the course of the licence campaign and particularly with its solution in September 1923, the RSGB lost considerable influence in the audience lobby. With the surge of new licence holders in October and November 1923, the amateurs were well and truly swamped. The number of affiliated societies began to decline and, by the end of 1925, total membership had fallen to approximately 10, 000. [48] They concerned themselves more and more with their own special problems, especially the shortage of free transmitter time. Dissentions emerged and considerable coaxing proved to be necessary to quell a rebellion within the RSGB.[49] Eventually, their minority position within the audience was digested and begrudgingly accepted.[50]

This change in role had become quite apparent with the publication of the Crawford Committee's Report on Broadcasting in 1926.[51] The amateurs were no longer an élite, leading opinion, but simply a lesser power amongst many. Other specialist societies had grown up and taken their place alongside the RSGB to represent those whose interest in wireless was less technically involved.[52] In fact the RSGB prevented the array of audience representatives from presenting a common front. The RSGB ran against the interests of all the other witnesses by requesting a silent period during peak listening times on weekday evenings. But, besides this important distinction, the RSGB, shared the view of most of the other wireless organisations: that public control and greater audience participation were essential for the future of broadcasting.[53] As Sir Capel Holden stated when presenting the Society's evidence:

> The Society considered that the following features in
> the constitution of the BBC were anomalous: (1) that
> there is no representation on the directorate of the
> public, who supply all the revenue, and (2) that the
> directorate consists solely of representatives of manu-
> facturing interests which are thereby in a position to
> dominate the direction of wireless development in this
> country ...... Seeing that broadcasting is or may be
> used as a powerful weapon for propaganda of any sort,
> the Society is strongly of the opinion that it should
> not be entrusted to the hands of a private Limited
> Liability Company.[54]

This was no more than what proved to be the prevailing orthodoxy. The contribution from Reith and the BBC proved to be far more decisive in winning over the Committee.[55]

The founding of the British Broadcasting Corporation in 1927 seemed to augur well for the RSGB. Continuous consultation appeared to be possible through the BBC's new Wireless Organisations' Advisory Committee. Unfortunately the Committee possessed no real influence during the course of its short existence. The influence of the RSGB rapidly fell away. It was now marked off from the rest of the audience by the barrier of the technical language which its members spoke and by the increasingly sophisticated knowledge of radio which was required of participating members.

By 1935, when the Ullswater Committee met to review
the BBC's Charter, the RSGB had so little to say about public
broadcasting that it was no longer amongst the list of those
giving evidence. [56] The weakness of the amateurs led them to
resume the role they had held in the era between 1918 and
1921. They returned to the area of experimental radio research, examining the capacity of radio waves over long
distances and at various frequencies, particularly in the short
wave bands. This work usefully covered areas neglected by
the public sector and was to have immense value in the post-
war years when very high frequency radio was used for public
broadcasting, and personal communication. The amateurs
were first to prove that it was possible to use such frequencies successfully.

The only direct beneficiaries of this work before 1939
were listeners overseas. In the earliest days, the work of
the radio amateurs had possessed a clear international
character. [57] They were also keen to extend their contribution to long distance reception and transmission. Public
imagination was soon captured by 'spectacular' feats of
listening to American stations such as KDKA Pittsburgh or
WJZ New Jersey purely because of the sheer distance
involved and the possible implications for international communications. [58] For amateur transmissions, the first transatlantic contact was made on the night of 8 to 9 December
1921, when a test held under the auspices of the WSL was a
great success, thanks mainly to the efforts of an American,
Paul Godley. From then on rapid progress was made and two-
way telephony achieved in the 'Transatlantic Test' held during
December 1923. [59]

With this success it was only a matter of time before
telephonic experiments extended the repertoire of those
broadcasting in the short wave bands. On 1 September 1927,
G. N. Marcuse, an amateur based in Caterham, Surrey, began broadcasting under a special GPO licence to many parts
of the world. [60] His station, G2NM, was heard as far away
as Australia. The BBC pressed by this example, began their
own tests in November 1927 with station G5SW at Chelmsford.[61]
The amateurs frequently claimed that it was only through
their pressure that BBC Empire broadcasting began at all.
Certainly the BBC appeared to procrastinate, since regular
broadcasting to the Empire commenced from Daventry as
late as December 1932. On the other hand, the BBC delayed
because it lacked political and financial support from the
government. When the final decision was made to go ahead

with the scheme, a considerable financial burden had to be borne by the BBC solely from its existing income. [62]

The primacy of the technical organisations was brief. Their influence was greatest in the period 1922-1926 when broadcasting was in flux. At that time the audience was uncertain and turned to such knowledgeable individuals and organisations for advice. The amateurs provided the nucleus for an expanding interest in radio; acting as a catalyst for the early growth of the audience by helping many to build sets or to purchase suitable equipment. After this initial stimulation, the BBC's authority was more effectively exerted and certain technical trends made the advice of amateurs largely superfluous. Sets became more complex, more efficient and more reliable. The cheaper, ready-made product rendered home construction unnecessary. This was matched by the increasing complexity of sets, particularly after the demise of crystal sets, which severely reduced the ability of many to handle the components. Manufacturers could now genuinely offer a viable commercial product which would not require any skill to operate and could be marketed in the same way as any other consumer durable. There was little room for the amateur here.

Moreover, after three or four years of broadcasting the audience began to consider the programme content rather more, especially since it was unfettered by the earlier obsessions with the sheer logistics of listening. The RSGB was wholly unsuited to commenting on programme content and hence other pressure groups, the press and other kinds of wireless organisations assumed a more important role in demonstrating audience interest in broadcasting. The amateurs reverted to their original role as a small, cohesive lobby of specialists and professional engineers committed to communications research.

Listener Organisations

In August 1922 another wireless organisation was founded in an attempt to bridge the gap between the broadcasting authorities and the technically unskilled listener - interested rather more in programme content than in the complexities of advanced wireless technology. This organisation, the Radio Association, was founded to lobby for a regular public broadcasting service. [63] Once this service was created, the Association was joined by several analogous organisations which emerged to represent those listening to the new British Broadcasting Company.

In this sense such bodies were subordinate to the broadcasting system - in complete contrast to the RSGB which would have survived reasonably happily without the BBC. Typical members of these non-specialist organisations generally did not have the transmitter capability to sustain themselves independently from the public broadcasting system. This was compensated by a keen devotion to broadcasting - the enthusiastic listener wanted some means of expressing his opinion on the quality, choice or arrangement of the output. There was considerable frustration at the lack of representation for listeners at the BBC and the BBC's failure to meet this emerging audience requirement stimulated the growth of these organisations. [64] Many were conscious of the monopoly control which the manufacturers held on public transmissions and desired the balanced representation of other interests on the board of control. [65]

Such opinions were held most strongly from 1922-1927 when the broadcasting system was seeking to establish itself. It was an experimental period with some uncertainty about the future course of broadcasting. It was in this period that this type of wireless organisation was born, reached its prime and began to wither. The Radio Association was reasonably typical. Under the chairmanship of Lieutenant-Commander J.M. Kenworthy MP, it grew slowly to a maximum strength of 3,000 members in 1925. It claimed to have 41 provincial and 12 metropolitan branches. [66] Essentially, it provided a service for ordinary non-technical members but had some unrequited aspirations to become the main professional association for wireless engineers and technicians.[67]

The Wireless League was an altogether larger affair, with a better eye for mass support and publicity. Originally it was a product of Lord Beaverbrook's fertile brain. Certainly it was meant to further his ambition to break the BBC monopoly and establish his own broadcasting station - but Beaverbrook changed his mind. By July 1925, the League was largely independent of the Daily Express and under the chairmanship of Sir Arthur Stanley. It now adopted a rather less hostile approach to the youthful BBC, supporting the public service character of broadcasting and cordially presenting its criticisms to the Managing Director. [68] The Wireless League had an extensive national network. At the end of 1925, the Wireless League claimed 80,000 members and 150 branches. [69] Socially, it was probably rather middle class, having a membership fee of two shillings per annum. However, this did not make it necessarily more articulate or exclusive.

One leader, Professor A. M. Low was anxious to deflect such criticisms: 'A large proportion of our members use the crystal set and they do not, as a class, express their opinions by letter to the BBC'.[70]

The other contemporary organisation was much smaller and less important. This was the Wireless Association of Great Britain formed under the chairmanship of Lord Drogheda. It was founded as a Limited Company on 21 January 1926, and claimed 1,000 members at the time of its unsuccessful bid to submit oral evidence in support of a rather gradiose memorandum to the Crawford Committee.[71.] Its organisation was rather more restrictive than the others, confined as it was to members able to pay for the £1 share in the company. Its aims seemed to be directed as much towards the interests of manufacturers as to listeners at large.

The lack of a clear two-way channel of communication with the BBC was an obvious frustration for listeners. The existence of the listener organisations owed a great deal to the public need to express their views on broadcasting - and receive a response from the BBC. As Sir Arthur Stanley remarked:

> I accepted the Chairmanship of the /Wireless7 League because I believe that it is essential for the efficiency of broadcasting that there should be some independent body representing the listeners; to focus their opinions, wishes and complaints; and to co-operate with the Broadcasting Authority by supplying useful criticisms and suggestions for the improvement of the Service. The need for some such body is the more pressing by the very nature of broadcasting. There is no effective method of communication by which the listener can express his approval or disapproval, except by means of a letter addressed to the BBC which is a much too cumbersome process to be useful.[72]

But that was a high-flown ideal when compared to the useful work done by the organisations to satisfy more mundane needs in the early, uncertain days of radio. All the societies offered some form of wireless set insurance in return for part of the membership fee. They also offered set maintenance advice to members - vitally necessary when sets were still delicate and temperamental, and where, for financial reasons, home construction was common amongst those lacking technical knowledge. Further action was undertaken by the Radio Association and jointly by the Wireless

League and RSGB to register radio dealers. [73] This served some purpose since large numbers of unskilled people were moving into the business of selling sets and registration helped to allay public fears that low trading standards would predominate.

The local branch of the Wireless League or the Radio Association also fulfilled an important social need. Meetings were important ways of gathering knowledge about listener ideas or criticisms and stimulating a sense of collective action. [74] Their distribution throughout England was reasonably broad but, as the Crawford Committee observed, most branches were in large towns, leaving rural areas largely unrepresented. As with any other pressure group, local branch meetings allowed members to vent their frustrations and, more constructively, prepare courses of action through discussion. Much of the Wireless League evidence to Crawford was derived from ideas developed in this form of debate. Items discussed included demands for more local programmes, the value of educational programmes and the possibility of using direct local action to prevent the dreaded 'oscillator'. Branch meetings also provided a valuable educative function. Men such as Professor Low toured the country, lecturing on broadcasting to many societies and organisations. This served to alleviate many listening problems and attracted local attention towards radio, publicising its value to non-listeners as well as listeners. [75]

The collection of members' opinions was pointless unless it could be matched by some effective and coherent means of expressing these opinions to the BBC. One method of applying pressure was to seek publicity for the cause and the Wireless League, with its Daily Express antecedents, was most adept at this form of action. The Wireless League's activities were widely reported in the national press and for two years between 1926 and 1928 the League produced a monthly four page supplement to the influential Wireless World. [76] All the organisations produced pamphlets and prospectuses to inform the public of their aims; they took stands at wireless exhibitions and both the Wireless League and the Radio Association produced their own handbooks. [77] The much maligned BBC also demonstrated some goodwill towards the organisations. In its Handbooks between 1928 and 1934, in a period when the wireless organisations were in decline, it continued to make a reference to them. [78]

Nonetheless, the organisations relied heavily on the reputation of their leaders to strengthen their political presence. Important patrons were sought and noted critics of radio, such as Ian Fraser and Filson Young, were enlisted to add a certain professional respectability to the cause. These leaders remained in power until January 1936 when there was a mass resignation. [79] At the BBC, W. E. Gladstone Murray was assigned the task of arranging personal contacts with the leaders. Relations were normally rather cordial, as he remarked to Stanley, 'your direct contact with us is so close and continuous that it is worth a dozen committees. '[80]

Another means of applying influence was through the GPO's ill-fated Programme Board. However the Board only met on six occasions between 9 April and 8 July 1924. It was formally wound up on 1 January 1927. [81] In 1926 the Postmaster-General argued that:

> the service has recently been working so smoothly and the questions submitted to the Post Office have been so few that it has not been necessary for some time past to call the Board together for its advice. [82]

In accordance with the Crawford Committee's recommendations the successor to the Board was the BBC's Wireless Organisations' Advisory Committee (WOAC). This had an equally brief and inauspicious career despite the high hopes for success at the outset. The brief for the Committee stated:

> The members of the Committee should prepare, through the machinery of the organisations which they represent, analytical reports based on the views of listeners regarding the composition of broadcast programmes. [83]

At first, Reith reported the discussions of the committee on issues to the Control Board but the tone of his reports soon became very dismissive and the Committee's recommendations were totally ignored. [84] In the face of this uncompromising resistance, the wireless groups lacked the resources and strength to apply firmer pressure. The WOAC faded away; meeting less and less, eventually ceasing to meet completely in 1931. [85] The main opportunity for presenting the views of the listeners was provided by the committees of inquiry on broadcasting. The Sykes Committee came too early for the listener organisations. Only the Radio Association gave evidence and the RSGB dominated the representation of listener interests during the licence 'war' and its aftermath in 1923. The period when the Crawford Committee was taking evidence during the winter of 1925 to 1926 marked the zenith of the organisations' influence. The Wireless League and Radio Association gave verbal evidence whilst all three listener organisations provided memoranda for the committee to examine.

All the organisations naturally wanted to extend their representation in the decision-making processes of broadcasting. The existing system was not condemned because it was a monopoly, indeed this was accepted by all the groups as essential to avoid chaos, but because the broadcasting monopoly allowed a private company to exclude other influences from the control of broadcasting. The reforms suggested by the organisations specifically excluded direct state control but advocated, instead, some form of governing board for the monopoly, representing the interests of many groups including the listeners and manufacturers. The Wireless League provided the most detailed and imaginative proposals along these lines. It suggested the creation of a British Broadcasting Commission to consist of ten members comprising: a chairman, a chief commissioner to represent MP's and a commissioner to represent each of: the GPO, the radio manufacturers, science, education, the arts, with two to represent the listeners. Each representative was to be in some way a nominee of the groups concerned. The added twist to the Wireless League's evidence was the provision of a Programme Advisory Committee. This would have represented the whole gamut of activity: education, the press, music, the stage, music halls, sport, commerce, industry and, of course, the Wireless League itself. [86]

In the shape of the British Broadcasting Corporation, the organisations got what they wanted in terms of a monopoly independent of state or private interest. Where they really failed was in democratising the BBC Governing Board. The Governors were purely political nominees and did not, therefore, necessarily have to represent the various interests. It was not easy for these interests to apply more than the most tenuous and indirect pressure to ensure that a political nominee for one of the five places on the Board might share any of the collective views of, for instance, the listeners' organisations. The Crawford Committee's report was therefore a tremendous rebuff for the organisations. They could not even claim credit for the creation of the Corporation, since this was a response to a clear consensus of opinion amongst most witnesses giving evidence before the Committee.

It would be unfair, however, to suggest that the wireless

organisations had served no useful purpose in the consultative process. The organisations made the views of their members known on many issues which were soon recognised by many other listeners to be of major importance. The poor provision of news broadcasts was one aspect raised. All the societies were anxious to see an extension of news programmes beyond the simple headline, news agency form; thus, implicitly, they were eager to break the grip of the press on news output. In the thirties such opinions were commonplace but the societies were the first to articulate listener concern on the question. They also wanted more alternative programmes. The Wireless League suggested a choice in favour of more popular programmes but it also advocated the introduction of more localised programmes for areas then only able to receive Daventry and the creation of a special network for the sole provision of educational material. [87]

The efforts of the BBC were not always adversely criticised. The general standard of programmes was broadly liked and the work done by the BBC in many output areas complimented. [88] Moreover, there was general contempt for the Post Office levy on licence revenue; the Wireless League and the Wireless Association of Great Britain soundly condemned the practice of extracting this money. In their opinion, the provision of a successful broadcasting system was significantly dependent on adequate financial support and, therefore, all the revenue should accrue to the BBC. [89]

This surge of involvement and the attainment of some influence was all too ephemeral. During the meetings of the Ullswater Committee, the sole gesture from the listeners' organisations was a letter, lamely urging: 'that the new Charter should retain the clause whereby the British Broadcasting Corporation are recommended to co-operate with listeners' organisations. ' This request was denied. [90]

In July 1936 the remnants of four organisations merged into the newly formed Listeners' League. There were only approximately 25,000 members remaining and whether many of these were active is doubtful. [91] The Listeners' League was suspected by the BBC to be no more than a thinly disguised lobby for radio advertisers or the relay exchanges. However, pressed by the BBC, the GPO investigated the League and discovered that it was little different in aims and structure to its predecessors. [92]

The demise of the organisations can be seen to have several causes. In the period 1927 to 1934 the BBC attempted to satisfy many of the grievances raised during the course of

Table 3.1: Guide to Listener Organisations

Organisation	Founded	Ended	Size	Other Details
Radio Association	August 1922	October 1936	3,000 in 1925	41 Provincial and 12 Metropolitan branches. Gave evidence to Sykes & Crawford. See BBC Yearbook, 1933, p. 73.
Wireless League	March 1925	October 1936. In January 1936, Dorgheda, Stanley and Fraser resigned	40,000 in June 1925 80,000 in Dec. 1925	150 Branches. Independent from Daily Express on 1 July 1925. Evidence to Crawford. See BBC Yearbook, 1933, p. 74.
Wireless Association of Great Britain	January 1926	1928. Amalgamated with the Wireless League.	1,000 in 1926	Memorandum to Crawford only.
Listeners' Association.	1932	October 1936	?	Suggested in Spectator, 23 January 1932.
Listeners' League	July 1936	31st December 1938	25,000 in 1939	Incorporated all the others. The Listeners' League was taken over by the Wireless Retailers' Association as the Listeners' Service Branch.

the proceedings of the Crawford Committee, thus undermining their main purpose. The news service was extended (albeit slowly until 1935), eyewitness accounts of major sporting and other national events were successfully included and there were more educational programmes. Most importantly, the expanding Regional Scheme provided a better geographical coverage and a choice of programme for many more listeners, although this did not exactly answer the demand for 'local' programmes specifically. The BBC also tried to usurp the role of the listener organisations by gathering its own information on listener opinion. It continued to operate the Programme Correspondence Section and maintained many other advisory committees, such as the Music Advisory Committee, to deal with important parts of the programme output. In 1935 this was extended with the creation of the General Advisory Council (GAC). This body closely accorded with suggestions made to Crawford but it was really a shadow of the idea since members were selected informally in a system very much under BBC control rather than through any semblance of proper democratic consultation with interested parties. [93] The GAC also served as a useful means of involving potentially dangerous critics within the BBC framework. If excluded, they might have become involved in reviving the flagging listener societies. Of course the creation of the GAC did at least imply a further acceptance by the BBC that the views of listeners were integral with the building of a successful broadcasting system.

Yet it took seven years to create the GAC and its existence might seem to be owed, from a cynical point of view at least, more to a desire to put the BBC shop window in order for the eyes of Ullswater than because of any undue audience pressure for involvement. Where the audience was concerned, increased apathy or, more precisely, resigned acceptance of the existence of the Corporation seemed to grow when the initial excitement of its formation had faded. The failure of the organisations to extract any substantial concessions through the work of the WOAC seems to have led quickly to disillusionment and a sense of powerlessness. Certainly the BBC did introduce some changes to answer its critics but it did so in its own time and on its own terms. It was difficult to see the BBC under Reith racing towards reforms at the insistence of listeners - in whatever form such pressure was applied.

There were other reasons for the inability to apply pressure successfully. Membership was always limited. A

maximum of 100,000 in a listening population for 1927 of
around nine million is respectable but not large and quite
possibly unrepresentative. The Crawford Committee was
not slow to notice this in the case of both the Wireless League
and the Radio Association. [94] Quite simply, the membership
never really 'took off'. The Wireless League had to admit
that it had not managed to win any more support after its
initial membership drive was over. Perhaps members felt
that the organisations were too élitist and did not permit
more than an illusion of democratic influence through their
leaderships' contacts at the BBC. The essential weakness
lay in the central idea of the societies. Wireless was a bad
choice if it was to be used as the rallying point for a collective movement. There were too many disparate opinions and
views on broadcasting to be represented adequately in one
organisation. Views about programme content and programme
balances could not be easily presented in a common front by
a society with such a fragile rationale for its existence. The
idea of the unaligned consumer consorting with similarly
minded individuals to provide a common front proved to be
unworkable. The listeners' societies and specialist technical societies were replaced by groups rooted in some other
vocation or interest. Usually these lobbies had a much
stronger interest in participation in programme production
and transmission. If the listener wanted to express his views
on programme policy he had to display his activism in one of
these other groups. For instance, the Crawford Committee
took evidence from musicians, music publishers, actors,
theatre owners, the Performing Right Society, the Incorporated Society of Authors, Playwrights and Composers, the
British National Opera Company and the London orchestras.
All clamoured for some share of control on broadcasting.
Moreover, they were attempting to challenge the grip of other
interests: the manufacturers, the press, press agencies and
the state, through its agent, the GPO. With all these powerful forces at work, it was clear that the listener organisations
would be swamped by much more cohesive and influential
interests. Indeed, it was these interests which dominated
the submission to the Ullswater Committee in 1937.
    In the end, the rump of the listener organisations - the
Listeners' League - itself suffered the humiliation of absorption in the Wireless Retailers' Association, not because it
had any political impact, but because, 'it represents a very
formidable buying power.'[95] This, more than anything else,
demonstrated the weakness of the organisations - they were

reduced to the role of a customer relations department for the radio industry. Their demise was complete.

Chapter Four

THE BROADCASTERS

Reith and his Audience

As the British Broadcasting Corporation developed it accumu-
lated a great deal of information about the 'void' into which
it broadcast. At first, knowledge of the audience was
acquired more by the accident of observation and correspondence than by a positive attempt to learn about the needs and
circumstances of listeners. Later, in the thirties, audience
research was formally permitted and a great deal of more
precise information was gathered. Despite the early limitations, these sources make a valuable contribution to an
analysis of the audience. To interpret the information which
was gathered, it is important to develop an understanding of
the early attitudes of the BBC, particularly the Reithian
philosophy of public service broadcasting which dominated
contact with the emerging audience. Then, it is necessary to
examine a gradual and interesting evolution in the attitude of
the BBC towards the audience as this philosophy came under
increasing pressure from inside and outside the BBC. A
closer relationship between the two sides of the microphone
was urged and, although Reith and his supporters did not
capitulate, some concessions were made. These concessions
deserve some investigation not only because they led to the
collection of more information about the audience, but also
because they had important social consequences.

A common reason for criticising the BBC in its formative period was its insularity. Critics argued that the
Director General, Sir John Reith, then indisputably the per-
sonification of British broadcasting, represented an organisation which relied entirely on independent judgements from its
hierarchy to establish moral and cultural standards for programmes and produced programmes based upon artistic

judgements that had little regard for the varied tastes of its audience. [1] However, even in its most introspective days, the BBC's contact with its audience ran deeper than the extreme statement might suggest. It possessed a limited method of contact which had some value but which was so inefficient and selective that it was capable of producing wholly misleading information. The best expression of these early arrangements can be found in Reith's book: Broadcast over Britain, written in 1924, when he was Managing Director of the British Broadcasting Company. The main purpose of the book was to establish the Company's position after eighteen months of service and it contained a detailed justification of monopoly public service broadcasting. In the book, Reith accepted the deficiencies in his knowledge about his audience but was defensive about existing policy and even pessimistic about the possibility of collecting more reliable evidence from the growing audience. Reith was anxious to stress the ultimate benefits of monopoly broadcasting with its insulation from commercial and any other dominant control. The manufacturers, he argued:

> have all come to the conclusion that, since the Broadcasting Company regards itself as a public service, and is catering for the public interest, it behoves the trade to adapt their manufacturing and selling policy to the requirements of the public as reflected in BBC policy.[2]

Yet a suggestion of a fully democratic broadcasting system which this statement implied was strictly limited by Reith. The public had to be firmly guided:

> I think it will be admitted by all, that to have exploited so great a scientific invention for the purpose and pursuit to 'entertainment' alone would have been a prostituion of its powers and an insult to the character and intelligence of the people. [3]

This sense of moral purpose pervades Broadcast over Britain. For instance, his firm opposition to gambling and religion was strongly expressed.

The idea of leading public taste and opinion was not subject to any considerable contemporary criticism, as such: what was attacked, was the direction which this leadership took, and the style of transmitting this to the audience. Few critics except the commercial lobby disputed the dangers of conceding to so-called popular taste. As Reith argued:

Figure 4.1: Sir John Reith by Low

New Statesman, 11 November 1933

Reproduced by permission of the Low Trustees and the
Evening Standard

> It is occasionally indicated to us that we are apparently
> setting out to give the public what we think they need -
> and not what they want - but few know what they want
> and very few what they need ...... In any case it is
> better to over-estimate the mentality of the public than
> to under-estimate it. [4]

In other words, Reith was prepared to respond to the
public only in the very broadest sense. He was interested in
audience opinion as it was expressed through established
representative bodies. These included advisory committees,
individual experts and members of the Board of Education,
the Ministries of Health and Agriculture, various learned
societies and the press. [5] More objective tests of audience
reaction were limited to the rising circulation of the Radio
Times and the boom in licence holding. Whatever the source
of information about the audience, the BBC was under no
obligation to accept it, for as Reith asserted:

> When it comes to questions of general policy - the
> fixing of standards and the setting up of ideals - to
> decisions as to what shall or shall not be broadcast,
> we are obviously on dangerous ground...... At the
> risk of being charged with posing as judge or educator,
> or with deciding matters outside our province, we must
> make the decision since ours is the responsibility for
> the conduct of the service. [6]

The intention was to rely on the capacity of the experienced
BBC production personnel. Their conception of broadcasting
policy was derived, not essentially from close contact with
the audience at large but rather more from the practice of
transmitting programmes, close cooperation with 'experts'
and, all too frequently from the advice of their own metropolitan, middle class circle of friends.

These 'experts' were sometimes called upon for advice
individually, the scientist Sir Oliver Lodge for instance, but
more frequently they participated in advisory committees.
Naturally, some were more influential and more useful than
others. The National Advisory Committee on Education,
formed on 6 October 1923 under the BBC Education Director
J. C. Stobart, had an important role to play. [7] The national
committee and its associated local committees later formed
the base for the more formal organisation, the Central
Council for Schools Broadcasting created by the new Corporation in February 1929. On the other hand, the GPO sponsored a Broadcasting Board which attempted to represent the

interests of groups such as the RSGB, the TUC and the press but so little contentious material was produced by the Board that Reith described the meetings as 'a ghastly waste of time.'[8]

Other Advisory Committees had slightly more value as a contact with the audience. These included the Religious Advisory Committee, formed in May 1923; the Advisory Committee on the Spoken Word, formed in April 1926; the Wireless Organisations Advisory Committee, created in January 1927; and the Musical Advisory Committee, begun in July 1925. Although these committees had varying degrees of success in creating closer contacts between the BBC and its audience, they all suffered from a common fault. The reliance on prominent citizens as representatives of their various fields drastically reduced the sense of wider participation. Indeed the collaboration between the committees and the BBC often became too close and their critical purpose was nullified.[9] These committees may have been of considerable value to the BBC but they stopped well short of significant democratic participation in the public service.

The advisory committees continued, uninterrupted by the creation of the Corporation. In fact in February 1935 a new committee was created: The General Advisory Council. As before, its personnel was selected by the BBC so that as many interests as possible should be represented. The secrecy in the selection automatically reduced the credibility of the committee and particularly when those such as Harold Laski or J. B. Priestley, with strong left-wing political sympathies, were deliberately excluded.

In Broadcast over Britain Reith outlined his other sources of contact, although with some qualifications about their usefulness. The contacts with Government Departments were often necessary to discover the details and demands of various groups. For instance, in the case of agricultural workers, the Ministry of Agriculture would be requested to delegate spokesmen to give talks on farming matters.[10] Again this was hardly a method of contact with audience opinions and could easily be interpreted as a means of disseminating official information.

Reith also made references to the rising circulation of Radio Times and the increase in licence holding but these were acceptable only as a broad guide to audience responses. Such statistics could reveal that the audience was certainly fascinated with broadcasting but could tell nothing about the views of the growing mass audience on details of broadcasting policy or programme content. Reith was prepared to accept these weaknesses: he admitted that close attention was paid to the circulation figures and a chart was plotted: 'on which is given the number of licences per thousand of the population at each broadcasting centre. Neither of these tests is definite enough.'[11]

Another source of contact was the Programme Correspondence Section (PCS): formed in May 1924, it was an important part of the BBC's organisation. Reith favoured it, not just because it opened the way for the audience to express opinions on broadcasting, and by this means effect change by the producers, but also because it gave the listener the sense and feeling that such changes were possible. The psychological satisfaction of contact was considered equally as important as the content of any letter or group of letters. As Reith argued: 'It all tends towards the establishment of some degree of confidence and intimacy between the broadcasting organisation and the public'.[12] By the thirties, the PCS could expect approximately 150,000 letters per year but this was still only 15-20 per programme on average - hardly enough on which to base any sound judgements.[13]

The character of this kind of approach stemmed from Reith's basically pessimistic view of his audience. He had no illusions about the selection process which led people to write to the BBC. 'The inarticulate portion of the audience is infinitely greater than the articulate.'[14] Yet his suspicions ran deeper than that. He visualised the audience to be so infinitely divided and separated by taste, so capricious in instinct, so limited in artistic appreciation and so selfish that it would be impossible to learn anything more from a more objective survey. Whilst paying due deference to the views of educated correspondents and his expert advisors, Reith was led to the conclusion that all too many letters: 'show neither acknowledgement of the existence of any kind of taste other than their own, nor the possibility of the existence of such, nor that it should have at least some measure of consideration.'[15]

One rather anomalous contact was with that strange person, the programme correspondent - a sort of official critic. Filson Young served in this role from 1926 until 1938 and was allowed to sit on the BBC's Programme Board to advise on the planning and organisation of programmes. Throughout the period he willingly offered criticism,[16] but his extremely close and friendly relationship with the staff at the BBC severely limited his value. He was hardly the typical man-in-the-street which he professed to be.[17]

The question now remains: what did all these methods of contact with the audience tell the BBC about its audience? The overall picture was sure to be distorted in favour of the opinions of articulate and powerful interest groups. The BBC discovered a good deal about the opinions of these dominant groups and there is no doubt that the information so acquired was put to use by BBC personnel in programme production, but on their own terms. This conformed very closely to Reith's avowed intention to set cultural standards and lead opinion rather than be seen to be led by it. Knowing too much about the uncertain and uneducated tastes of the audience might contaminate the programme builders. It was easy to accuse the BBC of ambiguity when it claimed to provide a public service but made no attempt to allow participation or provide any democratic access. Reith was determined to achieve higher cultural standards by the 'brute force of monopoly',[18] and answered criticisms of lack of responsiveness by pointing to consultation through the advisory committees and, ultimately, the regular reviews of the BBC Charter with ultimate democratic control in the shape of Parliamentary debate and reform. Nonetheless, with his reliance on experts and opinion leaders such as the national press for information, Reith missed the opportunity to gather details about less obvious groupings in the radio audience: age, sex, economic status and political opinion could provide an identity of interests which could not be discovered by the existing methods of contact. These groups, when viewed in aggregate, were certainly not as capricious as Reith might think. That is not to say that he ever accepted the idea of a 'standard listener' - Reith recognised the heterogeneous nature of society but argued that the BBC knew best how to guide it.

Matched against this, the BBC was especially handicapped by its choice of personnel and the pervading atmosphere of its organisation. The formality of the dinner jacket, invisible at the microphone, was merely a symbol of the public s.chool, Oxbridge backgrounds of many of the staff. This, along with the powerful establishment presence of characters like the deputy Director-General, Admiral Carpendale, laid the BBC open to criticism of being socially élitist. In this medium, the accent of the announcers alone was enough to mark the social distinctions between the broadcasters and most listeners. Where this distinction was felt by listeners, the BBC appeared to represent a part of the ruling establishment. This social barrier placed limits on Reith's understanding of his 'public' and weakened the validity of his reliance on committees as informed sources of contact with the audience as a whole. In mitigation, Robert Silvey, the first Head of Audience Research, recognised this criticism. Although a Fabian socialist himself, he defended the BBC on the grounds that: 'In those days, the people who had wireless sets were not a cross-section of the whole population, it was a section of the population which had a pretty strong middle-class bias.'[19] In this sense, the BBC represented the authentic voice of its audience but it had few means of discovering if potential working class listeners were deterred by the prevailing social image of the broadcasters.

Despite the refusal to seek out the detailed structure of its audience, it would be unfair to imply that the BBC made no attempt to provide for minorities. For instance, the ignorance about the needs and tastes of working people contrasted sharply with the social purpose of programmes such as 'Men Talking' and 'Time to Spare' which allowed the unemployed and others to speak for themselves on issues directly to the microphone. The BBC also permitted audience participation in social surveying organised by W. H. Beveridge as part of his series 'Changes in Family Life'.[20] These programmes revealed some interest at the BBC in hitherto unexplored areas, but the programmes could have been produced in a better form if largely inarticulate groups, such as the unemployed, had been consulted to discover their needs more precisely. It would not have been contradictory for the BBC to insist on setting standards whilst, at the same time, planning programmes with the fullest possible knowledge of the likely consumers. A tremendous sense of purpose, great self-confidence and not a little conceit, it seems, overwhelmed such thoughts.

There were few alternative sources of information about the audience to turn to. The BBC was not alone in lacking interest in the social activities of much of the population. Apart from the census returns and other official Government surveys, there was a serious deficiency of detailed institutional, commercial or academic social survey evidence to refer to. When the BBC finally decided to set out and survey the audience, it set the pace and most other authorities lagged a long way behind. Before this concession Reithian philosophy remained firm, partly, out of necessity - to preserve artistic integrity in the fight against intrusions from those less morally guided than the Director-General - particularly the commercial lobbies. However, once the organisation had firmly established its institutional position the question of closer audience contact could not be ignored indefinitely: perhaps a concession from strength might be possible - to help, not hinder the broadcaster at work.

The Case for Listener Research

Listener research by the BBC was formally accepted on 1 October 1936, when Robert Silvey was appointed to serve on the BBC's recently formed Listener Research Committee. The creation of the Committee owed much to the tireless work of Sir Stephen Tallents, the Controller of Public Relations since 1935, and to the pressure of the General Advisory Council. Tallents had shrewdly put the issue to the Council, won them to his side and, with their support, persuaded the Director-General to concede his opposition to research.

However, Tallents' final success was only achieved after many internal disputes and policy decisions which occurred before large-scale statistical surveying of the radio audience could begin. The debate, both inside and outside the BBC, on the merits of surveying revealed numerous interesting preconceptions about the audience and the methods of observing it.

When examining the internal debate over audience research, it is tempting to draw up battle lines inside the BBC: each side implacably opposed to the other: the radical subordinates against the establishment. In fact the struggle also took place inside the establishment. Heads of Departments in the traditional areas of audience response such as variety, drama and education felt the lack of audience contact as acutely as any of their subordinates. Val Gielgud, the Director of Drama, led the campaign. Taking his cue from a discussion on the possibilities for listener research at a programme meeting in May 1930, [21] Gielgud produced a detailed memorandum in favour of closer investigation of the audience. [22] His proposal was a reflection of growing anxiety amongst staff in the Drama Department at their ignorance of listener reactions to programmes:

> It must be a source of considerable disquiet to many people besides myself to think that it is quite possible that a very great deal of our money and time and effort may be expended on broadcasting into a void. I believe it is now generally agreed that the information to be gained from our correspondents is both inaccurate and

misleading. The plain listener is not a person who ever writes a letter, except under very startling circumstances, and we obviously do not wish to broadcast for the benefit of cranks and people with a great deal of spare time on their hands ...... It seems to me absolutely vital that some scheme should be put in hand - and such a scheme would have to be on a very large scale and one necessarily involving considerable expense - to survey our listening public.

He continued, stressing the positive benefits of a survey:

I do not suggest that popular opinion is or should be the last word as to whether our programmes are or are not good and should or should not be continued in any particular form; but a body of real information would be, speaking personally, of the most immense qualifying value to me in framing dramatic policy and controlling production methods and I cannot help feeling that such information could not fail to be of the same value to anyone else responsible for any type of programme activity. Again and again, one finds suggestions about programmes either pushed forward or opposed on the grounds that such and such a programme would or would not please the normal listener. There is the old slogan 'Remember the cabman's wife in Wigan'. But there is not the least use remembering her unless we know what she thinks; and at present I feel that we are allowing qualifications to be made on the grounds of what cabmen's wives think, when all we know is the opinion of X - member of Programme Board - as to what he thinks she thinks which is another story. [23]

Despite Gielgud's enthusiasm his views were largely ignored. The formal reason was the need for economy during the depression but the procrastination was partially the consequence of ignorance about the form of surveying. There was great distrust of sampling as a method of research, largely because of a failure to understand its mechanism and purpose. The only large-scale method of surveying then in use was the national census itself and BBC staff naturally quailed at the thought of a prohibitively expensive blanket survey. Those at the BBC who preferred a survey of this kind envisaged the addition of a questionnaire to the licence form but this would have been costly and presented tremendous

101

problems for any analysis. The use of sampling methods gained acceptance only slowly. After all, the most famous social surveyor of all, Rowntree, had no great love for sampling but it eventually became acceptable, partly because of dissatisfaction with the obvious selectivity of press survey samples and partly because of the good example set by commercial and advertising surveys in Britain and abroad. The future Head of the Listener Research Department, for instance, was selected on the basis of his commercial research into consumer behaviour for the London Press Exchange.[24] Nonetheless, even after his appointment Silvey still found problems in persuading BBC personnel to accept that samples could be representative. As he put it:

> Perplexities about sampling had their source in the innumeracy common among highly literate men. For example, I was asked again and again how big a sample should be. This frequently went along with a conviction that a sample which was small, in relation to the population it represented, was ipso facto suspect...... I would hear people say: 'How can this sample, numbering only five hundred, possibly tell you anything when it is supposed to represent a population of twenty million? It is only one in forty thousand'.[25]

This failure to comprehend the methods of random or quota sampling was not easily remedied. As late as 1935, for instance, Basil Nicolls, the Director of Internal Adminstration complained about one survey:

> If any surprising information came out of the plebiscite, we would not accept it, except in the case where the plebiscite was an absolutely complete one of every licence holder: otherwise we would say that it was a freak result.[26]

Such confusion was demonstrated by the first efforts to produce an ideal listener research questionnaire: where the Directors of Departments were asked to put their most urgent questions to their respective audiences. The desire for information was clear, as there were 115 items on the questionnaire. Cecil Graves, the Assistant Director of Programmes, discussed the plans with Professor Bowley of the London School of Economics, the doyen of inter-war social statisticians. Bowley demonstrated the naivety of this early BBC research by showing that 20 to 25 questions must be the maximum otherwise the survey would be too onerous for most listeners to answer and a good response prevented. [27]

A good deal of this early activity was induced by the demands of the Adult Education section. The Central Council for Broadcast Adult Education (CCBAE) badly needed audience research because its needs were so peculiarly related to the needs of its audience. Indeed, the poor performance of the CCBAE was in part attributable to ignorance of the educational needs of the audience. The Central Council had been the first to ask for more information in 1929 - well before Gielgud began his own campaign. At an Executive Committee meeting of the Council on 15 January 1930 the plan to employ a survey was formally introduced. The Council approved the expenditure of at least £1,000 on such a survey but it was delayed and eventually axed as an economy measure. [28] The CCBAE was very keen on the use of sampling and on the extension of the principle of audience research to all sections of the BBC. [29] In an undated memorandum, probably written in 1930, the CCBAE Executive Committee asserted: 'it would in many ways be wasteful if the surveys were rigidly confined to the sphere of adult education.'[30] Although this scheme was axed, the Education Department at the BBC had participated in one example of research: a survey undertaken in 1927 into schools' broadcasting in Kent. [31] This used the financial assistance of the Carnegie Trust and much useful material was gathered to support the successful school educational broadcasting programmes, helping to make them more relevant to actual needs before 1939. [32]

Despite the initial rebuff, the Drama Department continued to press its case for audience research. Gielgud eventually gathered allies inside the BBC, although most of them could not accept a full-blown statistical survey. Siepmann and Matheson, for instance, preferred more selective information from the audience. As Siepmann put it:

> I feel convinced that a statistical survey, i.e. anything in the nature of a mere numerical analysis of public opinion, whether widely or narrowly conceived, will prove futile and misleading. We are not out to count heads, but to collect a mass of information on which to base broad conclusions. [33]

This comment followed Gielgud's second attempt to get a decision on the principle of surveying the audience. In a memorandum to Roger Eckersley, the Director of Programmes in 1933, he again attacked the dependence on press comment and the PCS. The PCS, he envisaged, could fill a much wider role than its existing letter-box function. He advocated the use of regional headquarters as lines of contact with their respective audiences. He argued: 'it seems to me that a properly organised intelligence service is as urgent a need for a Broadcasting Corporation as it is for any War Office.'[34] His poignant appeal at the end of his memorandum was evidence of the kind of frustrations which afflicted the Directors of Departments who transmitted programmes traditionally associated with live audiences:

> . . . . . . from the point of view of my own department, nothing handicaps me more than the non-possession of anything in the nature of a thermometer which would correspond in the theatre to the acid test of box office returns. I am still entirely in the dark as to whether five thousand, ten thousand, a million, or twenty, people listen to the average play broadcast; I am still more in the dark as to what proportion listen from beginning to end, and as to what is the real opinion concerning them. It is, in fact, only when I occasionally give a lecture in public that I begin to have the slightest idea as to what listeners think of our dramatic work. The removal of this severe handicap could, it seems to me, be worth a very considerable sum of money, and almost any amount of necessary labour. [35]

Interestingly, this paragraph demonstrated a failure to define his demands precisely. He asked for a 'thermometer' of reaction but it is clear that his appeal was also for an audience 'barometer'; a purely quantitative assessment of the audience.

This confusion about intentions was shared by his critics. Lindsay Wellington, the Presentation Director, was broadly in favour of establishing a 'body of agreed data' about the audience but he feared that a single barometer of public opinion would stifle consideration of the tremendous variety of component groups within the audience. That surveying results would create the impression that the BBC had accepted the existence of an 'average listener' was a familiar criticism from inside the BBC. [36]

As if to scotch the critics, Gielgud launched a broadcast appeal for help from the audience in the construction of drama and feature programme policy. The appeal, broadcast on 8 and 9 March 1934, yielded 12,700 replies. The general opinion of this self-selected group was naturally more committed and better informed than any scientifically controlled sample but it produced some useful qualitative advice for Gielgud and was to form the basis for the first organised research by the Listener Research Section in 1937.

During 1934 and 1935, this search for more evidence was also pressed by the editor of the Radio Times, Maurice Gorham, who was anxious to use his pages to launch an appeal. He proposed the use of one page as a detachable questionnaire - a scheme which was later adopted. [37] On the other hand, Major Atkinson, the Director of Foreign Relations, was still pressing for a full survey, having been influenced by the apparent success of the Peace Ballot. The public, he claimed, had voted against the advice of the national press, and hence refuted the argument used against surveying: that during the period of research the electorate would be stampeded by the press and policy would be forced in directions where the BBC wished to preserve its liberty of action. [38] Both of these schemes reflected mis-conceptions about sampling which the uninitiated tended to hold: Gorham's appeal would have only produced qualitative results, derived from the more active readers of the Radio Times: Atkinson still assumed that a full survey necessarily had more validity than a sample.

One external influence on BBC policy came from the most important rival medium: the press. With its powerful vested interest, the press had a stronger influence on broadcasting policy than Reith would have liked. In the early days, it had taken the action of the American shop owner Gordon Selfridge to allow the printing of programme times in national papers: he broke a press ban by publishing the details in his own advertising space. [39] The competition to supply news was, however, the main battleground. The BBC was permitted to broadcast news only after 7 p.m. in the evening (6.30 p.m. in 1927 and 6 p.m. after 1928) and was forced to rely on the news agencies for the supply of material. Only for a short period during the General Strike and eventually in the thirties was the BBC able to break through this barrier and collect news for itself. After 1934, the News Section regained independent status from the Talks Department and rapidly expanded its own news collection and analysis. [40] Despite this mutual hostility, the BBC had some respect for the press as a source of criticism. Press influence could even be beneficial. It disliked radio advertising as much as Reith did, although the competition for revenue not a paternal concern for any damage to programme stand-

was the motive.

Of course, the BBC was itself involved in the business of publishing weekly magazines. The Radio Times, first issued on 28 September 1923, was not viewed solely as a means of providing programme details. It was also seen as a means of keeping in closer touch with the audience on a regular basis. Certainly, the emphasis was placed on the BBC informing the audience about its personalities, its programmes and its policies but correspondence from listeners was welcomed. As his interest in listener research showed, the editor Maurice Gorham was anxious to tilt the balance towards greater listener participation. [41] Priced at 2d., throughout the period, the circulation rose from 250,000 copies for the first issue to over a million by the end of the twenties and two million by 1934. The Coronation issue of 7 May 1937 sold 3,540,547 copies - a record for any weekly magazine. The readership was anything up to four times larger and the potential benefits from a closer relationship were, therefore, fairly significant. [42]

The Radio Times was the flagship but there were other magazines. World Radio, founded in 1926, was used to cover foreign programmes and eventually to support the new Empire Service. The Listener founded in January 1929, was meant to satisfy a more specialised market - listeners interested in adult education, literary or musical criticism. [43] Its publication was strenuously resisted by the newspaper proprietors and the New Statesman in particular, on the grounds that it would extend the Corporation's power and influence. [44] The Listener survived the crisis and settled down to a modest circulation of about 50,000 copies per week. It was aimed directly at a select and influential section of society, committed to better relations by informing and eliciting a critical response.

None of these magazines was a substitute for organised listener research but they suggested some involvement by the audience, albeit on the BBC's terms, and they kept the BBC staff informed of a very much wider range of critical responses to programmes and programme policy. [45]

The BBC underlined its interest in the press by making arrangements for cuttings to be taken from provincial and national dailies, periodicals and trade papers in the hope of discovering some local or national audience opinion. [46] Even when listener research was firmly established, current affairs and music producers still considered intelligent press criticism more useful than audience research, particularly when the audience was very small.

Some attempts by the press to discover information about the audience increased the pressure on the BBC to carry out its own research. Various dailies launched their own polls - where listeners wrote in to say which were their favourite programmes. Examples included the Daily Herald and the Daily Mail - which made frequent appeals for audience response - and some regional papers such as the Yorkshire Observer and the Birmingham Gazette. [47] The main purpose, besides helping to boost circulation and increase reader interest, was to provide ammunition to lobby the BBC for a change in programme planning. Despite their obvious unreliability, press polls gave an extra stimulus to the BBC hierarchy to accept more scientifically acceptable research as a means of defeating criticism. Robert Silvey certainly felt that this was the case. [48] If research was done scientifically it would be easy to demonstrate the accuracy of such methods in comparison with the poor quality, self-selected samples which the press produced.

Other forms of pressure on the BBC to organise research had a less definite effect. Commercial radio stations naturally had a much greater interest in audience size because of the competition for advertising revenue. Work done by the Institute of Incorporated Practitioners in Advertising (IIPA) into listeners' habits during the autumn of 1935 set an example of what was possible but, equally, it aroused hostility inside the BBC because of the inevitable intention of this sort of research - to pander to the audience as much as possible. [49] Nonetheless, a more sophisticated approach was adopted and the sample was carefully weighted to cover rural and urban areas throughout England, although, obviously, it produced the sort of material advertisers liked to see: it divided the audience rather crudely into economic groups and concentrated on listening to Radio Luxembourg. [50]

Earlier in November 1935, the Radio Manufacturers Association (RMA) had also put the case for more research. The RMA apparently related the approaching saturation of the market, expressed by the declining rate of new licence issues as though it were due instead to consumer resistance to the BBC's output. The Association's arguments were resisted by the BBC because of the RMA's clear conviction that the results could only sustain their assertion that 80% of the audience would fall into the group: 'who want entertainment which requires no special training to appreciate it', whilst 'those who have a cultivated capacity for appreciating serious

Table 4.1: Daily Mail Ballot, 1927[51]

How Listeners Voted:

	Subject	Votes Cast
1.	Variety and Concert Parties	238,489
2.	Light Orchestral Music	179,153
3.	Military Bands	164,613
4.	Dance Music	134,027
5.	Topical Sports and News	114,571
6.	Symphony Concerts	78,781
7.	Solos: Vocal and Instrumental	72,658
8.	Opera and Oratorio	60,983
9.	Outside Broadcasts	51,755
10.	Short Plays and Sketches	49,857
11.	Talks: Scientific and Informative	30,919
12.	Choruses and Sea Shanties	30,445
13.	Chamber Music	27,467
14.	Revues	27,059
15.	Long Plays	17,576
16.	Readings and Recitations	2,717
	Free Votes not recorded	4,013
		1,285,083

drama talks, grand opera, chamber music and symphonies represent no more than 20%'.[52] Such statements confirmed the worst fears of the BBC senior staff, that research material might be used by critics as a cudgel with which to beat the BBC and apply, instead, rule by the ratings.

Overseas examples of audience research may have had similar effects on the minds of BBC staff. The American example did not commend itself as a useful addition to the armoury of the programme planners because of its clear commercial intentions. German examples had even more distasteful overtones of marshalling the audience for anti-democratic, political purposes. Nevertheless, some members of the BBC examined these methods. The Chief Engineer, Noel Ashbridge, had examined German techniques in 1930 and the Director of Foreign Relations, C. F. Atkinson, kept the BBC constantly in touch with various systems throughout the world.[53]

The academic contribution to the arguments in favour of surveying were very limited, although some academics, such as Professor T. H. Pear, pressed the BBC to sponsor audience research - if only to compensate for the lack of alternative sources from their own profession.[54] The BBC consented to three very small, largely experimental surveys. For instance, H. C. Shearman was granted £40 to further research by the Cambridge University Extra-Mural Department into listening in six Bedfordshire villages. The financial axe fell on his survey before anything conclusive was produced. Consequently, the sponsored projects contributed little to the debate on audience research. Senior academics, such as Seebohm Rowntree and Professor Bowley, were sought out for advice whenever a scheme was discussed but their limited assistance does not appear to have significantly improved confidence in the value of statistical surveys.[55]

The Listener Research Committee

Despite the strength of the forces arrayed against them, support inside the BBC for listener research continued to rise. In 1935, the BBC hierarchy resorted to another subterfuge to quell the mounting criticism: The Director-General used blatant delaying tactics and held over the question pending the arrival of a public relations expert to fill the new office at the BBC. The appointment of Sir Stephen Tallents as Controller of Public Relations was a decisive stage in the establishment of systematic audience research. His arrival coincided with an increasing anxiety - even loss of confidence - at the BBC in the face of external criticism, especially from the press. This concern as much as anything else persuaded Reith and his deputy, Carpendale, to concede the initiation of research - at least it would help to improve the BBC's public image. Tallents already had experience of much closer contact with consumers when working in his previous appointment as Head of Public Relations at the GPO. He was actively in favour of listener research and began preparing a case soon after his arrival. He shrewdly pressed the case with Reith by having the problem discussed at the General Advisory Council meeting in January 1936.

The outcome was modest. In a memorandum to Carpendale, discussing the Council meeting, Tallents defined the three aims of listener research. First, more general sociological information was needed on the habits of listeners - a shortage of data shared with many other organisations. Secondly, research was needed on listeners' tastes. Thirdly, some empirical knowledge about the capacity of listeners' sets was required in order to judge reception patterns. Tallents pressed the second point particularly firmly: he aimed to build up a sensitive network of listeners throughout the country from which reports on programme tastes could be obtained.[56] This course was approved by the Control Board and an extra member of staff was permitted to help set up the work, although: 'Those concerned were reminded that research was to be selective, specialised and more or less informal.'[57] Reith was still apprehensive that quantitative analyses of public preferences should be used to subordinate programme policy. A Listener Research Committee was created soon after permission was granted in 1936 and Robert Silvey was appointed to prepare a programme of research.[58] He faced continued resistance by many senior BBC officials. Their objections were numerous but can be summed up in the aphorism, 'Look what happened to the Battleship Potemkin when the ratings took over'.[59] J. C. Stobart, despite his involvement in educational broadcasting, was consistently hostile,[60] and Lionel Fielden, of the Talks Department was positively antagonistic. He remarked: 'The real degradation of the BBC started with the invention of the hellish department which is called Listener Research'.[61]

It appears that these powerful opponents were only defeated because the supporters of listener research succeeded, crucially, in convincing Reith of the validity of their argument. His dominance over the Control Board, where such

policy decisions were ultimately made, meant that his attitude had to change before any concession could be made. However reluctantly, Reith had moved from his position in 1924.
He had final responsibility for appointing more personnel to
the Listener Research Committee as it grew in importance
and, noticeably, he saw fit to congratulate Silvey on the
results of the first effort in 1937. [62]

After his appointment, Silvey commenced work immediately and managed to produce his first Listener Research report (LR/1) in February 1937. His first task was, however,
to plan and prepare a much longer term of action for his
Committee. He had little BBC material to work on and was
no doubt expected to rely heavily on his experience in commercial research. [63] The only guide was a paper produced
by Maurice Farquharson of the Public Relations Department
outlining the proposed campaign on listener research. In his
memorandum he emphasised the contrasting methods which
were necessary to examine listeners' tastes and habits. [64]
Both types of information were in demand from many programme departments, but the latter form was hedged by the
ruling by the Control Board that research was to be selective,
specialised and informal. As Farquharson showed, this
restriction would not prevent the collection of valuable information on tastes but it would restrict research into habits:

> It would seem that information about habits, however,
> if it is to be useful, will need to be quantitatively re-
> liable to a far greater extent than information about
> listeners' reactions to programmes. Here we shall
> be in search of facts, as distinct from opinions, and
> it will be necessary to have quantitative rather than
> qualitative evidence. For this reason it will probably
> prove difficult to restrict ourselves to the informal
> small scale methods laid down in principle by the
> General Advisory Council.

Some, he asserted, could be learnt from public utilities,
where habits could be partially discerned from the noticeable
decline in electricity or water consumption observed during
the most popular broadcasts and the large increase observed
immediately afterwards. Early suggestions on research
methods were equally tentative. One was to invite five hundred selected listeners from their respective regions to
comment on BBC programmes. However Farquharson suspected that it would be impossible to weight these 'glowworms',
as they were called, to give a balanced cross-section of the

audience as a whole. Fortunately some information on tastes could be collected, possibly supplemented by material gathered by specially well-informed people such as social service workers, WEA tutors and even secretaries of Women's Institutes. These were to be called 'super glowworms' or 'searchlights'.

From this rather inadequate basis, Silvey set out to prepare more detailed plans for the first meeting of the Listener Research Committee on 15 October 1936. His initial intention was to strengthen the collection of material on the audience from other sources and exploit existing BBC activities such as the Programme Correspondence Section, press and trade connections more fully. [65] With this as the base, the Committee could embark on its essential task: the scientific surveying of the audience. These preparations clearly exposed the existing inadequacies, 'what was needed was a fresh start'. [66] Silvey stressed the experimental nature of this period but also emphasised that the accuracy of the results was not in any way lessened: rather it was a matter of exploiting the potential of the surveys more fully. It was also necessary to find the extent of public willingness to cooperate with the BBC and discover the most successful methods of surveying to satisfy the various needs of the programme planners - together with many other more routine points, such as the most attractive format for a questionnaire. In pioneering days, even the effect of the latter remained to be determined. The road ahead for Silvey and his colleagues was certainly perilous but also challenging. A considerable amount of entirely new ground would need to be covered and the foundations of BBC research would have to be laid very carefully to ensure a reliable supply of information.

Chapter Five

LISTENER RESEARCH

The Panel System

With the absence of alternative sources of information, the
methods and findings of BBC research are of considerable
interest in a study of the radio audience. Five basic methods
were used by the Listener Research Section, and it is possible to assess the contrasting purposes and techniques involved
and the information produced. Each method had something to
tell about the listening population and, invariably, even the
least scientific survey revealed much of social interest as
well as valuable raw material for the programme planners.

The approach used most frequently in the early days
was the panel system. The first and most important was the
Drama Reports Scheme. The panel system was chosen
because it was cheap and relatively easy to organise. Only
350 people were used on the panel, which was aimed at qualitative rather than quantitative results. With this in mind,
the small size of the panel was not as crucial as for a quantitative analysis, although a minimum size was chosen to
validate the conclusions. Drama was chosen because it was
a conveniently nucleated area of output which felt the lack of
an audience response most acutely. The Director of Drama
and Features, Val Gielgud, was of course the departmental
head most likely to cooperate with the work.

The panel had its limitations: it was only likely to produce restricted conclusions on listeners' opinions because it
was solely composed of those predisposed to listen to radio
drama. The BBC chose members from its programme
correspondence contacts and only a limited amount of weight-
ing was done, largely on the basis of occupation and area of
residence. [1]

The Listener Research Section justified this approach

on the grounds that:

> Until the composition and size of that part of the
> listening public which is interested in radio drama is
> known, it is impossible to find out statistically whether
> the present or any other panel is representative of the
> radio drama public.

The original selection was intended to produce a panel which
was broadly representative of those who normally listened to
radio drama; it being neither 'lowbrow' nor 'highbrow'. As
the scheme continued, it became clear that the opinions
gathered would be enhanced if the membership of the panel
could be arranged to contain fewer habitual and enthusiastic
listeners to dramatic productions. The scheme would then
resemble more closely the kind of 'box-office' which Gielgud
desired. [2] An appeal to the casual listener, it was felt, ought
to improve the representative nature of the qualitative judgements offered.

Despite these misgivings, some important evidence was
compiled from the replies to the numerous questionnaires
sent to the panel from January to June 1937. Cooperation,
for instance, proved to be no problem. A committed audience
responded with pleasure and it was the distortion due to
listening purely to please the enquiry, or 'duty listening',
rather than apathy which presented the major problem to this
and many subsequent enquiries. The response averaged 55%
with a steady decline from 75% for the first few weeks down
to 35% in May and June. [3] The shape and frequency of the
questionnaires was also established. Free comment sections
provided a useful counterbalance to the limiting rigidity of
the question structure, with its demand for a definite rather
than a qualified response. [4] Several other lessons of general
surveying relevance were also learnt. The style of the
questions was varied and the panel split into two groups to
compare the results. It was found that a straight 'Yes/No'
choice of answer was open to confusion as 'No' often meant
'No option'. [5] On the other hand, a limited choice of answers
did not produce significantly different overall results when
compared with a broader selection of alternative answers. [6]
This sort of detail provided lessons for improving the quality
of later surveys; largely because of the greater understanding
of the psychology of those who responded to questionnaires.

The scheme also provided an opportunity to compare
the results of listener research with the more primitive
methods hitherto used with apparent equanimity. In a direct

comparison with the Programme Correspondence Section
(PCS), the Listener Research Section demonstrated the superiority of its most limited method of research over the correspondence method of opinion gathering: 8,000 reports clearly
outweighed the 600 letters on the same topic received during
the operation of the scheme. Letters to the PCS seized
upon the less well received programmes and clearly provided
a much poorer and certainly deceptive guide to the way
individual plays had been received. One of the least remarkable plays according to the panel was, The Emperor Jones
broadcast in 1937, but it actually received the most letters
simply because bad language was used.[7] Clearly this 'goat-
getter' might normally have overshadowed the generally
favourable response to the drama productions and hence,
deceived the programme planners.

A good deal of the Drama Report Scheme material was
hardly of world-shattering importance, but it was a solid
beginning and some light was cast on the technical problems
of surveying. To the Drama Department, very little of the
response could have been entirely surprising but it was
obviously important to have suspicions established and confirmed.

The panel method was successful enough for its future
to be secure although, before 1939, it was largely confined to
research for the Talks Department.[8] The BBC appointed
panels to listen to talks on the cinema[9] and a series of talks
on various subjects from October to December 1938. The
information gathered was of great assistance to the programme planners, giving guidance on preferences for programme content and convenience of broadcasting times.
Furthermore, the talks in which people were permitted to
talk for themselves about their lives, jobs and opinions were
confirmed as immensely popular. Two series - 'Men Talking'
and the BBC response to the Munich crisis 'Everyman and
the Crisis' - were particularly well received because they
used this technique, although there were some suspicions:

> Several listeners made remarks which suggest the
> prevalence of the view that the BBC is not always
> free from official interference. One said: 'How
> many of the talks were given in their original form?
> Was there much Blue Pencil used?'[10]

The BBC was nonetheless interested to observe that the series
had such broad appeal and that many of the panels argued for
the principle of direct access in this form to be extended.

Two other methods of acquiring qualitative information were used to a limited extent before 1939. Both methods relied on opinions gathered by specialists in the fields covered by the surveys. The smallest and most specialised was the Roster of Music critics undertaken by fifteen 'experts' between November 1937 and January 1938. [11] Each critic was asked to produce ad lib comments on Chamber Music and Studio Orchestral Concerts. These minority programmes were obviously suited to this more detailed and informed criticism but the roster paralleled press criticism too closely and soon fell out of use. [12]

A much larger affair was the 'Searchlight' on 'Children's Hour' programmes. In March 1938, 2,561 teachers were asked to elicit the views of the 79,341 children under their charge. The selection of teachers was balanced to represent the spread of population in the BBC regions. The report set out to discover the quantity of listening and programme preferences. The results were interesting, although the reliability of the sampling left something to be desired and they had to be used with care. It appears that 6 out of 10 children aged between 5 and 13 listened to 'Children's Hour' and of the remainder 2 out of 10 could not listen because they had no access to a set. Extrapolated to the whole population, this would give 1.2 million children who could not hear the programme because they had no set and 3.75 million who listened regularly or occasionally - out of a total elementary school population of 6 million - a very considerable section of the community. These estimates cannot have been too far away from the actual position and tell something about the popularity of at least one BBC programme and the considerable number of families which still did not possess a set in 1938. [13]

The Variety Listening Barometer

The main deficiency in the Drama Reports Scheme was that it did not entirely satisfy the demand from the Drama Department for a 'box-office' because there was insufficient attention to the quantitative aspect of listening. To remedy this weakness, the Listener Research Section proposed a wider scheme which was to become the 'Variety Listening Barometer'. [14] In its ultimate form, a 'barometer' would measure the rise and fall in the total size of audience for a programme. If this was completed, the results made generally available and, most important of all, used in the compilation of programme

plans, then one of the bastions of Reith's philosophy would
have fallen.

The plan was issued in August 1937. Variety was
chosen because, like drama, it was a well defined area of
programmes which had a strong need for audience reaction.
It was meant to be confined only to regular listeners to
variety - not the audience as a whole - but as variety attracted such a large part of the audience, those selected would be
fairly representative of the whole listening population. The
original intentions for research were clearly indicated:

> It ought to be pointed out, first, that listening barom-
> eters are visualised as centering round different
> departments. A Variety Listening Barometer would
> be quite separate from an Outside Broadcast Barom-
> eter or a Music Listening Barometer. Secondly, that
> a listening barometer will not show how large an
> audience is in terms of thousands of listeners, what it
> is hoped it will show is the relative sizes of audiences
> to different types of output from a given department. [15]

This experimental stage was intended to check simple
details in the mechanics of surveying: to establish the best
method of organisation, to check the value of the information
for planners and to see whether an adequate number of
thoroughly representative listeners could be induced to participate for the duration of the survey.

To construct the barometer an appeal was launched for
volunteers willing to complete the weekly listening logs.
Originally it was intended to use only 1, 000 volunteers but so
vast was the response to the microphone appeal by John Watt,
the Head of Variety, after a Saturday night 'Music Hall' on 18
September 1937, that 2, 000 were used instead. In all, 47, 000
people responded to the broadcast appeal and the appeals in
the Radio Times and The Listener. The excellent response
quickly removed fears about the lack of public goodwill. The
scheme ran from 11 October 1937 to 1 January 1938 and
involved the participants in completing weekly listening logs,
supplemented with extra questionnaires requesting opinions
on the programmes. These supplementary questions covered
broader issues of great importance to the BBC, especially
the extent of listening to foreign stations on Sundays. The
data was processed in a series of interim reports, issued
between January and May 1938, so that when the main report
was produced in November 1938 most of the results were
already well distributed inside the BBC.

The inevitable pre-selection of the volunteers suggests that the survey represented only the more eloquent and active listeners to variety. This criticism was anticipated:

> The recruitment of logkeepers by means of invitation from the Corporation is open to the possible objection that those who respond may not be really representative of the variety public. The greatest safeguard against this danger lies in the way in which the appeal for volunteers is made and the simplicity of the work which they are asked to do.[16]

In fact a control group was employed to check that the sample was broadly representative.[17] Fortunately the virtual identity of the variety-loving public with the radio audience as a whole meant that a large response from volunteers was achieved and the Listener Research Section was able to weight the sample according to age, sex, region and social class with much greater freedom than expected. The actual representativeness of the 2,000 logkeepers was examined in detail. There were more male than female logkeepers and their average age was lower than that for the whole population. The social composition was over-weighted towards the middle class listener, 45% of the logkeepers compared with 49% who were working class: for the whole population it was more like 33% to 66%. This assumed that working class people were those earning less than £5 per week and middle class people those earning £5 to £12 per week. This may represent the relative willingness of the two classes to cooperate and also the extent of set ownership, roughly at least, amongst working class people. The geographical distribution of the logkeepers compared with licence holders over-represented the London area at the expense of most of the other parts of the country, particularly Scotland and Wales.[18]

The only other substantial problem, which also afflicted the Drama Reports Scheme, had potentially more serious consequences for a quantitatively orientated survey: 'duty listening'. The overall effect was to increase the amount of listening by members of the barometer, partially out of a mistaken sense of duty to the BBC but also out of interest in broadcasting aroused by participation. The net effect was probably less serious:

> Briefly, the conclusion arrived at .... is that while the 2,000 logkeepers undoubtedly listen to more programmes than the average listener does, their choice

of programmes is probably typical of the great mass of listeners who like broadcast light entertainment.[19]

The barometer discovered some interesting facts about the habits of the radio audience as represented by the log-keepers: there was much to be learnt about the main times for listening, the daily variations in these times and also the overall quantity of listening in these periods. Some discoveries were obvious. For instance, Saturday evenings drew the largest audiences and revealed the greatest number of people listening until a late hour - after 11 p.m. This was due to the leisure available on the following day but also to the skill of the radio producers in transmitting the most attractive programmes on that evening. This was suggested when the 'Palace of Varieties' programme was moved to a Tuesday for one week. It still managed to draw a loyal audience of 82% of the logkeepers. On the other hand, the timing of Saturday programmes produced some surprise. Twice as many preferred 8-9 p.m. as the best time for 'Music Hall' - then the most popular programme - as compared with 9.20 - 10.20 p.m. As might be expected there was much less late evening listening on weekdays but even on a Saturday the audience declined very rapidly after 10 p.m. Relevant figures were derived from a question to the panel in November 1937.

Table 5.1: Variety Listening Barometer: Listening Levels.[20]

Proportion of logkeepers who listen to radio in any form:	Weekdays %	Saturday %
Up to 9.30 p.m.	97	97
9.30 - 10.00 p.m.	91	94
10.00 - 10.30 p.m.	54	79
10.30 - 11.00 p.m.	25	57
11.00 - 11.30 p.m.	7	29
11.30 - midnight	3	16

The Listener Research Section also attempted to use the barometer to quantify one of the most contentious issues - the amount of listening to foreign stations. About 20% of the audience for light entertainment listened to them on weekdays - mostly before 10. 30 a.m. when there was no BBC competition - and 66% listened at some time on Sundays. Approximately 33% of the panel would be listening to foreign stations at any time during the period 10. 00 a.m. to 7. 30 p.m. on a Sunday. [21] Even when the BBC was in competition, the relative popularity of the two alternatives on Sunday was hardly in doubt since, 'the proportion of listeners to foreign stations at 6. 00 p.m. is higher than at any time during the day.'[22] Obviously there was a need for more corroborative surveying but the results were the first solid manifestations of the extent of listening to foreign stations and the first concrete proof - established by BBC personnel - of widespread dissatisfaction with BBC programmes on Sunday. In addition, the barometer revealed the stations listened to. On Sundays 70% of those who said they listened to foreign stations - that was nearly 50% of the panel - listened to Radio Luxembourg. Radio Normandie was second in popularity, followed well behind by Lyons and Hilversum. As the BBC now observed, Luxembourg's programmes on Sunday had some extra attraction since:

> Apart from the fact that regular foreign station listening is three times as frequent on Sundays as on weekdays it is noteworthy that whereas Normandie slightly exceeds Luxembourg in popularity on weekdays, Luxembourg is nearly twice as popular as Normandie on Sundays. [23]

The component elements of the barometer's aggregate view of the habits of the panel revealed more interesting aspects of the audience. The audience was markedly differentiated in habits by age: for every 100 listeners aged 16 to 20 there were 121 aged 40 to 49. On the other hand, young people tended to listen later in the evening than the average. There were also differences in the quantity of listening between men and women. Female listening was consistently higher than male listening. Obviously work patterns were influential and the survey clearly showed that the most numerous daytime listeners during the weekdays were working class housewives. Only in listening to foreign stations did male significantly exceed female listening.

Table 5. 2: Variety Listening Barometer:
          Listening by Men and Women. [24]

Shows beginning between (average for the whole week)	Ratio	
	Women	Men
12. 00 - 2. 30 p. m.	100	58
4. 00 - 4. 59 p. m.	100	62
5. 00 - 5. 59 p. m.	100	79
6. 00 - 7. 59 p. m.	100	95
8. 00 - 8. 59 p. m.	100	98
9. 00 p. m. and after	100	96

Probably the most interesting result of all was the small variation between the regions which was discovered. Probably the only major difference was that, listeners in the BBC's North Region tended to listen later in the evening in greater numbers than those in the London Region. This was the first real evidence that audience behaviour was dictated primarily by the age, sex and social class of the listener. These early findings were to be consistently supported by later research and it served to make research into local behaviour a high priority - to see why this similarity should occur. All kinds of imponderable factors were aroused by these results and needed to be scrutinised. Had broadcasting, since its inception in 1922, wrought the basis for this similarity or had regional habits and tastes been fairly uniform before the arrival of broadcasting? Equally there were graduations between these two outer limits. If broadcasting had some influence, it may have been heavily modified by other social forces. It could not be assumed that broadcasting was the sole agent in creating such a position; other persuasive forces towards better communications, such as the press and, indirectly, the internal combustion engine, need to be considered.

Variations according to social class were more marked. If middle and working class listening was taken separately, proportionately more of the working class with sets listened than their middle class counterparts, particularly on Saturdays and to foreign stations on Sundays. [25] The Listener Research Section commented on the Sunday listening with some interest:

> If the habits of middle class and working class listeners
> are considered separately it is found that the curves
> run approximately parallel throughout the day - the
> working class curve, however, being some 10 to 15%
> higher than the middle class curve. This position is
> only reversed after the Corporation has closed down at
> 10.30 p.m. [26]

Of course, the working class listening group was already
<u>numerically</u> greater than the middle class group. It was only
on weekdays that the proportion of middle class listeners
exceeded the proportion of working class listeners. The
Listener Research Section was prepared to comment on these
figures but it did not seek an explanation. Clearly, the differences were slight but there was a noticeable and persistent
variation of 10-20% except on weekdays. This was hardly
due to sampling error and was probably attributable to the
contrasting leisure patterns of the respective income groups.
The differing hours of work may explain, for instance, why
working class listening was so much lower on weekdays than
the middle class, whilst the greater tendency to seek cheaper
home-based entertainment may explain the greater degree of
listening at weekends.
    The research into the programme preferences of the
2,000 also proved to be fruitful. Before pursuing the discoveries further it will be useful to explain what the BBC
meant by 'taste' in audience research particularly when
compared with 'habits'. A barometer was meant to be
essentially concerned with pressure rather than heat. That
is, it was meant to be concerned with quantities of listening
not with the enjoyment of the programmes. In this case only
a limited attempt was made to discover the opinions and preferences of the logkeepers. 'Tastes' are extraordinarily
difficult to measure. There can be no foolproof method of
measuring them collectively. Any questionnaire must expect
firm answers - usually a blunt yes or no - to its questions on
tastes. This is contrary to normal experience where taste
is graduated almost infinitely between the two extremes of
liking and disliking. However, a wider choice of answers
will probably introduce confusion and certainly lead to results
which are difficult to analyse. Programme categorisation is
no easier - there is no agreed definition of what is 'serious'
as opposed to 'popular' music. It could be asked, too, where
'taste' ended and 'habit' began. The Listener Research
Section resorted to one definition and shut out the blurring at

the edges for the sake of convenience. The surveying of 'habits' concerned those available to listen at various times of the day. This part of the research became almost a general social survey, simply because so many other daily activities influenced the hours at which people could listen. The surveying of 'tastes' was restricted to the liking for specific programmes or groups of programmes.

In fact some interrelation has to be ignored because it would be so difficult to demonstrate anything more than speculative conclusions - habits can influence tastes. If, say, a listener is available to listen for a specific period of time each day, he may begin by disliking the programme then available but eventually acquire the taste simply by the act of listening. This, after all, was an essential aim of the BBC. The only way to measure this change in taste is to carry out a regular census of taste at fairly frequent intervals and, even then, the mechanics of the change could elude the surveyors. It was equally true that taste could influence habit. If the same listener could not hear the programme at all, he might resort to another leisure activity - hence being lost to broadcasting for that period of time regardless of any future change in the programme. There was possibly an element of this in Sunday listening: part of the audience may have chosen to abstain habitually because of the unattractive BBC programmes and a reluctance to listen to foreign stations.

In the Variety Listening Barometer, the analysis of 'taste' relied on a pre-selected group, with the risk that only the opinions and preferences of the more committed would be discovered. Tables of the most popular programmes were constructed and the category 'Straight Variety' was easily the most popular. 'Vaudeville' always drew enormous audiences, with the Royal Command Performance attracting the largest audience when 94% of the logkeepers listened. A supplementary questionnaire put to the audience produced a useful confirmation of the most popular types of programme. Although these figures were only true for the more committed, evidence from the control group for the barometer did suggest that, although their liking for the various programmes was a good deal less, the order of popularity was roughly similar. As the variety audience represented the largest part of the whole audience, it seemed probable that there would have been little change if the logkeepers had been chosen entirely at random.

Audiences were capable of behaving differently towards programmes of the same basic type. So called 'background'

Table 5.3: Variety Listening Barometer: Popular Programmes[27]

Type	like more %	like less %	satisfied %
Straight Variety (Music Hall etc.)	70	1	29
Reginald Foort at the Theatre Organ	55	5	40
Comedy Shows	54	5	41
Concert Parties	44	8	48
'Interest Programmes' (Scrapbook)	41	7	52
Cinema Organs	41	8	50
Serials (The Plums)	31	12	51
Musical Comedy	29	19	52
Dance Music	17	28	54
Relays from the United States etc.	8	57	34
Average	39	15	46

music programmes broadcast during the daytime, such as gramophone record broadcasts, were listened to by roughly the same number of people regardless of content - the size of the audience being related far more to the time of the broadcast.[28] In the evenings the 'foreground' programmes attracted a more discriminating audience. A programme such as 'Monday at Seven' varied somewhat according to content. This was a limited challenge to the theory of undiscriminating 'tap listening' by the audience. Nonetheless, previously unperceived evidence could be produced in support of this theory. It was noticed that the rise or fall in size of audience for a programme, such as 'Monday at Seven', heavily influenced the size for the following programme. One report observed the behaviour of a group of intermittent listeners: 'Whether the smaller group should or should not listen to 'The Plums' does not appear to have had anything to do with that programme but to have depended upon the attractiveness of 'Monday at Seven' which preceded it.'[29] As with the habits of the audience, opinions differed most markedly according to age. The main report on the Variety Listening Barometer stated rather bluntly: 'Differences in taste were more often correlated with differences in age than with differences either in sex, social class or region but even these were less than might have been expected.' For the really big variety broadcasts the structure of the audience was almost identical to the social composition of the entire audience, but, as might be expected, the programmes appealing to the physically active, such as dance music, drew decidedly more of their audience from young rather than middle aged people.

Variations in taste according to sex were hidden by the inability of men to hear many of the daytime programmes; these were therefore confined largely to female audiences because of the limitations of the working day rather than from any free programme selection. Regional preferences varied much less than might have been expected. The classic case used to demonstrate this similarity was the serial 'The Plums'. As the main report argued: 'It is interesting to note that although 'The Plums' were North country characters, the proportion of logkeepers who listened to them was as high in the London Region as in the North.' Class differences in taste were also less prominent than might have been expected. The report had few speculations to make on the influence of social class on tastes but those differences which were discernable were closely related to the habits of listeners already observed. In their greater willingness to listen to foreign stations, working people demonstrated a lower tolerance to BBC Sunday programmes and probably shared a greater affinity for the variety and popular music broadcasts produced by Luxembourg and Normandie.

General Listening Barometer

The Variety Listening Barometer was so successful that it was decided to expand the method to cover the entire output of BBC programmes. The new panel was in operation from 4 December 1936 to 1 April 1939 and produced a continuous listening log of great value to the programme planners. The panel was composed partly of volunteers and partly of those pre-selected by the Listener Research Section to produce a more accurate balance by age, sex, region, class and occupation. Of the total 4,205 on the panel, roughly 500 middle class people and 500 working class came from each of the four English BBC regions: London, North, Midland and West. Questionnaires were used, although the surveyors looked to the future when the expensive, but more reliable, method of personal interviewing could be used. As Silvey explained:

> Volunteers had again to be used, for the days when we could conduct a survey based on personal interviews were still to come, and it was clearly understood that we would be estimating no more than the relative audiences of programmes. [30]

The results were issued in two forms: special reports dealt with the specific issues which most excited the attention of the BBC planners, while information on listening to foreign stations was issued in interim reports as soon after collection as possible. One special report covered religious broadcasts and in the process told something about contemporary attitudes towards religion generally. For instance, 33% of the panel listened to at least one of the Sunday evening broadcasts - the most successful being the monthly broadcast from St. Martin-in-the-Fields. Working class listeners listened more than middle class ones and listening was greatest in the West Region and least in the London area. [31] Other reports dealt with such disparate topics as listening to news, music and sport[32] but the most interesting analysis reflected the increasing concern for the European situation. One report covered the extent of listening to German bulletins in English. [33] The group was asked if they listened to broadcasts from Hamburg or Cologne at 7.15 p.m. each evening. The results revealed little listening - or few who would admit to listening.

Table 5.4: General Listening Barometer: Listening to German Broadcasts

Question	Yes %	No %
Reception of them possible?	64	36
Did you know of them?	49	51
Have you heard them?	29	71
Do you listen regularly?	7	93

The North Region's Public Relations Officer included some of the volunteers' comments to provide colour to these results:

> I think that the German broadcasts were listened to rather extensively at first, but now they seem to have fallen quite flat .... In spite of this there are some, shall we say, thoughtful people who listen periodically to try to detect any reactions that may be registered in response to important speeches or events.

One man argued: 'I felt, what is the use of all this, its only a pack of lies - we can only get the truth from our own stations, and of course did not listen again.' This disbelief seemed to have been shared by many listeners in the North.

The interim reports also contained interesting material. Several paralleled the earlier work on listening to foreign stations - rather confirming the original impression. Since the previous investigation, the BBC had managed to make some inroads on Sunday listening by opening transmissions other than for religious broadcasts at 10.45 a.m. instead of 12.30 p.m. However, weekday listening to other stations had actually increased and there were several prominent points of resistance to the BBC's output. On weekdays the peaks were from 8 - 9 a.m. when 10% of the logkeepers listened to foreign stations (with no BBC competition) and from 10 - 11 p.m. when 8% listened. Luxembourg was the most popular station throughout the week. On Sundays the trends were much as before, although there was one particular body of large scale listening which lingered between 4 and 6 p. m. The reason was common knowledge at the BBC - one report explained the popularity of the rival programmes for the uninitiated:

> From 4. 00 to 5. 00 p. m. both Luxembourg and Normandie broadcast a Horlick's Tea Hour, and from 5. 30 to 6. 00 p. m. Luxembourg broadcasts the "Ovaltineys" which is primarily a children's programme. [34]

Another report examined the impact of talks on the audience: 45% considered them to be too cautious, 39% felt that they did not deal with contemporary issues, whilst a considerable minority felt that they were not interesting enough. [35] Noticeably, few of those cooperating with the questionnaire used the section for free comment to criticise political bias in BBC news broadcasts. Reticence was not responsible as many, especially working class listeners, took the opportunity to vehemently condemn the dull Sunday programmes.

One interim report looked at sport. [36] A table of the most popular sports was composed. The top six sporting commentaries were:

Table 5. 5: General Listening Barometer: Sports Programmes

	Sport	Liked by % of the panel
1.	The Boat Race	70
2.	Championship Boxing	51
3.	Soccer	50
4.	Cricket	50
5.	Lawn Tennis	34
6.	Horse Racing	33

Compared with the middle class sample, the working class correspondents were more interested in broadcast sport and liked soccer and boxing noticeably more. There were some predictable regional variations: the London Region liked the Boat Race and speedway more than the average, whilst the North liked Rugby League more. The Welsh Region preferred Rugby Union and soccer was more popular in the North and

Midlands than elsewhere.

Overall, this barometer was successful enough to persuade the Listener Research Section to press for its development as a continuous survey using personal interviews rather
than questionnaires. [37] Ironically, September 1939 was to be
the starting date and the war delayed its introduction: of
course war conditions, where the study of morale was crucial,
actually made it more necessary than ever to discover audience preferences and after the initial hesitation, the 'Continuous Survey of Listening' was rushed into service. It began
work in December 1939. [38]

Random Samples

After the work on the Variety Listening Barometer, the
Listener Research Section moved on to the random sample
method of surveying. Once again one of the main problems
was to persuade BBC personnel that the sampling method was
reliable. There were two random samples in 1938; the first
searched for 'Winter Listening Habits', the other, 'Summer
Listening Habits'. The First Random Sample, published in
September 1938, chose 3,000 homes at random from GPO
licence files covering all the BBC Regions: 8,200 persons
over 16 years old were reached by this method and 3,152
replied - a response rate of 44%. The Second Random
Sample, published in February 1939, also looked at households rather than individuals and reached 4,700 households
or 12,700 listeners in all: 4,500 replied, a response rate of
35%.

Overall, the two surveys were much more reliable than
any previously undertaken: the pre-selection was carried out
as much as possible by the samplers and even the lowest
response at 35% was good by existing precedents with a
negligible effect on the accuracy of the results. The report
attached to the First Random Sample observed:

> Had a full 100% response been received the results so
> given would possibly have been on a slightly lower
> level all round though it is not thought that there would
> have been any material change in the relative positions
> of the various programmes or times which were com-
> pared.

The report was also keen to emphasise that the size of the
sample was not necessarily concomitant with its accuracy:

> In order to double the accuracy of a sample it is

129

necessary to quadruple its size; to quadruple the
accuracy, the sample must be multiplied by sixteen,
and so on. This can be put another way: if accuracy
to within 3% is sufficient for the job in hand, a sample
of 1,000 is just as good as a sample of 10,000.

Silvey also sought to reassure the unilluminated about the
theory of probability upon which the sample depended:

> We are concerned not with the theoretical <u>possibility</u>
> of getting the right answer from a sample, but with
> the <u>probability</u> of doing so, which is a very different
> matter. The important point is that though those 501
> different answers are all equally <u>possible</u> they are
> certainly not all equally <u>probable</u>. [39]

The surveys were fairly representative of the population, by age, sex and location. The only main divergence
was that of the social class of the listener. The First Random
Sample again used income levels to estimate broad class
assignation and gave figures of 42.9% middle class, 51.2%
working class, with 5.9% unknown. The report noted this
over-representation of the middle class in the sample but
stressed that it was unsafe to assume that the composition of
the listening population should be similar to that of the population as a whole:

> Indeed there is every reason to suppose that the social
> grade composition of the listening public is radically
> different from that of the population as a whole, for it
> is highly probable that the principal factor preventing
> families from having sets is poverty. It has been
> estimated that approximately 70% of the population is
> working class ... If we assume that 90% of the fami-
> lies without sets are working class (a legitimate
> assumption in the circumstances) this would mean that
> the listening public consists of 40% middle class and
> 60% working class.

Consequently the report asserted:

> it seems probable that the sample is subject to two
> biases - an under-representation of the less enthusi-
> astic listeners and an over-representation of the
> middle class. But since we know that more listening
> is done in the average working class home, than in the
> average middle class home, it may well be that these
> two biases to some extent cancel one another out. [40]

Perhaps the questionnaire was too formidable for working class listeners (despite the popularity of football pools) or probably there was a connection between more listening than average and a greater willingness to cooperate.

Between them, the two surveys examined four major facets of the amount and type of listening. The first indicator of the quantity of listening was the time when listeners normally switched on their sets in both summer and winter. The second naturally involved looking at the time they switched them off. Thirdly, for the purposes of comparison, the samples examined the level of listening each day at half-hour intervals. The Second Random Sample also asked listeners to judge for themselves whether they listened more or less in summer than in winter. The fourth part of each sample analysed the audience for the various types of programme. In addition, the Second Random Sample included the first real attempt to discover more about the things which listeners actually liked by using a separate questionnaire devoted to 'tastes'.

The time when listeners switched on their sets provided the first basis by which the levels of listening could be measured and a comparison can be made between the two samples. An absolute comparison between the samples was not possible because the base levels at 9 p.m. were higher in winter than in summer. Accepting this, contrasts in listening are still evident. Winter listening was always higher at an earlier time for all groups, almost certainly due to the darkness and inclement weather which reduced alternative leisure pursuits. The young listened consistently less than the old, although as the evening progressed, especially in winter, the difference was reduced. Women could listen consistently more than men whatever the season or time of day. More of the working class could listen at any time. Regionally there was little contrast. Significantly the London Region showed slightly less listening than the other areas at 6 p.m. This was probably due to the longer distance from work to home and the consequently increased travelling times. The most complex variation was that between urban and rural listening. In the First Random Sample, urban listening was definitely less than rural listening. In the summer the position for early evening listening was exactly reversed. This may have reflected the increase in agricultural work during the summer evenings.

In addition, the Second Random Sample demonstrated the contrast between summer and winter listening in a differ-

Table 5.6: Random Samples: Listening in Summer and Winter[41]

Proportion of those listening at 9 p.m. who usually start listening about:	Winter First Random Sample Base at 9 p.m. = 100			Summer Second Random Sample Base at 9 p.m. = 100 (Base levels are not comparable between samples)		
	6 p.m.	7 p.m.	8 p.m.	6 p.m.	7 p.m.	8 p.m.
Grand Total	83	93	99	66	71	91
Men	78	91	98	61	67	87
Women	89	95	100	70	74	93
Middle Class	80	91	98	59	65	88
Working Class	86	95	99	70	74	93
Aged 20-29	80	91	99	62	67	89
Aged 50-59	88	95	99	72	75	93
Urban	83	92	98	66	71	90
Rural	89	97	100	61	66	90
London Region	80	92	99	63	69	92
North Region	85	93	98	67	72	90
Midland Region	86	94	99	65	70	92
West Region	86	94	99	67	72	88
Welsh Region	89	94	98	74	76	93
Scottish Region	88	94	97	65	70	85
N. Ireland Region	84	99	100	71	80	89

ent way. It asked its listeners to say for themselves whether they listened more, less or about the same amount in the summer. Two periods were suggested: from 6 - 8 p.m., 42% claimed they listened less, 3% claimed they listened more and a majority, 55%, claimed they listened about the same amount. By 8 - 10.30 p.m., 20% claimed they listened less, 8% more and 66% the same amount.[42] The report commented:

> early and later, there is less seasonal change in women's listening than in men's. It is the young and the middle class listeners, too, rather than the elderly and the working class, who tend to listen less in the summer. As between different regions, there is little worth remark ......

The statement continued:

> But a comparison of the answers of urban, with those of rural listeners shows that whereas in the early evening in the summer many more listeners in the country are kept away from their wireless sets than in the town, after 8.00 p.m., the position changes. For between 8.00 and 10.30, not only is the shrinkage in the audience no greater in the country than the town, but there is a substantial minority of country listeners (13%) who say that they listen more in the summer than in the winter.

The time when listeners switched off can also be compared. The question in both samples was: 'At what time in the evening do you usually stop listening on weekdays (excluding Saturday)?'. The results are displayed in Table 5.7. Again, absolute comparisons between the samples were not possible because the summer base levels were lower. Nonetheless, some comparisons are possible and some interesting differences emerge. The difference in listening between the classes was, for instance, influenced by the seasonal change. On summer weekdays the audience contained more of the middle class than of working class listeners - in contrast to the winter when the classes listened in roughly the same proportions. Men listened later than women, although over the rest of the day women listened in greater proportions. At both times of the year, urban dwellers listened later than rural inhabitants. The regional variations revealed a new feature of listening which had not been appreciated before. The report argued the point clearly enough:

Table 5.7: Random Samples: Time When Listening Ends in Summer and Winter 43

Proportion of those listening at 9 p.m. on weekdays (not Saturdays) who usually listen up to:	Winter First Random Sample Base at 9 p.m. = 100					Summer Second Random Sample Base at 9 p.m. = 100 (Base levels are not comparable between samples)				
	10.00 p.m.	10.30 p.m.	11.00 p.m.	11.30 p.m.	12.00 p.m.	10.00 p.m.	10.30 p.m.	11.00 p.m.	11.30 p.m.	12.00 p.m.
Grand Total	92	62	31	9	4	93	65	32	12	6
Men	93	66	33	11	5	93	69	36	14	8
Women	90	57	29	8	4	92	61	29	10	4
Middle Class	92	64	30	9	5	94	70	36	13	7
Working Class	92	61	32	10	4	91	63	30	11	5
Aged: Under 20	86	56	27	11	3	91	64	31	13	6
20-29	96	70	43	17	8	95	71	43	19	9
30-39	92	65	30	9	6	94	67	31	10	5
40-49	93	61	30	8	3	94	69	34	12	6
50-59	92	60	29	6	2	92	64	32	12	7
60-69	91	56	22	5	2	89	59	27	7	3
70+	78	28	6	- -	- -	81	43	16	3	3
Urban	93	64	33	11	5	93	66	33	13	6
Rural	85	51	19	3	1	91	42	25	9	4

London Region	89	58	27	8	4	91	60	27	8	4
North Region	92	64	33	8	3	94	70	38	15	7
Midland Region	95	59	30	10	6	92	61	28	9	4
West Region	92	54	19	7	5	93	57	23	7	3
Welsh Region	93	66	37	10	4	92	73	32	19	16
Scotland	95	75	43	16	5	95	76	49	25	11
N. Ireland	99	83	55	23	11	96	87	66	30	11

These figures suggest that no matter what the season or the day, the greater the distance of a region from the South of England, the later do its listeners switch off in the evening. This result is so unexpected that one might be excused for suspecting it to be a statistical freak were it not for the fact that it is corroborated by three separate questions in two distinct enquiries.

Other questions on the same basis asked listeners when they switched off on Saturdays and Sundays. Broadly speaking, there was little seasonal variation: in both periods of the year, there was more listening on Saturdays at a later time, whilst there was less on Sunday than for a normal weekday. The most obvious contrast was the confirmation that, regardless of the season, working class listeners listened much later on Saturday than on weekdays, whereas marginally more of the middle class listened later on weekdays. The pattern of switching off later in the provinces was maintained on Saturdays throughout the year, although listening in the West of England appears to have ended earliest of all. Sunday listening was considerably less: the BBC closed down at 10. 30 p. m. on Sunday and hence any listening recorded after this time must have been to foreign stations. [44]

The main tendency unearthed by the surveys was that there was definitely less listening in summer but it was a much smaller reduction than had been thought previously. Technically, the reduction took place almost entirely before 9 p. m. The report on the Second Random Sample was anxious to demonstrate that the blocks of figures and percentages might hide a varied composition. The conclusion was tempered by this:

Listening less in the summer may take the form of listening fewer evenings per week, of being more selective when one is listening, of switching on later, or of switching off earlier. The available evidence suggests that listeners certainly do not switch off their sets earlier in the summer. That they are more selective in their listening is possible, though unlikely. At the time of writing we have no evidence on the question of whether listeners listen fewer evenings per week in the summer. But there is evidence to support the view that to a large extent that minority who do less listening in the summer are in the main listeners who begin their evening listening at about 8. 00 p. m. , rather than at about 6. 00 p. m. or 6. 30 p. m.

In the First Random Sample there were some interesting observations on the quantity of listening in the daytime before 6 p.m. It was observed that the largest increase in listening took place, naturally enough, as people came home from work between 5 and 6 p.m.:

> This means that from the time BBC transmissions begin at 10.00 a.m. until 6 o'clock, the normal audience is never less than about 4,000,000 persons. At the peak of lunchtime it rises to about 8,000,000 and between 5 and 6 it passes the 10,000,000 mark.

The audience was predominantly female, forming 75% of the audience from 10 a.m. to 12 noon and from 2 to 5 p.m. Male listening only increased in the period 12 to 2 p.m. Then it was noticeable that working class lunches ran more frequently from 12 until 1 p.m., whilst middle class lunchtimes normally ran from 1 to 2 p.m. [45] In rural areas, daytime listening was significantly higher than in urban areas. The gap was greatest between 10 and 11 a.m., when the morning service and women's talk attracted 40% of women listening in rural areas but only 27% of women in towns. There were also regional differences. In Wales and the West of England, listening was consistently higher throughout the day. The report added:

> this is not a repetition in different words of the fact that rural daytime listening is greater than that in towns, for urban areas were strongly represented in both Wales and the West of England. [46]

Some research was also done on the audience for evening news programmes. Basically, there were two main news bulletins in the evening on the National wavelength and two on the Regional Programmes. The first news programme was easily the most popular, being the earliest permitted bulletin of the day. It contained much of the news which would escape the press until the next day and it contained a very popular sports section. A table composed of the results in the First Random Sample can be drawn as shown in Table 5.8.

A rather different sort of research was done in the Second Random Sample, where a questionnaire was devoted to listener's tastes over the whole output. It is useful to turn to Silvey's definition and description:

> This was the first of a number of attempts we made during my time at the BBC to carry out a census of

what we came to call 'tastes'. (For convenience we
confined the term 'tastes' to attitudes towards broad
categories of output as distinct from particular broadcasts.)[47]

Table 5. 8: First Random Sample: Listening to News

News	Regular	Occasional
1st News 6 p. m. National + Sport	58	16
2nd News 7 p. m. Regional. No Sport	14	24
3rd News 9 p. m. National. No Sport	33	25
News Summary 10 p. m. Regional + Sport and Talks	21	24

Altogether there were 21 categories of existing programmes to choose from and tables were composed to show
the numerical support for each of them. It was not the intention to provide a guide to the quantity or quality of programmes which the audience might desire in the future.
Variety naturally topped the list, with cinema and theatre
organ music following closely. The categorisation of the
programmes was the weakest point of the sample, due to the
varied interpretations which participants made of the definitions used, but a broad order of popularity was indicated,
with musical programmes having a clear lead over the spoken
word.

For all the programmes, the average number marked
as 'liked' was 9. 9 out of 21. In other words, the average
listener liked about half of the 21 major categories of programmes. Middle class people had more catholic tastes than
working class listeners, choosing 10. 2 on average compared
with 9. 8 selections. Of course, this could have meant that
middle class correspondents marked the questionnaire more
liberally. A clear divergence in programme appeal was
apparent between young and old listeners. Older listeners,
say from 40 to 49, chose 10. 5 programmes on average, compared with 9. 3 for those under 20. This might be expected,
as would be the divergence of taste between the two age
groups on particular types of programmes. Dance music
appealed to 88% of the under twenties and, hardly surprisingly,

to only 38% of those between 60 and 69. The reverse was
true of the relative popularity of talks and discussions, which
were liked by 25% and 60% respectively. Other programmes
showed less divergence.

Table 5.9: Second Random Sample:
          Programme Preferences of the Sample [48]

Programme	%
Variety	93
Theatre and Cinema Organs	82
Military Bands	72
Musical Comedy	69
Dance Music	68
Plays	68
Light Music	66
Orchestral Music	55
Brass Bands	55
Talks	53
Discussions	49
Cricket Commentaries	48
Serial Plays	41
Light Opera	38
Vocal Recitals	32
Tennis Commentaries	26
Piano Recitals	21
Grand Opera	21
Violin Recitals	19
Serial Readings	12
Chamber Music	8

The variation according to sex was reasonably predict-
able. Two-thirds of the men liked cricket commentaries,
compared with only a third of the women. Men also liked
brass band music and discussions significantly more than
women. In contrast, women liked plays, serial plays and
serial readings a good deal more than men. Regional variations were much less than expected. Cricket commentaries
were not liked as much in Scotland or Northern Ireland - for
the obvious reason that the game was played less there. The
Scots, Irish, Welsh and North Region listeners preferred
vocal recitals more than elsewhere, whilst listeners in the
North Region showed an expected affinity for brass bands.

This useful quantification of taste had a fairly predict-able impact on the BBC hierarchy. Of course, planners already knew that variety was more popular than chamber music and this led many to reject the findings of surveys as unnecessary. However, as Silvey asserted, 'by no means everyone would have predicted that men's and women's pre-ferences were as similar as they proved to be.' Fortunately Silvey could see that the number of those in the BBC who preferred 'facts to folklore' was increasing. On its own, the survey did have limits but these were largely due to the lack of corroboration:

> We saw it as merely the first of a series, much of the value of which would come from comparisons. Was it true, as was so often said at the time, that broadcasting would raise public tastes? A series of inquiries on these lines should, we thought, contribute to the even-tual finding of an answer. [49]

In fact the results of subsequent series did not differ marked-ly and, hence, the earliest conclusions about tastes in the thirties can be used as valuable guides to audience behaviour.

Commercial Research

One of Silvey's first principles of action had been to ensure that other social surveys of relevance to the BBC were sent in as a matter of course. Surveys for commercial purposes had inspired some of the methods used in research and, of course, Silvey's early experience lay in such work. As in the USA, the primary incentive for commercial broadcasting organisations to engage in research was the lure of attracting advertising revenue. To sell prime time at higher rates and to attract commercial interest, it was essential to discover the peak viewing hours.

American influence was strongly impressed on the British market. Firms engaged in research by the opinion poll method included Gallup and Crossley from the United States. [50] They were first employed by the two European rivals broadcasting to Britain - Radio Luxembourg and Radio Normandie. Nielson's mechanical set recorder also had its attractions. Although not used in Britain before the war, it was interesting enough to persuade Silvey to visit Nielson and investigate the potential of his method when on a tour of the States to try and learn more about the techniques of survey-ing. [51] The relevance of this commercial research was that it provided invaluable supplementary evidence on audience behaviour - evidence which corroborated BBC research conclusions.

The International Broadcasting Company's station, Radio Normandie, had collected material on the audience as early as 1935. In evidence to Ullswater, the proprietor of the IBC, Captain Plugge, cited this survey in support of his case. At that time he had a team of twelve making personal calls throughout the country. The survey was of 8,800 homes, of which 79% had a set: 62% of those with sets claimed to listen to IBC, although no details were specified. [52] Plugge put the case deceptively. His argument that the greatest concentrations of listeners were in the South and South Coast, where proximity to the transmitter made listening easy, slipped over the fact that in the North, where reception was poor or non-existent, there were hardly any listeners to IBC. [53]

In 1938, Radio Normandie offered a research contract to Crossley Incorporated. This produced evidence of more value. Also using personal, next-day interviewing, 5,785 interviews were carried out. The results were analysed by day and by hour. On weekdays 64% of those listening before 11.30 a.m. listened to commercial stations, although the audience was only 30% of the maximum size at that time. Between 2 - 6 p.m., 44% of sets were in use, only 36% of these were listening to foreign stations.

It was on Sundays that the really large-scale listening occurred - as the Variety Listening Barometer had shown. In the morning 52% of sets were in use, of which a massive 82.1% were listening to foreign stations. After noon more sets, 66%, were in use and before 6 p.m., 70.3% were listening to commercial broadcasts. This amply confirmed BBC research. The survey concluded that the concentration for Normandie was in London and the Home Counties; Luxembourg, having a more powerful transmitter, had a much wider reception area. On weekdays these two stations had roughly equivalent levels of listening - if anything Normandie had the most listeners - but on Sundays, Luxembourg had easily the largest audience in Britain. [54]

The need to sell advertising airtime meant that the time of listening was always more important to the commercial stations than to the BBC. It was imperative for commercial stations to give their advertisers a clear idea of the market which they offered: the size and composition of their audience. In ideal circumstances, the commercial stations could monop-

olise this market and hence attract more prime time advertisers. It was therefore to their advantage that there was a
serious imperfection in the provision of a regular daily
broadcasting service by the BBC. That was the restriction
on the hours of broadcasting. At no time before 1939 did
BBC broadcasting begin before 10.30 a.m. thus giving the
commercial and other foreign stations free play in the early
morning. In 1923, the starting time had only been at 3.30
p.m. and even when this was moved to the earlier time,
there were frequent gaps during the rest of the day. These
gaps were between 10.45 a.m. and noon and from 2.00 p.m.
to 2.25 p.m. each weekday. Weekends were the main black-
spot. Only in 1932 was there non-stop broadcasting from
noon to midnight on Saturdays. On Sundays, it was not until
1933 that the period between 6.15 p.m. and 8.00 p.m. was
filled. [55]

Many of these limits were imposed as concessions to
outside groups, including the Press Agencies' ban on early
news summaries, and the Radio Manufacturers' insistence on
a test period each day. The self-imposed restriction was on
Sunday to avoid a clash with church services.

Commercial broadcasting companies realised that these
limitations presented them with a fine opportunity to provide
a service at times when people were normally able to listen
but were not provided with BBC broadcasts. Some simple
research exposed the potential for broadcasting to a considerable part of the listening population, unchallenged by a
rival domestic service for many hours each day. The IBC,
for instance, issued a pamphlet to advertisers in an attempt
to attract buyers for their period of 'broadcasting time' on
Radio Normandie. The evidence for early morning listening
was based on the following advice:

> We asked the electricity engineer of a thriving London
> suburb and he, very kindly, had a look at his supply
> loading chart which, to our surprise, indicated that
> 74% of the population in his district got up between 7
> and 8.00 a.m., while 24% got up before 7.00 a.m.
> This certainly seemed interesting, so we went to his
> competitor - (one of Mr. Therm's engineers), and he
> told us that 75% of the gas consumers were up before
> 8 o'clock. [56]

Of course, these figures were measuring potential audiences
but information derived from public utilities was an extremely
useful guide to the general pattern of social activity which

influenced the size of the audience throughout the day.

Another similar example of research also yielded some information on the times at which the audience was able to listen. The People's Food, by Crawford and Broadley produced survey material of general social interest which could be used as valuable raw material for estimating the potential audience. The survey was, however, limited by its restriction to households in major urban areas throughout the country. The book openly noted the importance of meal times to the broadcaster since this was a likely time for listening. The time of breakfast was discovered to be commonly shared by all social classes in the hour from 8.00 a.m. to 9.00 a.m. This was, moreover, increasingly taken at home by working men: formerly they had taken breakfast at work because the working day started much earlier, particularly before the First World War. This potential listening period was never served by the BBC before 1939 and the market was left completely open to commercial stations which duly filled the gap.

The only specific time which was shared by all social classes as a meal time was 1.00 p.m. Everywhere else there was some disparity, particularly between those earning less than £5 per week and those earning more. Crawford and Broadley noted the failure of all the broadcasting stations to meet the needs of the audience at this common meal time:

> It is interesting to note that whereas the foreign stations which provide commercial broadcasts for the English market have developed extensive programmes before, during, and following the breakfast period, they have as yet done little to provide similar entertainment for the midday break. It is true that programmes provided during the luncheon interval would not reach those who lunch in restaurants and factories, but it must be remembered that the great majority of the population take their midday meal at home. [57]

The most interesting disparity from the point of view of the broadcaster was the contrast between the working class 'high tea', usually taken from 5 to 5.30 p.m., immediately after work, and the upper class 'tea' which was most often eaten between 4.30 and 5.00 p.m. This variation continued with the 'upper' class 'dinner' being normally taken between 7.30 and 8.00 p.m., whilst the more numerous working class generally ate 'supper' between 9.00 and 9.30 p.m. It was noticed that the 'high tea' had moved to a considerably earlier

time than before the First World War - when 6.00 to 6.30
p.m. was the most popular time - a change also caused by
the reduction in the length of the working day. The book outlined the significance of the new position for broadcasters:

> The hour of the tea-time meal is even more important
> to wireless broadcasters than breakfast and lunch. The
> Children's Hour must be fitted in between their return
> from school and tea-time or postponed until tea is well
> over. A programme of special appeal to housewives
> will not secure its maximum listening public if it
> clashes with the preparation of tea or the washing up.[58]

Crawford and Broadley did not go further and examine
the consequences of the BBC's limits on the hours of broadcasting and the net effect of the restricted service is hard to
estimate. Some potential daytime listeners, out of range for
good foreign station reception, may have been discouraged
from owning a set by the gaps in the BBC service. However,
the provision of a full evening programme was maintained,
except on Sundays, and this was probably the decisive influence on set ownership, since that was the time when most of
the population was free to listen.[59] Silvey made use of the
People's Food in the preparation of his own research work
and many of the Listener Research Section's reports supported the main findings.[60]

The Use of Listener Research

The decision to undertake audience research appeared to
indicate a complete change in policy, but if the BBC was to
prove that this was a genuine change of heart, the research
material actually had to be used in programme planning. If
it was not, then the research would only have served to
satiate the superficial need to improve public relations: granting only the illusion of deeper consultation.

In fact, the use of the material varied considerably
from department to department throughout the Corporation.
The Variety Department used it extensively, as might be
expected with its greater commitment to the audience, whilst
the Talks Department employed the information much less.
The nature of the output seemed to be a decisive influence on
the level of interest shown by a department; Silvey noted the
response to the Variety Listening Barometer by the Head of
Variety: 'John Watt used the results extensively when planning this winter's programmes.'[61] Otherwise the implementation of findings was more desultory and their value was not

properly appreciated before the outbreak of war. Publicity
was certainly an essential aim and the Listener Research
Section remained a part of the Public Relations Department
before 1939. A paper from the Section to the General Advisory Council made the position clear:

> Another by-product of the work lies in the goodwill
> which it has evidently created among the listening
> public. Appeals for cooperation from listeners have
> met in every case with a most encouraging response,
> and sustained help has been given by those selected to
> take part in the various schemes described. News-
> paper comment has been friendly. Goodwill of this kind,
> while not the primary object of the work, is helpful to
> the BBC in many ways. [62]

Actually, some of the press were not so easily placated.
Whereas most newspapers had demanded formal listener research, with typical perfidiousness some papers actually
attacked the results of the first efforts, and even advocated
a return to dependence on correspondence. [63]

Despite the lack of interest in some departments there
had been some change in BBC policy and the relationship between the broadcaster and the listener had moved marginally
closer. Horizons had been broadened and there was no longer
any need to rely on letters or personal contact. As Maurice
Gorham remarked:

> To study these figures, as we did, day by day, seven
> days a week, gave you a feeling of being in touch with
> your audience and much more satisfying than depending
> on letters, which are often written by minorities, or
> by taking the opinions of the comparatively few people
> around London who you can meet yourself. [64]

BBC personnel began to accept that knowing more about
the audience would not necessarily challenge the prerogative
of the producer and consequently lower programme standards.
Some began to realise that knowing more about less conspicu-
ous social groups might actually help in programme planning
and production. There appeared to be less harm than expected in discovering more precise information about the time
when listeners were able to use the radio during the day: perhaps programmes could be timed more effectively.

There was, no doubt, some satisfaction that listener
research findings often confirmed existing opinions at Portland Place about the habits and tastes of the audience. None-

theless, it must also have been valuable for broadcasting staff to discover that some of their confidently held preconceptions about the audience were, surprisingly, not supported by listener research. Regional variations were much less marked than anyone expected and there were far fewer contrasts between male and female tastes than it had been assumed. Age and social class often proved to be the most important guides to contrasts in the habits and tastes of listeners.

Chapter Six

BROADCASTING AND SOCIETY

The Local Community

 The speed at which sound travels is a constant source
of amazement to those who take even the slightest
interest in wireless. The boom of Big Ben, which is
rung in London and heard by us in Derby almost any
night we care to listen, is one of the wireless stunts
which creates an impression. Of course, we have become so used to the wonder of wireless (when it is not
playing tricks) that we are apt to say, "Oh, it is
nothing; we often hear that." Yes, but ten years ago,
if you had been told that such a thing would be possible
in a million British homes, you would have been very
hesitant to believe such scientific progress probable. [1]

This extract from the columns of a local newspaper in 1924
effectively captures something of the flavour of the audience
attitude towards radio. There is still a sense of awe at the
power of the waves through the ether, but, at the same time,
there is already a certain familiarity with the medium. All
too often, the audience became blasé as the novelty of the
medium passed and was largely unconscious of many of its
effects or, at least, felt less inclined to record the part
which radio played in everyday life. This raises many difficulties for further investigation of the social influence of
broadcasting. Fortunately, the quotation provides a starting
point. Its essential spirit is of a locality responding to the
sense of national community which radio created. It is in
the local community where the atmosphere of listening - the
nuance and detail - is most likely to be observed in an enlightening way.
 The decision to end local stations, to increase the use
of simultaneous broadcasting and, eventually, to launch a

national programme with a series of regional alternatives
determined a national pattern. This national basis for broadcasting, beginning with the long-wave transmitter in 1925
and thereafter more firmly entrenched with each new station,
raised many questions about the effect which it would have on
British social life, particularly the response of local communities. Would it help to produce a common culture,
through extensive broadcasting of the national news, information, the arts, music and drama using a standardized form
of speech? Would it, as a consequence, usurp alternative
cultural activities entirely to produce tedious uniformity?
Were there any forces in the localities which would resist
such an apparently inexorable force?

To answer some of these questions, the first consideration is to examine the work of contemporary social surveyors
and other commentators on British society. Unfortunately,
between the wars there was a general lack of interest in the
social effects of broadcasting. Any interest that was shown
by academics or social surveyors was usually confined to
sweeping statements on the relationship between radio and its
audience with the vague but confident assertion - rather than
detailed proof - that this revolution in communication produced profound social effects. [2]

The explanation for this lack of contemporary interest
in broadcasting appears to lie in neglect, as part of a blind-
spot in social sciences at British universities before 1939.
There was a great deficiency of data collection and analysis
on most social questions before the Second World War. Where,
broadcasting is concerned, the field is even more narrowly
confined. Licence statistics were publicly available but not
used very thoroughly except to point blandly at the marvellous
national growth with little apparent interest in the structure
or composition. [3] Sadly, there are only three major social
surveys in the period which even touch on radio and only then
in such a peripheral way as to be of strictly limited value.
They are, Rowntree's study of York, Poverty and Progress,
Llewellyn Smith's project, New Survey of London Life and
Labour and Caradog Jones' work, Survey of Merseyside.
Only one contemporary work of value concentrated entirely on
the social effects of broadcasting. The BBC offered £250 to
sponsor the work. [4] Tom Harrisson was suggested but declined due to the pressure of his Mass-Observation work
(Mass-Observation only vaguely touched on broadcasting before 1939)[5] and the choice fell upon Hilda Jennings and Wini-
fred Gill. Their findings on listening in the Bristol area were

published by the BBC in July 1939.

Some social scientists realised the value of broadcasting as an aid to research in social questions. The best example was William Beveridge's series 'Changes in Family Life' which was on the air in 1931. He argued, 'The ways of getting essential fact for social science are so limited that no way which offers any chance ought to be neglected'. Hence, to support the programmes, listeners were asked to take part in a social survey. Many welcomed the opportunity to involve themselves in a programme and there was a good response. 50,000 listeners completed a questionnaire but, unfortunately, radio was of peripheral interest to the main thrust of the survey and little knowledge about radio's relationship with changes in the family was gained. [6]

Academics also gave broadcast talks on social questions with some success, but what was lacking was a sustained concentration of resources applied to data collection. More questionnaires and samples would have done something to answer specific questions about broadcasting and the response of the audience, reducing the risk of confusion with the influences of the multiplicity of other media. Of course, good questionnaires were expensive and, even assuming that sufficient interest existed before 1939, it must be said that few British universities were financially provided to carry out such work.

Several problems arise when the work of the social surveyors is used to examine the local response to broadcasting. One is that most of them started with the uncritical assumption that the extension of a uniform, national service was inherently good. This judgement rested on the belief that radio would act as a desirable social weapon in the war against social distinctions and antagonisms. Jennings and Gill set out to look for this tendency. They asked themselves, 'Are the greater possibilities of common cultural enjoyments tending to decrease class barriers and making social unity more possible?' After their research they concluded:

> The prevalent habit of daily listening to the news, the opportunities for cultural enjoyments, such as music and drama, which were formerly denied to the poorer sections of the population, the increased familiarity with a standardised diction and a greater vocabulary, tend to do away with those class barriers which are the result of paucity of common interests. Broadcasting is thus an equalising and unifying factor in national life. [7]

They appeared to be oblivious of the risk that they may have ignored some of the less desirable, enervating consequences of a national system leading to dull cultural uniformity.

There are further limitations in the methods used by the inter-war social surveyors. Although Rowntree employed a house-to-house survey technique in York and the others used questionnaires, the scale of their surveys was very limited - in terms of the methods and their restricted geographical scope. Since each survey concentrated on a particular urban area, there was a lack of comparison or perspective, particularly with smaller communities. Moreover, broadcasting was decidedly peripheral to the main purpose of the surveyors and this produced generalisations and rather casual remarks about broadcasting. For these reasons, the temptation to place great store on their observations must be resisted. Large areas of the relationship between broadcasters and their audience were not addressed by them. What they can provide, is a body of educated observations and impressions on some of the most important changes in the life and leisure of the growing radio audience.

In view of its limitations, social survey evidence must be supported by further observation - not only to corroborate BBC research but also to look further into the questions about local audience responses to broadcasting. In particular, it is important to examine the social influence of broadcasting on rural and urban communities: to see the effects of radio on local politics, the local press, the spoken word, education, religious observance and social concern.

The immediacy of a nationally available news and information service had many implications for the local community, not least for the press which had previously dominated the supply of news.

Jennings and Gill found that all but a small minority gave more credence to the political objectivity of the broadcast news when compared with the coverage of the press. [8] But there was no sign that overall newspaper consumption fell: the reinforcement value of the written word was still important, although in the case of local newspapers there was rather less competition from news bulletins. Local news was not covered in any detail by radio and radio could not satisfy the need of local advertising at that time - neither the Corporation because of its Charter, nor the nationally orientated commercial stations. The immediacy of news bulletins was of more relevance to the national press but throughout the newspaper industry there was a decided change in format to meet the competition of radio. After the creation of the BBC news service in 1934 and a certain relaxation of some press agency restrictions, this competition with broadcasting was intensified, although this should not be overstressed. Even after a modus vivendi had been reached with the press, the advantage of broadcasting for speed in reporting remained under the considerable artificial restriction of a daytime ban on news programmes before 6 p.m. Even with its own news service, the BBC could not then risk a breach of the concession for fear of losing the press agency service.[9] Moreover, other causes were partly responsible for the changes: there was heavy competition within the newspaper business, better technology allowed much higher quality reproduction for photography on newsprint and the newsreels, which came to the cinemas in the thirties, created a sharper visual impression of the news. Despite all of these considerations, the most influential cause seems to have been listening to radio news bulletins. Newspapers gradually realised that their role had to change. They had to assume that readers had already heard the news and concentrate on recapitulation, amplification, interpretation and comment.[10] Radio bulletins, out of necessity, were briefer and sharper than newspaper reports. The mere fact of speech reduced the amount of news that could be conveyed within a reasonable time. The press competed by reducing the amount of fine print: headlines became bolder, columns were doubled and articles in the more popular papers were frequently supported by photographs. The stress was placed on shorter sentences, concise paragraphs and bolder presentation. The contrast between the style of the twenties, with tightly-knit, fine print, covering all the pages of both national and local newspapers, and the thirties, with a much lower density of print on each page, is easily the most noticeable feature of the inter-war press. Radio helped to create the taste for such a change.

The nature of broadcasting, particularly its ephemerality, makes it very difficult to discover direct reference to it and its supposed effects. Without the local press, there would be an extreme shortage of information which could not be supplemented easily by alternatives such as oral history. The primary purpose of the local newspaper was, naturally enough, to provide information for its readership and, therefore, its absence would have made the publicising of broadcasting much more difficult. For example, there would have been less opportunity for wireless clubs to publish their activities and less opportunity for radio retailers to advertise.

Fortunately, local newspapers were comparatively sympathetic towards stories about radio and have left a reasonably solid historical trace.

If the local press had seen broadcasting as a more serious rival, there might have been a serious misrepresentation of its role especially because of omission to avoid attracting favourable attention towards a competitor. Although overall newspaper sales held up well before 1939, many local weekly newspapers were forced to close. The overtly partisan phase of the local daily press came to an end as competitors went out of business or, more frequently, chose to merge and adopt a guise of neutrality. No blame was attributed to broadcasting for this change, rather the local press adopted a very positive attitude towards the growing BBC and also the service from continental stations. Whenever the national press attempted to ban publication of programme times and details, the local press leaped at the chance. As early as 1923, it was usually possible to find the programme details and wavelengths for all the BBC stations then broadcasting as well as the details for many continental stations, particularly the French stations such as Radiola, Paris and Eiffel Tower. [11]

Local papers frequently showed their interest in broadcasting by publishing weekly technical columns dealing with elementary construction or radio equipment developments, often in the form of answers to readers' questions. [12] These columns were often written by local amateurs who clearly influenced editorial opinions on broadcasting. The local press often gave support to plans for silent periods in the evenings so that amateurs could experiment alongside public broadcasting - in recognition of their past achievements in making broadcasting popular and the possibility that their work in short wave or long distance communication could alleviate the overcrowding of the airways. [13] This opinion contained a populist element of support for the little man against big brother - the GPO or the BBC.

Nevertheless, the local press was overwhelmingly sympathetic to the BBC in the majority of its reporting and was normally anxious to do all that it could to help. For instance, licence evaders generally came in for strong criticism. The local press did not see the pattern of local broadcasting which initially existed or the national and regional broadcasting which eventually emerged as a threat to their newspapers. The demand for their specifically local news service and the strength of the printed word itself were

considered to be sufficient to resist any possibility of damage
to their circulations. Indeed the local press was a strong
defender of radio at times when the national press was not.
As the Oxford Chronicle asserted:

> It is now becoming a popular pastime with the London
> daily press to unfavourably criticise wireless broad-
> casting with many sarcastic references and half-veiled
> sneers. This attitude, however, will not affect those
> who possess wireless receivers or are well acquainted
> with wireless reception. They will understand that one
> particular evening's entertainment, or one item of a
> programme, cannot be taken as representative of broad-
> casting as a whole. [14]

Local papers recognised that broadcasting supplied a largely
untapped area of demand for information. Rowntree was
impressed by the appetite for immediacy and the good knowledge of national and international questions:

> As important as the entertainment value of wireless is
> its value in giving the news of the day. Whatever else
> is missed, one or other of the news summaries is
> generally listened to. Different parts of the news may
> appeal to different listeners, the weather forecast to
> the cyclist or the gardener; the fat stock prices to the
> farmer; the results of sporting events to the majority
> of men; but there is also a general desire to know what
> is happening at home and abroad. [15]

The desire for contact with national and international
questions was present from the very beginning. With the
coming of war in 1939, the news bulletin was highlighted more
than it had ever been - even during the General Strike or, in
the recent past, the Munich crisis. The Spectator praised the
contribution of radio news above that of the press:

> whereas press news is imbibed singly, radio news is
> imbibed in groups. You can walk down a street and
> hear the same voice busy in every house. Thus radio
> news is community news: it is a united gesture of a
> society listening at the same time. [16]

Radio was often attributed as the cause of a national
obsession with another, very specialised type of information:
precise time. The validity of this argument seems to be
somewhat wanting. The tyranny of the machine, the demands
of industrial production following the industrial revolution

seems to have been more fundamental in this respect. In fact, attempts by the BBC to 'change' time, as it were, met with absolute failure. The logic of the BBC's case for the 'change' was that a twenty-four hour clock would reduce the amount of confusion in programme timetabling - and at the same time have wider implications. On this occasion the resentment of the patronising, paternalist tone of the BBC and the dislike of 'Big Brother' so openly applying its social engineering policy led to defeat for the BBC at the hands of a concerted press and public campaign. The trial lasted only three months and was terminated forthwith during the summer of 1934. [17]

Rowntree referred to the interest in broadcast weather forecasts. Mundane items such as weather forecasts were immeasureably more effective when broadcast than when covered in print and there was a clear demand for them, predominantly in rural areas. Indeed, in rural areas broadcasting was quickly seen to have much greater virtues. Radio could be used as the keystone of a coordinated campaign by public and voluntary bodies to strengthen the rural community. For instance, in Oxfordshire, the Earl of Macclesfield was very keen to use radio as a means of reinvigorating the existing village clubs, then threatened financially by the agricultural depression and failing in their purpose to bring the community closer together. The emphasis was on radio as a general social aid - to encourage a community spirit by assisting the organisation of community entertainment rather than any specifically educational gathering. The Earl and a local retailer toured the villages to demonstrate the possibilities of radio and emphasising the economy of this method of rejuvenation. [18]

In Derbyshire this form of action could also be seen in action. Here the Rural Community Council used radio as the mainstay of a coordinated policy to revive village culture. The Council set up a pilot listening group in one village, Eyam, in an attempt to strengthen communal spirit and integrated this trial with programmes to build or repair village halls, provide a better county library facility, encourage electrification and then draw Women's Institutes, Drama Clubs and other social gatherings back into the village halls throughout the county. The group leader of the listening group was a school master and the thirty or so participants came in roughly equal numbers from those already engaged in some form of education and ordinary working people, with equal proportions of men and women. The size was, therefore, small but manageable. An article in the <u>Manchester Guardian</u> explained the practice of the group:

> Their method is to listen to the wireless speaker, then spend a week in thinking over the lecture, and on the following week meet an hour before the next installment is due and spend the waiting-time in discussing what they heard a week before.

There was also some enthusiasm for future prospects - as the article remarked:

> The Derbyshire Rural Community Council, which launched Eyam on this movement, has recently secured, well in advance, from the BBC the syllabus of its educational talks, and has circulated this to the 165 villages with which it has now established some link. It is hoped to start other study groups in the near future. [19]

The fate of this policy and the number of groups formed is less certain. Local evidence is elusive. Nationally there seems to be little doubt that these paternalistic, formal attempts to use wireless to revive village life, were of indifferent or negligible effect.

The groups which were formed were reasonably well spread over the rural areas but memberships were usually small. Direct participation seems to have been limited to those already interested or involved in education. Precise statements are difficult because the groups formed and reformed very rapidly as each lecture series began and ended. Normally a course was pursued for an eight week period, and was usually held in the winter months.

It is evident that the isolation of rural dwellers and their communities, coupled with their inferior facilities for entertainment and education, led to heightened interest in broadcasting as a means of filling the void. The National Federation of Women's Institutes could also be seen at work in the rural shires with their campaign to fit sets in village halls. The Women's Institutes were specifically created to provide for women in communities with populations under 4,000. In the evidence to the Crawford Committee, on behalf of the Institutes, Mrs. Nugent Harris noted the friendliness which she felt radio had created in rural areas:

> When one person has got wireless it means that they ask neighbours to drop in, or neighbours ask if they

> may drop in, and it has created friendliness. It has
> kept the young people in, they do not go so much to the
> Town for cinemas and other things when they have
> wireless and everywhere they spoke of the pleasure it
> gives to old people and invalids. [20]

These facets of broadcasting may have been felt more
acutely in rural areas but it was also reasonably true of behaviour in urban areas. More obvious contrasts in the
response of the respective audiences lay elsewhere. The
strength of the agricultural lobby was the key, pressing for
better weather forecasting details and more live-stock
prices. [21] In a series of articles syndicated to the local press,
A. Lancaster Smith outlined the obvious advantages:

> The farmer is an isolated unit in the community and
> especially during the long autumn and winter evenings,
> the fact that he can be brought into touch with 'Broad-
> cast concerts', important news, educative lectures
> and 101 items of interest, renders it desirable that
> more agriculturalists should be able to 'listen-in'. [22]

In a second article, Smith argued that inate conservatism
rather than expense or poor reception was responsible for
the reluctance of rural inhabitants to listen to radio. 'Around
the Metropolis and other large towns almost everybody is
going in for receiving sets, whilst in country districts the
sight of outside aerials is not so common.'[23] Smith compared
the impact of the internal combustion engine with that of the
radio as a means of speeding communications in rural areas.
He stressed the value to farmers of weather forecasts and
the social benefits of broadcast music for village life.

Of course the influences of poverty and poor reception
should not be disregarded as deterrents too readily. They
must have had some role to play in keeping the total level of
listening lower than in urban areas. This is a particularly
interesting phenomenon since the incentive for owning a set
was otherwise so strong. For instance, the seasonal pattern
of listening was often remarked to have a much greater
effect on rural communities without the rival attractions of
the town. By 1924 the Oxford Chronicle was certain that:

> With the coming of winter wireless will reign practi-
> cally supreme in the countryside as an evening enter-
> tainment. It is not difficult to imagine that in a short
> time country people will wonder how they managed to
> beguile their time before wireless became a popular

pastime.

Even with mass listening in village halls this seems to have been rather premature. [24]

Radio provided a substitute community for isolated villages and, therefore, emphasised the sense of contact with the nation rather more than for urban dwellers, who had many other more substantial means of celebrating major occasions. It is worth noting that as late as 1937 during the Coronation festivities, rural inhabitants had not quite thrown off the astonishment at the achievement of broadcasting - an emotion long lost by many urban dwellers. Phrases such as 'The Wonder of Wireless' or the 'Miracle of Radio' still flew about. There was still an element of novelty in sitting by a fireside, turning a knob and being brought almost instantly into close contact with the Ceremony in Westminster Abbey. [25] By 1937 the majority of rural homes were equipped with a set but until then there was a noticeable divergence between the seemingly greater need of rural dwellers to listen to radio compared with the relatively low proportion who actually had sets. It is hard to resolve whether this was due to a suspicion of new technology and a preference for traditional pastimes or a reflection of enthusiasm frustrated by poverty and poor reception.

It seems that the level of listening in rural communities was often influenced by technical factors. Poor signal strength, difficult topography and low population densities were not condusive to a high level of licence holding. [26] This was frequently demonstrated by the licence returns where the rural areas of English counties such as Staffordshire and Northumberland showed very low levels of licence holding whereas those counties within range of the metropolis showed a much greater propensity to listen. The proximity of such a high density of population seems to have exposed potential listeners to wireless more quickly and given them a stronger desire to listen. For example, Oxfordshire showed consistently higher levels of licence holding than most other rural counties and was one of the first parts of the country to approach saturation point in 1936. [27] There may have been a marked contrast in the expansion of listening between rural and urban areas but perhaps one of the most interesting aspects of rural listening was revealed by the BBC's Random Samples. Once a rural household acquired a set, its habits and tastes were not markedly different from urban listeners. Apart from minor differences in the time of listening, the similarities in behaviour came as some surprise to the BBC.

The common interest of urban and rural communities was confirmed by the obvious delight which they derived from any involvement in radio programmes. This was exemplified by the 'Microphone at Large' series where the presenter toured the country and recorded his conversations with local people. The BBC found everyone more than willing to participate and eager to hear the resulting broadcasts. [28]

The expansion of broadcasting quickly involved local municipalities, urban and rural district councils. A profusion of wireless aerials, many of them reaching the full 100ft., extent permitted, was erected to receive signals for crystal and early valve sets. They could be a public nuisance, particularly where they were stretched across public highways. The attitude of local authorities varied greatly towards them. In some places they were strictly forbidden: requests to erect them were refused and those which were erected without authorisation were ordered to be dismantled.[29] In other places such as Oxford it was possible to erect them if a good case could be made. [30]

Similarly, local authorities had responsibility for dealing with local relay exchanges. Again the strengths of interests in each area varied, and these produced different reactions. For example, in Chiswick requests to establish such exchanges were persistently refused before 1939. A special sub-committee of the Council's Works and Highways Committee was created to investigate the application and it advised that the request be denied on the grounds of the unsightly proliferation of overhead cables which would result.[31] Many councils shared this opinion, but some other towns took a different view. On the coast, normal reception was difficult and, apparently, the resistance to cables was less acute when a reasonable service was at stake. Hull, Newcastle and Plymouth were good examples of a sympathetic approach to relays. Inland, towns with good reception seemed to have no objection to the cables and allowed relays to be installed, particularly in Nottinghamshire and Lancashire. Some authorities actively supported a relay service, often because it could be readily installed in flats and new council housing estates.

On the question of the nuisance caused by excessive loudspeaker noise, local authorities also had responsibility to act. Those that had not already taken action by approving the relevant byelaw were recommended to do so by the Ullswater Committee in 1935 [32] and a sample was attached to the Report for guidance. In any case, many local authorities had already taken such a course under the powers granted by Section 249 of the Local Government Act 1933. [33]

Municipal authorities were disappointingly slow to respond to the new medium. With some notable exceptions, there was little sign of a speedy and positive response to exploit the advantages of broadcasting - whether formally in schools or indirectly by cooperation through the library and museum services. Normally, broadcasting was ignored or actually despised. The lack of rapid action is quite clearly emphasised by the uncharacteristically slow moves to apply restrictive measures on aerials, relay exchanges and noise. In sharp contrast to the enthusiasm of local listeners, broadcasting usually had a very low priority in local government activity before 1939.

The Spoken Word

The response to the Regional Scheme suggested that it was well received wherever it expanded the range and quality of the BBC programme service and that this appeared to substantially offset any disappointment at the loss of a local station or a sense that national or regional conformity threatened the local community. Even in the case of spoken English, where there was plenty of scope for conflict between local and national preferences, there was little discernable resistance and it does not seem to have been a major issue.

This lack of response is rather surprising. Perhaps the influence of the new, and readily available, form of model speech was sufficiently imperceptible for any changes to go unnoticed. Certainly dialects remained reasonably unchanged by the BBC service. As Hilda Jennings discovered in her survey of Bristol:

> Syntax remains unaffected, and in ordinary conversations in the home, especially among older people, the local colloquial mode of speech with its native raciness holds its own. In some instances, whether as a result mainly of broadcasting or of education in the schools there appears to be a conscious use of two distinct modes of speech in the homes and at business or for social purposes. [34]

Twenty years later, Tom Harrisson revisited Worktown (Bolton) the scene of his most famous Mass-Observation project and came to very much the same conclusions:

> No voice change can be detected between 1937 and 1960.

> Radio, television and other outside impacts orientated
> to a more standard English appear to have had little
> or no effect. A tiny minority have consciously altered
> their voices. But elocution and speech training are
> still not important here. An English master at one of
> the big local schools, a friend of 1937 and 1960, gave
> his considered opinion that if anything the standard of
> speaking what he called "King's English" had gone
> down. [35]

This was not for want of trying by the BBC. The Advisory Committee on Spoken English was formed in April 1926
with a lecturer in phonetics, A. Lloyd James, as honorary
secretary. [36] In one guise or another, this committee continued with Lloyd James at the helm throughout this period.
Advice on the preferred BBC pronunciation of words was
freely given to BBC staff and even passed on directly to the
public in the form of a series of pamphlets on Broadcast
English. First issued in 1928, these pamphlets covered
important and controversial words, including British place
names. [37] Of course, the public could also hear the results
of the Committee's efforts. They were informed that the
correct usage for broadcasting terms were 'listen' not 'listen-
in' and that the past tense of broadcast was 'broadcast' not
'broadcasted'. Daventry was not to be pronounced
'Daintry'. [38] Many listeners resented the BBC's presump-
tion.

They could hardly avoid listening to the announcers who
most closely reflected the aural image of the BBC. The
announcers were supposed to be anonymous to resist the
growth of a personality cult. In fact their identities were
open secrets. [39] They were carefully selected and drilled to
intone as well as pronounce English in the preferred BBC
manner. Lloyd James always denied that the BBC was
dictating 'correct' English rather,

> it is quite evident that we are not entitled to conclude
> that there is one standard pronunciation, one and only
> one right way of speaking English. There are varieties
> that are acceptable throughout the country and others
> that are not. [40]

Notwithstanding his assertion, the BBC came close to
insisting that its speakers, members of staff or otherwise,
should speak what Lloyd James described as a variety of
educated Southern English:

> It may be the educated English spoken by a Scotsman,
> or a Welshman, or an Irishman, or an Englishman,
> but it has to be educated, unless there are any very
> powerful reasons, political or social, why this proviso
> should not apply. [41]

Moreover, it appears that the apparent failure of this
approach to convert the audience to any substantial degree
frustrated a profound sense of moral purpose. Lloyd James
was determined to prevent what he saw as the disintegration
of spoken English in Britain and the Empire into,

> a series of mutually unintelligible dialects; the forces
> of disintegration fed by local prejudice, parochial
> patriotism, and petty nationalisms are a menace not
> only to the unity of the language but to the unity of the
> English-speaking peoples.

There was a strong didactic element in pronunciation,
stress and even the mechanics of the language. The committee and BBC staff had high ideals. Broadcasters were
told that they,

> must insist on high standards of clarity and intelligi-
> bility, for whether they like it or not, they are in the
> process of determining the future form of our spoken
> language as surely as the printer and type designer
> determined the form of our printed language. [42]

Almost certainly, it would take longer than the period up to
1939 for the results of this strong sense of purpose to
emerge. It appears that the BBC's efforts were treated
largely with indifference. The general, rather ill-defined
hostility to the accent of the announcers, particularly in the
North of England, Scotland and Wales was not translated into
an active and coordinated resistance movement.

In fact, the spoken word was more likely to arouse
controversy in the national press. Where pronunciation is
concerned, the press had a complete change of heart. At
first there was support for the clarity of speech broadcast
and an idealistic belief in the wider consequences of BBC
pronunciation. [43] Commenting in 1929 on the BBC pamphlet,
Broadcast English I, which gave recommendations for pro-
nouncing doubtful words, the Spectator argued:

> Everything that makes our speech a conscious heritage
> and spreads this heritage as widely as possible is a
> communal good. In this way, too, the BBC can diffuse

> a high standard of culture, can assimilate classes and
> can help to provide equality of opportunity. [44]

This idealism quickly evaporated: indeed the uniform
BBC pronunciation became a positively undesirable goal.
Robert Lynd, of the New Statesman was outraged by BBC
advice for 'correct' pronunciation:

> When the BBC takes upon itself to tell us how to pro-
> nounce the language that we have more or less mis-
> pronounced from the nursery, the blood mounts to our
> heads in indignation, and nothing short of a letter of
> protest to a newspaper can restore us to our accustom-
> ed calm. [45]

The volte-face by the Spectator was equally strenuously underlined: 'I cannot help viewing with distaste the day when every
child from Land's End to John o'Groats speaks the same
broadcast English. '[46]

Sunday newspapers such as the People was no less keen
to resist paternalistic advice of this kind. It, too, defended
the dialects of Britain but its main criticisms were aimed at
the class bias implicit in the pronunciation used for the model
BBC voice. In parody of their efforts the People chose to
emphasise the phonetic spelling of their words. Thus there
were 'Uxford'and 'Keambridge' at the Boat Race. The target
was not just the tone of the voices but the whole social milieu
which they stood for - an obsession with varsity sports and
old school tie acquaintances at the expense of the soccer or
horse racing results which interested the common man. [47]

Religion and Philanthropy

The decline in religious observance was often attributed by
critics to the arrival of radio. The social surveyors were
less certain of this. They pointed out the advantages of
exposing the invalids and the aged to religious broadcasts.
This was a considerable social contribution. Rowntree
realised the difficulty of assessment:

> To what extent the fact that people can listen at home
> to a service is affecting church attendance it is im-
> possible to say, for one does not know how many of
> those listening-in to services would have attended
> church had there been no wireless.

His questionnaire showed that about half of those replying did
listen to a religious broadcast each week and thought that, on

balance, radio had served 'to bring religious teaching to
many homes whose members seldom, if ever, attend a place
of worship.'[48] Jennings and Gill supported the view that
religious attendance fell only slightly, and largely because
the elderly and infirm stayed at home:

> It seems that churchgoers felt that personal participa-
> tion in the service, worship in fellowship with others,
> and a suitable environment were fundamental needs
> which could not be met by listening to broadcast
> services.[49]

They felt that the real effect was neutral - radio brought
more into contact with religion but neither discouraged attendance nor stimulated new membership of congregations. A
more generally accepted view was that there was some contribution to a decline in attendances, but there is little trace
of any firm local action in response.[50] Certainly the programmes themselves were rarely criticised. Most listeners
had a good word to say for Revd. Dick Sheppard and his
broadcasts from St. Martin-in-the-Fields and radio sermons
were seen everywhere as valuable aids to the elderly and
disabled who were unable to attend normal services.[51] On
great occasions, such as the Coronation, more advanced
clergymen even brought the set into the church so that both
ceremonies could be enjoyed simultaneously.[52] It is worth
mentioning here that the general dislike of the solemnity of
the BBC's Sunday programmes should be seen in the context
of a general ban on Sunday entertainments. It was only in the
late twenties that cinemas and other similar establishments
were allowed by local authorities to show performances on
Sundays in many towns throughout Britain.

The national press recognised that criticism of BBC
Sunday programmes was part of a general campaign to relax
restrictions on Sunday entertainments, nevertheless, attacks
on the BBC were quite unrestrained. Raymond Postgate put
the socialist case in his pamphlet, 'What to do with the
BBC'.[53] He went as far as to argue that the BBC had abne-
gated the terms of its Charter by handing over effective
control of the airways to the English manufacturers who paid
for airtime on the commercial stations. The New Statesman
raised a further objection:

> the Sunday programmes of the BBC have long become
> something of a joke. It seemed to be thrusting religion
> upon one to have both the Regional and National wave-

lengths almost exclusively devoted to various brands of orthodoxy. [54]

The columnist 'Critic' added tartly: 'I believe that the BBC has never yet invited anyone to broadcast a moral case for disbelief. '[55]

After some earlier mumblings, the campaign really got under way in 1931. The popular press bemoaned the prospect of endless Bach cantatas every Sunday[56] and attempted to persuade listeners to boycott the BBC and tune into the foreign stations on Sundays. One critic, Sydney Moseley, led the attack on the BBC. Moseley was a member of a growing circle of journalists who made their reputations out of broadcasting criticism. With the demise of the wireless organisations and the technical press, these critics assumed far more importance, alleging that they closely represented public opinion on broadcasting. Beginning in 1932, Moseley and his fellow critics claimed a whole series of victories in their campaign to change BBC policy. Progress was slow and in 1936 he was still arguing that:

> Most folks must especially find our Sunday programmes a nightmare, with their doleful contraltos, sopranos and chamber music. For my part, after putting in my dutiful attendance at church, I rush abroad to escape the doldrums of British stations. [57]

Listener research showed the widespread sympathy for his view and the question of Sunday programmes was a persistent theme. The BBC conceded to very few of the arguments for a change, being content to extend the hours of broadcasting and offer programme alternatives.

Radio was an excellent aid for philanthropy. Fitting sets in hospitals was a favoured form of help. Local charitable organisations and wireless enthusiasts frequently coordinated their efforts. In Oxford, the Oxford Times gave financial support to a local retailer, Captain Shirley, and with the help of other voluntary contributions he succeeded in installing sets in a hundred hospitals in the county by May 1926. [58] Similar achievements were seen elsewhere. A typical installation worked on the relay principle with a large central set connected to the headphones at the bedside by cable. The cost would be approximately £500 per hundred beds - no mean feat for a local charitable action to achieve.[59] Other popular institutions for support included almshouses and homes for the aged. [60] The Spectator magazine even ran a short campaign in 1938 to raise money for wireless sets in prisons. Despite some protests from readers, the paper persevered and raised over £130. [61]

The blind benefited most from the growth of broadcasting and attracted a great deal of support from philanthropists. Fund raising at sponsored balls, concerts or whist drives was a typical method of attracting funds. [62] At national level, one charitable organisation, the British Wireless for the Blind Fund, deserves attention because it was the classic example of an area of social concern which the mere existence of radio generated. It was immediately realised that radio was the ideal medium for this handicap. Blind listeners were exempt from the licence payment - largely through the efforts of Captain Ian Fraser. Blinded in the First World War, he became a leading member of the Wireless Society of London and had close links with St. Dunstan's - the institute for blinded soldiers. He was a member of the Crawford Committee and agitated for the blind incessantly, eventually from his seat in Parliament. [63] Because of his efforts, the licence fee was waived when royal assent was granted to an Act of December 1926. [64] Nonetheless, the expense of a set was a considerable barrier before that privilege could be enjoyed. The fund was founded in 1929 to break down this barrier and the most successful mode of appeal proved to be radio itself. Many charities were permitted to broadcast appeals but only this fund had the privilege of Christmas Day appeals, beginning in 1929 with Winston Churchill as the speaker. By 1931, £37,000 had been raised and 17,000 sets supplied to blind listeners. [65] Because of this scheme, most blind listeners obtained a set if they wanted one, although Christmas Day appeals continued throughout the thirties and, as late as 1938, Lord Southwood broke the record for a radio charities' appeal when £40,000 was raised for the fund after his broadcast. Of course, broadcasting was a great solace to most of the housebound handicapped or invalid but, with help of this charity, it was with the blind that radio formed a special and enduring relationship.

Broadcast Education

The backbone of the BBC's policy of social engineering was undoubtedly its attempt at formal education. Contemporary press comment invariably referred to this service in the most glowing terms. Newspapers seemed to lapse into reams of rhetorical excess. In its educational role, radio was seen as a 'social revolution', 'a great force for enlightenment' and the 'most important essential for an educated democracy'. Idealistically, the press saw broadcast education as a powerful force for 'cultural uplift', the service of minority interests and the defence of democratic institutions. In fact, apart from schools broadcasting, these broadcasts were a failure and their influence on communities was decidedly limited. The listening groups organised by the BBC's Central Council for Broadcast Adult Education (CCBAE) did not attract widespread support despite the efforts of academics such as Sir Henry Hadow, T. H. Pear and T. H. Searls.[66] Possibly, the medium was an inadequate method of teaching, with the lack of the normal two way teacher - pupil relationship being difficult for students to accept. Certainly there was no lack of interest in acquiring further knowledge amongst a large part of the population. Many listeners had left school at thirteen or fourteen and consequently had plenty of untapped potential. Perhaps the competition from the many existing further educational opportunities reduced involvement. Llewellyn Smith felt that this was the case:

> Of these newer agencies one of the most powerful is Broadcasting House, which offers its excellent educational talks to all and sundry who wish to listen and are able to listen at the right moment. But up to the present there has not been in London any organisation of 'listening groups' under leaders, such as have been found to be of value in some other parts of the country. This is ascribed to the fact that in London the ground is so well covered by the various types of institutes.[67]

Of course, cooperation between the BBC and educational institutions did take place. The Carnegie Trust provided money for radio sets and helped to form listening groups amongst the unemployed in four areas of Britain: Lanarkshire, Yorkshire, the West Midlands and Kent.[68] Despite the Trust's sponsorship these schemes were not successful. The reports made by the organising committees shed some light on their failings. First there was some suspicion of officialdom and the possibility that attendance at a group might lead to trouble from the Labour Exchanges 'for not genuinely seeking work.'[69] There was also the inevitable demoralisation amongst the unemployed which left them apathetic and difficult to organise.[70] Of more significance was the question of speech. In Scotland this was a very serious problem but even in Yorkshire there was a difficulty:

There is still much room for improvement both in
simplification of language and speed of delivery. The
terms employed are still too academic and though
their unfamiliarity put a double strain upon the un-
trained listener of having to interpret the language,
and of following the line of thought of the speaker. [71]

The topics chosen for talks also came under attack.
From Yorkshire came the recommendation that:

Unemployed men have on the whole a hum-drum and
sometimes squalid existence especially in the cities
and talks should be devised which relate to the hobbies
and pastimes in which they engage. [72]

In the West Midlands the lack of empathy between the subject
matter and working-class men was also observed:

The talks most suitable for discussion are those connected with everyday life and interests of members to
which they can make their own contributions from
personal knowledge; but many talks which are not
suitable for discussion are welcome as a means of
acquiring knowledge. [73]

These criticisms go some way towards an explanation
for the failure to get fuller participation. The BBC eventually recognised this and in a Press Release of 14 December
1934 announced the demise of the CCBAE. Although cooperation with adult education was not entirely terminated, the
active role of the BBC in helping the listening groups was
very much diminished. [74]

Despite this failure, local communities often sought to
ease the problems of the unemployed with their enforced
poverty and leisure. Even in the normally affluent Nottinghamshire and Derbyshire coalfield, the Miners' Welfare
Adult Education Joint Committee held listening classes at the
height of the slump - helped considerably by the extra-mural
departments of the Universities of Sheffield and Nottingham. [75]
At Staveley near Chesterfield the branch library ran a listening group and provided books for BBC talks in centres
specially set up for the unemployed in the towns and villages
in the vicinity. This listening group continued to meet as
late as the winter of 1937-38, when the group listened to the
very popular 'Men Talking' series. [76]

As the work of the University extra-mural departments
shows, Further Education authorities were not completely

oblivious to the potential of broadcasting and many colleges
and polytechnics ran courses on wireless telegraphy or
telephony, although the greatest use of broadcasting was in
the evening classes which used public educational facilities,
under the auspices of voluntary groups. The Workers'
Educational Association (WEA), certainly used radio as an
aid to study. In Oxfordshire there was some enthusiasm for
starting WEA listening groups if not for keeping them running
and they usually lacked durability. Noting the publication of
the BBC 'Aids to Study' for the use of adult education groups,
Mr. G. H. L. Fear, the Chairman of the Oxford branch of
the WEA took the opportunity to explain the WEA's proposed
role and provided some practical advice:

> Now while individuals as such may acquire a wealth of
> information from radio lectures such as these, the
> maximum harvest is only garnered, I suggest, by
> studying in groups, and the Workers' Educational
> Association will be delighted to lend its organisation
> to the formation of groups for this purpose. The WEA
> has already considered such a scheme, the main
> features of which are as follows: A group should con-
> sist of, say, from twelve to thirty members of either
> sex and should meet in a room situated centrally for
> its members. The WEA would undertake to place the
> necessary books on loan to any groups studying under
> its auspices. Each student would do a certain amount
> of reading prior to the radio lecture, and make notes
> at the time it is broadcast. A discussion would follow,
> in which the views, ideas and criticisms of each would
> be pooled, to the benefit of all. [77]

This description accurately reflected the style of listening adopted by the WEA and many other groups in the countryside.

When the CCBAE was disbanded in July 1934 very few
localities had actually come under its full administrative
control. The intention had been to create area councils
throughout the country but only four of these were formed.
The CCBAE failed because of lack of support even though
some listening groups did emerge successfully in the localities. Their ultimate demise was more a reflection of the
informal, ad hoc and ephemeral nature of many of the listening groups. They grew up to meet specific needs and ceased
once the local spark of interest faded. Indeed, there was
some hostility towards larger organisations which attempted

to use radio listening as a means of adult education. The left-wing newspaper, <u>Plebs</u>, for instance, saw both the CCBAE and even the <u>WEA</u> as an instrument of reactionary state control:

> Our rulers and governors have not been slow to profit by the lesson they learned during the General Strike as to the usefulness of broadcasting. An Adult Educational Section of the BBC has been set up, and a prominent WEA er put in charge. So that, as J. P. M. Millar pointed out in his letter to the Daily Herald the other day, 'the workers will now be educated by wireless on lines that have governing-class approval.' Let us, to avoid misunderstanding frankly admit that a series of talks on English working-class history by a WEA lecturer which were broadcasted early this year were very good. But if anyone deduces from that that the general tone of the lessons-by-wireless which are now to be given under Government control is likely to be satisfactory from the workers' point of view, he must be an optimist indeed. It is one more proof, if such were needed, of the entire failure of the WEA to grasp the fundamental facts about the position of the workers under capitalism, and about their educational needs, that such a scheme under such auspices, should receive its sympathetic support. [78]

This was an extreme and largely political objection to educational broadcasting in this form, but much of the practice seems to have been based on a feeling that local needs were better met by the spontaneous voluntary action and more flexible coordination of local groups with a broad commitment to adult education and leisure rather than by a centralised structure. Thus the main evidence for adult education listening groups came from those such as the YMCA in Burton-on-Trent, where their wireless set was used to provide the facilities for a listening group, [79] and in Oxfordshire from the Federation of Women's Institutes, where a Ford van was fitted up with a set so that it could tour from village to village, 'entertaining and educating.' [80]

The educational use of broadcasting for school children was particularly important because it increased awareness amongst the young of radio's potential and also because it exposed an impressionable age group to the BBC's centrally generated cultural and social values. For a brief period, educational broadcasting was the responsibility of the local

stations: from the first broadcasts in 1924, [81] until the simultaneous broadcasting network was fully established. The
main output was, however, very quickly centralised in
London and, hence, the tendency for programmes to encourage uniformity was soon established. Whether this potential
was realised is difficult to verify but two factors in the chain
of possible influences can be examined. Did schools actually
equip themselves to listen to broadcast educational programmes and, if they did, how much use was made of the
service provided?

In Brentford and Chiswick, listening in schools began
almost immediately. There were several good reasons for
this. It was due partly to the inspiration of local teachers
but equally it owed a good deal to the proximity of 2LO at
Savoy Hill and the relationship between Middlesex County
Council and J. C. Stobart, the newly appointed Director of
Educational Broadcasting. Stobart had been an Inspector of
Schools in the county. The initial action by senior schools in
the area was entirely voluntary. In April 1924, the headmaster of Hogarth School in Chiswick recorded this interesting account in the school log book:

> A broadcasting test organised by the British B. C.
> Company /sic/ was was /sic/ heard this afternoon by
> boys of standard IIIa and VIb with the apparatus pro-
> vided by Mr. Varley. It consisted of a lecture on
> school music given by Sir Henry Walford Davies at
> the Savoy Hill studio of the BBC. [82]

In Brentford, the Rothschild School recorded listening
for the first time in May 1924, having been lent a five valve
set. [83] Later there is evidence at both schools of regular
listening to BBC programmes - including participation in
essay tests and examinations organised by the BBC. Some
pupils even accompanied their Headmaster on a visit to Savoy
Hill. [84] All of this activity was due to the initiative of each
school and the local authority was not involved. Formal
authorisation to purchase sets only came from the UDC's
Education Committee for the first time in November 1924 and
uniformly throughout the senior schools in the area much
later in March 1931. [85]

This pattern of publicly funded support following the
original voluntary initiative was followed fairly closely elsewhere - but with a wide divergence in the timing. In Derbyshire, fewer schools appear to have had their own sets, although some had possessed school radio societies from a very

early date. [86] The lack of official or wider public support
for broadcasting as an aid to school education was ruefully
noted by the Derby Evening Telegraph as late as 1939, when
it heard of Burton-on-Trent's decision to fit radio sets as a
standard provision for a school rather than a 'privilege':

> Praise ye Burton's progressive Education Committee,
> the first local authority properly to appreciate the
> importance of Broadcasts to Schools .... It is true
> that in Derby the senior schools have wireless sets
> and that they are used regularly, but it is true also
> that in only one case has the apparatus been supplied
> entirely by the Education Committee - and that these
> benefits are denied the great majority of the junior
> schools in the town - why? [87]

The general rule for the period was, therefore, that schools
only possessed sets through the energy of masters and
pupils, [88] or through expenditure squeezed out of the block
grant to the school. The minutes of several Education
Committees make it fairly obvious that there was little
official interest in broadcasting for schools in many places.
No special funds were set aside and some direct requests
for financial assistance for radio purchases were turned
down - despite representations from the BBC to relax the
policy - although moneys for gramophones and pianos were
specifically allowed. BBC demonstrations at schools throughout the country during 1929 could not convince the committee
members to authorise any expenditure. [89]

It is doubtful, therefore, whether the use of broadcasting in formal education had much impact, simply because
sets were not provided in any numbers. Broadcast programmes rarely formed a regular part of the timetable. If
they were used at all, they were far more likely to serve as
a novelty or special treat. Only occasionally was the full
potential of broadcast education realised and exploited,
before 1939.

The response of the local community shows that broadcasting was generally welcomed and the supply of news and
information was greatly appreciated. Certainly, there was
little interest in formal broadcast education and some,
largely unfounded, fears of damage to local dialects and
customs, but it is equally evident that local communities saw
broadcasting as a positive aid to the sick, elderly and disadvantaged. Particularly in rural areas, it was seen as a
means of actually strengthening local life and culture, even

to the point where it could do something to resist the trend
to depopulation.

Chapter Seven

MASS LISTENING

Radio and the Crowd

Evidence revealing the influence of radio on local social life
is normally most elusive. One exception is the profusion of
contemporary observations on the significant changes in the
manner of listening. In the beginning, much of the listening
was done in groups or even in large crowds. By the mid-
thirties, enormous audiences for programmes were
commonplace but listening had been translated into a private
activity, limited to the individual or the family within the
confines of the home. Mass listening had a great influence
on the local community, particularly in the context of commercial activity, political life and the relations between
listeners and the nation.

The earliest examples of listening by crowds were
usually advertising stunts organised by shops wishing to
sell wireless sets. There was a significant element of
natural curiosity in the crowds which gathered since this
was usually the first means of coming into contact with broadcasting. This advertising by local retailers must not be
underrated as a means of influencing people to become listeners. A strong local effort was essential if sales were to be
encouraged. Even in the late thirties it was important for
local retailers to back up national press advertising by
manufacturers and advertise their goods and supplementary
services in the local newspaper. [1]

On the whole, the shops were slow in seizing the opportunity to advertise. This may reflect the state of the market
or simply a lack of local initiative. At first, advertisements
were terse and unimaginative, but eventually, competitiveness between rival retailers encouraged more inventive
advertisements, including photographs and detailed descrip-

tions of the sets and components. National or religious occasions were the best selling points. Besides general elections, it was usually a speech by the King, or more uniquely, the Coronation which provided the inspiration for an advertisement. The onset of autumn or the pre-Christmas period were also favourite advertising periods. [2]

Retailers employed similar tactics to the local wireless societies to gain publicity. One publicity stunt carried out by two firms in Oxford included a return journey to London by charabancs fitted with wireless receivers. The Oxford Chronicle described the event:

> Oxonians who went by charabanc to London on Whit Monday had music on the way. There are rival services of coaches and rival wireless firms, and each coach had its wireless equipment from one or other of these firms. It was a matter for debate which set of passengers heard the music best.

The travellers had time to go to a London theatre and then return in the late evening to the strains of an opera broadcast from 2LO. When one of the coaches stopped at Maidenhead, a crowd of more than 300 gathered around the vehicle - such was the novelty of the occasion. [3]

This competitiveness created a good deal of interest and excitement but even day-to-day activities attracted considerable attention from large crowds. The Oxford Wireless Telephony Company made a wireless tour throughout the county in 1923, giving evening demonstrations in many Oxfordshire villages and towns which would not otherwise have heard broadcasting. [4] At one demonstration in Henley, the Oxford Chronicle observed:

> The reality of the reception may be realised when it is known that a large portion of the audience actually clapped and applauded . . . . . The dance music was so greatly appreciated and was so loud and distinct that many couples danced to it. [5]

This rather effectively captures the sense of surprise which the early broadcasts created.

Retailers often gave wireless concerts in the evenings. One example in Oxford took place in October 1922 - before the foundation of the BBC. The local press observed the mixture of awe and astonishment which the audience displayed as they listened to a broadcast of music and speech from London. [6] Local trade exhibitions gave radio shops the opportunity to demonstrate their wares. They rarely failed to up-stage all the other exhibitors by attracting enormous crowds and heavy local press coverage. [7]

These forms of publicity were valuable but the most consistent contribution to public awareness was provided by the normal service in each shop. Such was the attention which wireless shops attracted, that almost every evening, for the first two or three years of public broadcasting, large crowds would gather just to hear broadcasts outside the shops. This contribution, through mass listening, must have made radio very familiar to most urban dwellers within months of the formation of the BBC.

Since most people could best listen after work and, as a consequence, most programmes were broadcast in the evening, then the shops also stayed open in the evenings to attract commuters as they journeyed home. In Oxford, mass listening was a regular activity. Crowds gathered just to hear news summaries or sporting results during the evening demonstration given by the two rival wireless shops. The public listened in the street to such diverse things as opera broadcasts, including Dame Nellie Melba, the news, the running commentary on the Boat Race and eye witness accounts of the F.A. Cup Final. The Boat Race was so popular in Oxford that large crowds gathered every year after the first broadcast in 1923 and a reasonable crowd could still be seen listening to the broadcast in the street as late as 1937. [8] Most of these events could draw anything from 300 to 800 people in Queen Street and High Street, although less auspicious occasions could still cause large crowds to gather. In April 1923, for instance, the crowd which was only listening to a normal BBC programme of music became so large that the police were called to keep the road clear. [9]

The General Strike

Although party political broadcasting began in 1924 with three broadcast speeches by the main party leaders, [10] the first political event in which broadcasting played a serious part was not a straightforward party political clash. The General Strike of 1926 gave broadcasting an important opportunity to impress itself on the public. The role of broadcasting in this event has often been underrated partly because of the relatively low number of licence holders existent at that time. Such a view misunderstands the mechanisms of early listening.

The audience response to BBC broadcasts during the General Strike has to be seen in the context of the relations between the BBC and a government which heavily controlled the content of the news bulletins which were issued. [11] Reith was able to resist Churchill's design to commandeer the BBC and apply the same propaganda techniques to broadcasting which he used in the British Gazette but the threat was held over him by Baldwin and his lieutenant, J. C. C. Davidson, that this course could not be resisted in Cabinet if the BBC did not follow the government's instructions. [12] The effect was that leaders in the Labour Party and the trade unions were not allowed to speak over the air, whereas government ministers were allowed to make their appeals directly to the public. [13]

After the strike, Reith insisted that the BBC had had to be, 'for the Government in the crisis' but although the Cabinet would not allow him to declare this enforced position publicly, he did ensure that the BBC adopted a more moderate (if not independent) approach to the news. [14] The BBC refused to use intemperate language to describe the strikers in the manner of the British Gazette, and showed itself willing to broadcast messages from the TUC General Council. There was news coverage of the activities of the strikers and the speeches of Labour leaders, even if they were not allowed to broadcast for themselves. [15] Nevertheless, the tenor of most news items was unashamedly that of support for the government. News to boost the morale of the government and its supporters attracted the greatest weight in bulletins - the arrival and movement of food or fuel supplies to various locations received detailed comment, as did reports of strikers returning to work. Some of these reports were quite inaccurate but corrections requested by the TUC were not broadcast. [16] The BBC's position was cruelly exposed by its coverage of an appeal for the resumption of negotiations between the strikers and the government. It was made by churchmen led by the Archbishop of Canterbury but Baldwin and Davidson pressurised Reith and he refused to broadcast the Archbishop's appeal until after the end of the strike. Instead, the appeal had to be read from the pulpit on the Archbishop's behalf in churches throughout the country. On the other hand, publicity was given to a sermon given on the 9 May by Cardinal Bourne, the Roman Catholic Archbishop of Westminster, where he declared that the strike was, 'a sin against the obedience which we owe to God.' This inconsistency in reporting did not go unnoticed during the strike.[17]

Broadcasting was playing its part even before the strike was formally announced. After the NATSOPA dispute at the Daily Mail very few papers emerged on 3 May and the BBC news was quickly highlighted, providing information where other sources ceased to exist and setting the scene for the strike. The Oxford Chronicle captured the atmosphere which radio helped to generate at the beginning of the strike:

> The air of uncertainty hung over Oxford throughout the day, and in the evening when the evening papers, with the exception of the Star failed to appear, owing to the compositors having taken exception to certain passages in the strike comments,anxiety deepened. The wireless bulletins were eagerly listened to, and the voice from the ether announcing the successive stages in the crisis had a dramatic quality. In the middle of the evening there was a hopeful note and it was announced that the general feeling in the House of Commons was that a settlement might be reached before midnight. Further bulletins rather dampened these hopes and at 11.15 the announcer's voice said: "I'm afraid this is the final news regarding the coal situation. All negotiations have broken down and the strike is fixed for 12 o'clock tonight". [18]

The BBC broadcast five bulletins a day at 10 a.m., 1 p.m., 4 p.m., 7 p.m. and 9.30 p.m. Very little news was collected by the BBC itself and bulletins relied heavily on official Government statements and the press agencies which relaxed their normal restrictions. [19] On 4 May, editorials were also added. These were permitted during the course of the strike and for a short period afterwards. Eventually, a combination of pressure from the press and a government suspicion of radical comment ensured their demise. [20]

In estimating the extent of listening to these bulletins and editorials, the indirect influence of wireless has to be taken into account. Even if there were less than two million licence holders out of a population of forty-five million in 1926, it seems safe to say that most of the population could have had contact with radio. People could listen in groups, read bulletins printed with radio as a source or, more crudely, exchange news heard on the radio by word of mouth. Indeed, word of mouth was still the most important means of exchanging information, particularly with the frequent lack

of the press, and regular news bulletins ensured that any
gossip could be better informed and rumour nipped in the bud.

During the strike, listeners fell into three broad categories. There were those who were solidly behind the government's position and welcomed the BBC's broadcasts wholeheartedly and uncritically. There were the neutrals and
waverers who generally seemed to have appreciated the
BBC's output. Finally, there were the strikers and labour
supporters who frequently listened to the broadcasts but
treated them almost universally with suspicion and hostility.

Apart from Churchill and one or two other ultras, the
government, employers and their supporters were well
pleased with the service they received. The extremists
were certainly not satisfied - Churchill thought it 'monstrous
not to use such an instrument to the best possible advantage.'[21]
Most of the Cabinet, on the other hand, realised that the
BBC's position, under threat of being commandeered, produced the right product: an apparent independence with
careful behind the scenes control of its bulletins. The airways were open for Ministers to make formal statements and
certainly to make their position clear. The Home Secretary,
Joynson-Hicks appealed for special constables and far more
came forward than could be readily signed on for useful
work.[22] Certainly, the government's supporters were often
introduced to broadcasting for the first time and gained a
favourable impression. Some London clubs installed a set
for the occasion so that members could listen to bulletins in
comfort.[23] When the strike was over, letters poured into
the BBC, the vast majority proclaiming their gratitude for
the BBC's news coverage. Nearly 3,700 people obviously
felt that the medium had firmly established itself as a useful
public service.[24]

The politically neutral listening population was obviously composed of many different types - some remained completely unsure of their position, some were eventually
persuaded to join one side or another, whilst others were
rather more detached, cynical observers of the scene. There
seems no doubt that the BBC got the government's message
across to such people and that many were reassured by the
achievement. The semblance of objectivity and fairness was
very seductive.[25] The editorials and bulletins were consci-
ously designed to be uplifting in an attempt to persuade the
confused and bewildered to have more confidence. This
calmness was exemplified by Reith's careful prompting and
Baldwin's natural style in his famous broadcast appeal for a

settlement on Saturday evening, the eighth day of the strike. It was widely considered to be a successful morale booster, convincing many waverers to stand firm. [26]

The BBC increased its signal strength during the strike to make sure that as many people as possible could listen and this was particularly important for scattered, small communities which did not normally enjoy good reception from the urban based local transmitters or Daventry. [27]

Beatrice Webb wrote in her diary, a little sardonically perhaps: 'The sensation of a General Strike, which stops the press as witnessed from a cottage in the country, centres round the headphones of the wireless set.' [28] Throughout the country this sense of contact with events suppressed the rumour and raised the morale of the perplexed. Many communities, particularly the small and isolated ones lost all of their alternative sources of communications during the strike but the existence of a single set acted as a magnet for the whole community - keeping listeners and their neighbours well informed about national events.

The local press was convinced of the value of radio. The Oxford Chronicle asserted:

> The situation was saved of course by wireless. Perhaps the BBC bulletins under Government control were unduly optimistic now and then, but they did give the news, and on the whole gave it fairly. And this news came regularly into hundreds of Oxford homes, many of them the homes of very humble people. [29]

The local press was hard hit by the strike. Like the national press, many papers failed to appear because of union action and, where they did succeed in producing an issue, it was normally in a truncated form. News was scarce and frequently the emergency editions unashamedly took information straight from the BBC bulletins as well as their normal correspondents or press agency wire supplies - not even seeking to disguise their new source. [30] By this means, and ingenuity from proprietors and managers, some local editions appeared in short runs. The strike did not last long enough to restrict newsprint, although distribution problems were probably almost as effective as the strike by printers in obstructing the supply of papers to readers. [31]

Radio news could fill the gap even when no edition was possible. Radio news bulletins were printed and displayed in local newspaper office windows. Similarly, radio shops printed bulletins for issue to passers-by. The General Radio

Company in Regent Street, London, claimed to have succeeded in printing 80,000 copies of a bulletin within thirty minutes of a broadcast. [32] Where local newspapers could not appear, or editions were limited, the demand for day to day news had to be met by the local authority. This happened in Chiswick:

> A four-valve wireless set has been installed in the Town Hall. Six shorthand-typists, two at a time, working three shifts per day, take down all the wireless information. It is then printed and put on two posters outside the Town Hall. By this system the district is kept well informed of the situation from hour to hour. [33]

It must be emphasised that the sense of stability which the BBC gave to the waverers during the strike was exemplified by the determination to maintain a normal service around the bulletins. A calming output of music and talks maintained the sense of normality. Robert Lynd of the New Statesman observed:

> A good many people, I am sure, were charmed when, on the first day of the first General Strike that this island has known, they turned to the wireless for news of what was happening to themselves and their civilisation and found themselves, having heard all the news that was fit to transmit, invited to listen to a talk on 'holidays with ants and grasshoppers.' Since Drake played out his game of bowls while the Armada was approaching, there have been few things more pleasantly characteristic of the English attitude to a crisis. [34]

This contract gave the new listeners a chance to discover something about other values of broadcasting and may explain much of the 32% increase in licence holding during 1926 [35]

A considerable section of the audience during the strike did not enjoy the BBC's coverage; rather news bulletins were received with a mixture of hostility, resentment and suspicion. The BBC realised that many listeners had taken to using the term BFC (British Falsehood Corporation) to express their disgust. [36] Ellen Wilkinson MP, later to become a Cabinet Minister in the 1945 Labour Government, toured the country during the strike and afterwards wrote to the Radio Times to complain that the attitude of the BBC:

caused pain and indignation to many subscribers. I travelled by car over two thousand miles during the strike and addressed very many meetings. Everywhere the complaints were bitter that a national service subscribed to by every class should have given only one side during the dispute. Personally, I feel like asking the Postmaster-General for my licence fee back. [37]

Notwithstanding her protestations and the undisguised susicions of her supporters, there is strong evidence that those on strike, or sympathetic to it, listened to BBC broadcasts in one way or another and murmured threats to disrupt broadcasts by oscillation did not materialise.

There are several reasons for this apparent paradox. First, the order by the General Council of the TUC for the strike of the printers hampered the cause of the unions far more than the government side. All over the country unionised printers remained out on strike, even when asked to help in the preparation of local strike bulletins or newsheets by strike committees. They were afraid that their loyalty would be brought into question and that they would be labelled 'blacklegs'. The printers even raised objections to the printing of regional editions of the British Worker. [38] Coupled with the utter lack of preparedness for action before the strike, local strike committees failed to establish alternative sources of communication quickly. Strikers frequently had to turn to the BBC for a good supply of information about the strike to supplement the scraps of information which they could glean from the strike breaking editions of the press or non-unionised local papers, neither of which was likely to be at all sympathetic to the strikers' cause. Production and distribution problems afflicted the strikers' own bulletins and they were often unable to provide an adequate alternative - leaving the BBC to dominate the supply of information. The staff of the British Worker decided to arrange regional printing because of the distribution problems faced by the early editions run off in the Daily Herald machine room, but it was the 10 May before printing began in the provinces (appearing as the Scottish Worker in Scotland) and it was widely argued that copies did not get through to eager readers until it was too late. Complaints came from such important cities as Manchester, in the early part of the strike, and places only a few miles from Glasgow or Newcastle were not receiving copies. [39]

A further important reason for the success of the BBC
in attracting strikers to listen was that the coverage of the
national pattern of events was left open to the broadcasters
even where their own strike bulletins were available in
reasonable quantities. The established local press was not
afraid to reprint news from the BBC or the British Gazette
but, of course, the strike bulletins could not do this except
in articles challenging such sources. Local strike newspapers could not hope to compete with the BBC's national
news and the British Worker made a deliberate policy
decision not to. Hamilton Fyfe, editor of the Daily Herald,
suggested that the British Worker should cover general news
but the TUC Publicity Committee determined from the outset
that the paper would concentrate singlemindedly on the control and operation of the strike. High morale, loyalty to the
General Council and denunciation of government-inspired
information were the main tasks.

Local bulletins did not have the option. They had no
apparatus for gathering national news and concentrated almost
entirely on local needs. [40] In the North East, the Northern
Light in Chopwell and the Workers' Chronicle in Newcastle
were particularly good examples of local bulletins which
concentrated on the immediate needs of organisation, picket-
ing, public meetings and local communication. These
bulletins saw their main purpose as raising the morale of the
strikers, particularly by satirical denunciations of the government and the coal owners. They gave little idea of the
national position of the strikers or the opposing Organisation
for the Maintenance of Supply (OMS) and other government
forces. Like many other local bulletins and even the British
Worker the threat of impoundment of the press and newsprint
was a real consideration - several issues suffered confisca-
tion - and this tempered the tone of the most passionate
supporters of the strike. The editor of the Northern Light
used a new headquarters every night in an unsuccessful
attempt to avoid arrest and, similarly, the Workers'
Chronicle staff set up a shadow editor with his own duplicator
in case of a police raid on the printing press. [41] Most local
bulletins lacked even this cover. Largely because of a lack
of preparedness, they faced serious cash shortages, problems with newsprint, equipment or distribution. In Middles-
brough, for instance, the strike was actually over before
preparations for the production of a daily bulletin were completed. Most places managed better than this and despatch
riders or postal contact ensure that TUC messages or bulletins

were available for display or reprinting in local bulletins. [42]
Even in the best cases, however, the distribution of
local bulletins was limited. Although the British Worker was
sometimes available to supplement the local effort, the
strikers could not generally match the circulations achieved
by the established local press. [43] The Workers' Chronicle
rarely managed to produce more than 3,000 copies at a time
and on an irregular basis, while the local press in Newcastle
managed 150,000 copies of their emergency editions between
them. [44] In Derby, the strike bulletin was sold daily from the
first day of the strike to the last; costing 1d, it was estimated to have sold 50,000 copies although it only raised
£92.17s.6d in income. [45] In Oxford a similar course was
taken, distribution being arranged by the University Labour
Club and Ruskin College and 18,000 to 20,000 copies were
sold. [46] Even assuming more than one reader for each issue -
for instance where bulletins were pinned up at strike committee rooms - this was not particularly impressive competition for the BBC and the local press.

The British Worker recognised that the paper's readers
were listening to the BBC. The obstruction of the Archbishop
of Canterbury's appeal and the broadcast speech by Sir John
Simon condemning the strikers were given front page coverage. [47] It was accepted that supporters and waverers alike
were relying on the BBC for an immediacy and breadth of
coverage with which the TUC Publicity Committee could not
compete. Contemporary photographic evidence clearly show
mass listening to bulletins by strikers. [48] Even local strike
committees felt the need to use radio in bulletin preparation.
The Sheffield Forward supplemented its local news network
in this way - if only to attack what was broadcast. [49]

The British Worker also corrected BBC misreporting
of returns to work and after the strike, the Publicity Committee, rather over-confidently considered that radio news
had been successfully countered. [50] The Committee could not
stop workers listening - it could only provide a corrective to
what was heard and, if it was not already present, this
critical approach was well instilled into the minds of the
strikers. Strikers at Littlemore near Cowley condemned
'the meagre and one-sided information given by the BBC.'[51]
Immediately after the strike, Émile Burns reviewed the local
strike bulletins in his book for the Labour Research Department on the work of the Trades Councils:

> The warning not to believe the wireless or capitalist
> publications is a universal feature, and there are also

many denials of particular statements by the BBC, the British Gazette, or other papers. [52]

At 1 p.m. on Wednesday, 12 May, the ninth day of the strike, Reith was the first to announce the end of the strike and relayed a message from the General Council to the strikers. [53] The response of the public to the announcement emphasised the growing dependence which had been placed on the BBC during the course of the strike and, equally strongly, indicated the divergent ways in which this radio news was received. The Chiswick Times reported:

'Thank God for that'. This was the phrase reverently on many lips in Chiswick shortly after one o'clock on Wednesday, when rumours that had been floating around all the morning were confirmed by the announcement over the wireless. Those people who had gathered in large numbers outside premises which had served a good purpose during the past week by broadcasting the official news of the great strike came up against an interruption of music from one of the London restaurants. A voice said, 'The general strike was declared off at one o'clock', and immediately after the restaurant orchestra played the National Anthem and enthusiastic cheers came over the wire. There was little or no cheering by the listeners; it all seemed too sudden to be true. [54]

Strike committees throughout the country heard the news in the same way but received it with a mixture of suspicion and disbelief. [55] The response in Pontypridd was typical: the strikers waiting outside the strike headquarters refused to believe the broadcast and only accepted the end of the strike when the official telegrams from the TUC began to arrive from London. [56]

At the end of the strike, radio was confirmed as essential equipment for the coverage of national political events, even if the manner of reporting was not accepted by everyone uncritically. The style of reporting and the omissions in the coverage during the strike cost the BBC some of the goodwill which it had determinedly built up before the strike but it retained a great deal of support and even secured many new listeners from the ranks of those who had barely taken any notice of the medium before May 1926.

Figure 7.1: Advertising and the General Strike

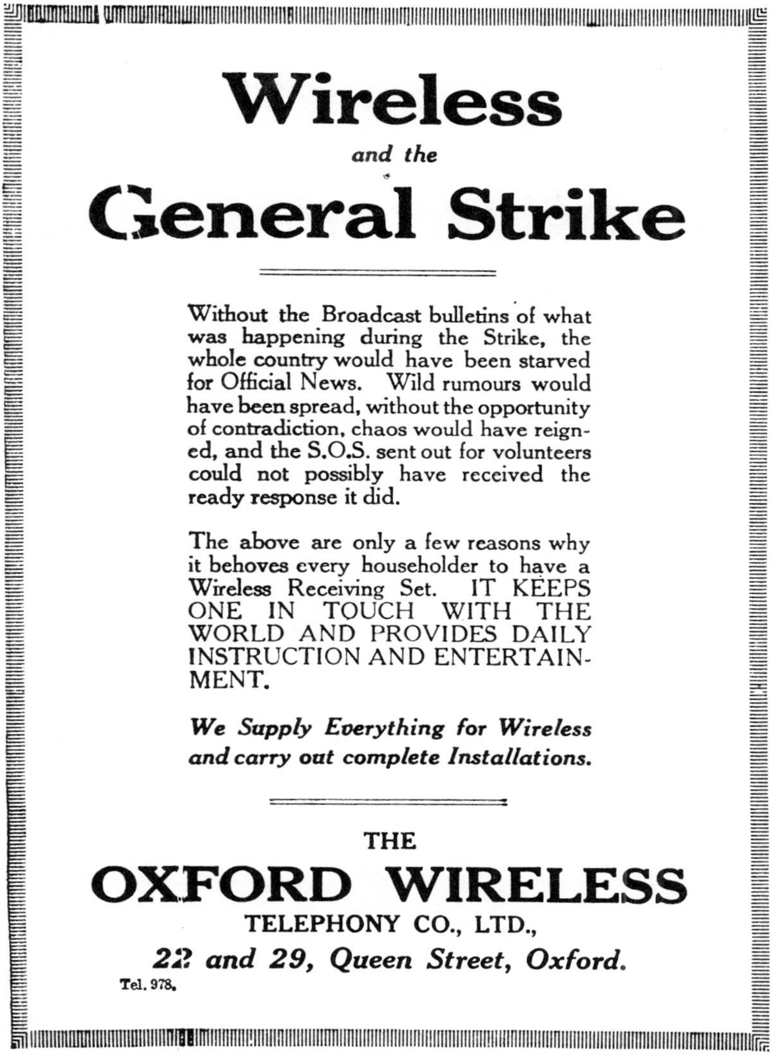

Wireless

and the

General Strike

Without the Broadcast bulletins of what was happening during the Strike, the whole country would have been starved for Official News. Wild rumours would have been spread, without the opportunity of contradiction, chaos would have reigned, and the S.O.S. sent out for volunteers could not possibly have received the ready response it did.

The above are only a few reasons why it behoves every householder to have a Wireless Receiving Set. IT KEEPS ONE IN TOUCH WITH THE WORLD AND PROVIDES DAILY INSTRUCTION AND ENTERTAINMENT.

We Supply Everything for Wireless and carry out complete Installations.

THE

OXFORD WIRELESS

TELEPHONY CO., LTD.,

22 and 29, Queen Street, Oxford.

Tel. 978.

Oxford Times, 21 May 1926, p. 16.

Reproduced by permission of the British Library.

Local Political Activity

The influence of broadcasting on local political activity did
not concern the social surveyors. They had little to contribute beyond the observation that public meetings were
attended less well and that, more vaguely, 'many people who
would not go to a meeting to hear a political opponent will
listen to what he has to say on the air and afterwards discuss
his point of view.'[57] Lacking detailed proof they could only
speculate that people might be more eager to listen to
national leaders when they broadcast rather than go out to
hear their local political figures. Although these general
observations are accurate, the influence of broadcasting on
politics was a great deal more complicated.

The BBC's coverage of political matters had a decidedly mixed effect on local society. The BBC was fettered in
its coverage by the rule on controversial broadcasting imposed by the government before 1928 and, after its relaxation by
various written and unwritten agreements made with the
government, press and press agencies. The Charter laid
down terms which restricted political news coverage and,
furthermore, the Regional Scheme prevented the detailed
reporting of local government elections. It was in the case
of general elections that broadcasting was able to produce
noticeable changes. After the 1918 Representation of the
People Act, the electorate increased in size quite considerably and was expanded further with the enfranchisement of
women aged 21 to 30 in 1928. Many groups, not least the
local press, were looking at ways in which candidates could
get their message across before broadcasting became a
reality.[58] For this reason, radio was seen to be an absolutely essential aid to the traditional methods of expressing
political comment or debate and, normally, it was welcomed
by the local press and certainly by the local community.[59]

At first broadcasting tended to supplement rather than
replace existing means of bringing election news - particularly on election nights. Normally, crowds would gather
outside the Town Hall where the count was being undertaken
and greet the candidates at the announcement of the result.
This crowd was kept in touch with other results brought by
wire from the press agencies and displayed by lantern slide
shows on a large screen, either in the open air - by courtesy
of the local newspaper - or else indoors at the local cinema
or theatre. Radio simply accelerated the process of providing this news, whilst the facilities remained the same.[60]

In Chiswick, for instance, the local paper reviewed the
activities of supporters during the 1931 Election. Outside
the Town Hall, things were much quieter than in past elections and the paper assumed that:

> The supporters of the National Conservative [sic]
> candidate were content, having recorded their opinion,
> to sit quietly at home and wait for the announcement
> of the results through the medium of wireless.

At the count inside the Town Hall party activists and supporters were also listening; a portable set was used to keep
them in touch with other results. [61]

There was some optimism that radio would bring many
beneficial qualities to electoral practice. Local newspapers
hoped, as did the BBC, that the proceedings of Parliament
would be broadcast. [62] There was also great expectancy when
the first speeches by national leaders were broadcast. Then
disillusionment set in. In 1929 a squabble over airtime for
the first full series of party political broadcasts soured the
taste of these broadcasts. The local press, however, concentrated less on the political significance of this dispute
rather on the appalling quality of the broadcasts. As the
Oxford Mail observed: 'The most comprehensive method of
attracting the people has its limitations. Mr. Arthur Hender-
son on the wireless last night was not the same as the prime
organiser of the Labour Party on the platform.' The Postmaster-General, Worthington-Evans was also written off - in
this case as, 'insufferably dull'. [63] Thus, the early novelty
of these national broadcasts wore off very quickly. In 1926
the local press was excitedly greeting the first broadcast by
Lloyd George, by 1931 they were forced to conclude that the
Liberal leader, 'though a capital platform speaker is not a
good microphone subject.' The only leading figures to escape
condemnation were Baldwin and particularly Snowden, whose
speech on the Gold Standard in September 1931 was generally
credited with attracting 'at least ninety per cent of homes
equipped with wireless receiving sets.' [64]

The early idealism faded and the realisation that radio
had wrought some unwelcome changes on electoral activity
was now bemoaned powerlessly by the local papers. Their
own grip on the electoral publicity machine was waning.
People no longer stayed in the streets to view the press displays - they stayed at home. Election night consequently
become a lot quieter: the trend was observable as early as
1929. At first the cause perplexed local observers: perhaps

the presence of female voters had calmed down the unruly elements in the electorate; perhaps the damp weather was to blame for the empty streets?[65] The local press was already raising the familiar complaint about the ability of party political broadcasts to penetrate the Englishman's castle but, as one paper put it, 'after all, we console ourselves; we can switch off when we have had enough.'[66] One or two papers vainly exhorted listeners to leave the comfort of the fireside and go to meetings to hear the candidates for themselves. In fact, all the local newspapers observed that the election had been the quietest for years.[67] This could have been quite unrelated to the influence of broadcasting but in subsequent elections the connection became clearer and the pattern more firmly fixed. This is not to say that broadcasting cured the rowdism and violence previously associated with elections. Before broadcasting had made any impression, it was widely accepted that contemporary standards of behaviour compared most favourably with nineteenth century elections.[68]

In 1931 the controversial circumstances generally failed to arrest the trend. It was observed that: 'A great many people, of course, preferred the comfort of their own fireside, listening to the news by wireless, the BBC having made special arrangements for sending the figures through the ether.'[69] In 1935 heavy rainfall made election night quieter still. Some Town Halls attracted fairly large gatherings for the result but this was exceptional. In general, the streets were deserted and meetings poorly attended throughout the campaign.[70] The close physical contact between the electorate and parliamentary candidates had been considerably diluted by the appeal from the party leadership, using radio to speak directly to voters over the heads of their party colleagues. Of course, canvassing and public meetings had continued during the course of the election campaign, but they were increasingly badly attended and their influence suffered a commensurate decline.

As radio took over the task of communicating the policies and beliefs of politicians to the nation, so the control of these statements became more important. After the end of the ruling on controversial broadcasts in 1928, the BBC was still very vulnerable to political interference. The ideal - to use the power of the airways to nurture an enlightened, participative democracy - was not easy to achieve in the face of pressures applied from all sides.[71]

The strongest criticism was aimed at the BBC for

failing to stimulate the political awareness which it was
hoped would defend and strengthen democracy in Britain.
These criticisms gained extra impetus with the rise of the
European dictators who had, of course, shown the political
power of radio when it was manipulated for more malevolent
purposes. From the other side of the political arena came
the charge that the BBC was 'pink', that the Talks Department in particular had a bias to the left. [72]

E. M. Forster described the BBC's growing dilemma
in 1931:

> Nemesis has descended, bringing all the powers of
> darkness in her train. For the easy days are over,
> brightness falls from the air, and the conflict has
> begun. The BBC because of its success and growing
> importance, is being constantly attacked, in the pul-
> pit, in Parliament, in the Press, and the attack is on
> new and dangerous lines. The aim is suppression. [73]

He appealed for the silent supporters to rally round and make
their views known to counterbalance these critics.

Other critics treated the BBC's position less sympa-
thetically. The left denounced the 'timid authoritarianism'
of the BBC, accusing it of cravenly conceding to official and
orthodox pressure and excluding the expression of new
ideas. [74] Harold Nicolson deplored the BBC's pusillanimous
tendency to pursue the line of least resistance: 'Even though
that line leads them to the Rectory sofa of 1887.'[75] Many
shared this view, most of them agreeing that the best solution was to permit as many views as possible to broadcast
rather than dilute or censor broadcasts on political issues.
As one of the BBC's founding fathers, Cecil Lewis, put it:

> If your job is holding a balance, you can keep the
> pointer steady by putting nothing in either scale, but
> you can also keep it steady by putting a ton in either
> scale. [76]

In this way, the attempt to provide an educated democracy became a balancing act. The BBC preferred caution to
adventure. Speakers were banned from appearing if they
intended to express views hostile to the Government. In 1934,
William Ferrie caused a furore when he cast aside his
approved script, denounced the prior censorship of his broadcast and proceeded to express his real views on behalf of the
common man. The press reaction was interestingly sympathetic:

heavily censored opinions have no value. If Mr. Ferrie had not been a rebel we should have listened to him and imagined that we were getting a working man's views, whereas, actually, we should have been merely swallowing the usual cautious dope approved by the pundits as suitable food for a public of infants and invalids .... [77]

At the other end of the social and political spectrum, Churchill was forbidden to broadcast his views on the Government's policy towards India. The New Statesman was forced to come to the unlikely defence of a political opponent in his efforts to break this brand of censorship:

> The right way of dealing with speakers as irritating and mischief-making as Mr. Churchill is to put them up against others of their own kind. Why not let Mr. Churchill broadcast, Mr. Saklatvala reply, and some sane person to sum up - all on the same occasion? It would be instructive and entertaining, and it would leave Mr. Churchill with no grievance.

The man himself needed little assistance in expressing his views, denouncing the whole business as 'pontifical mugwum-pery'. [78]

Critics continued to press for greater support from the broadcasters in developing an educated democracy. A regular broadcaster, Stephen King-Hall put the case in its most basic form:

> The school broadcast talk brings the child in the rural school into direct relationship with Mr. Baldwin defending democracy. It could - and if I had my way it would - bring that same child into a similar relationship with Mr. Lansbury on socialism and Sir Oswald Mosley defending fascism, and Mr. Pollitt or Mr. Tom Mann making the case for communism. [79]

The BBC was prepared to try this course but was frustrated by political interference. Reith's plan for broadcasting parliamentary debates was rejected out of hand and even individual talks came under fierce attack. [80] An attempt to organise a series of talks, 'A Citizen and his Government' was scrapped after a secret Cabinet intervention because it proposed the inclusion of talks by Pollitt and Mosley. [81]

As eyes and ears turned increasingly towards the deteriorating European situation, the BBC continued to come under fire. In 1933, Vernon Bartlett had caused a controversy when his talk on Germany leaving the disarmament talks was construed as causing 'great embarrassment' for the government. [82] Churchill continued to complain at his continued exclusion from the airways. [83] After Munich, the BBC did, however, begin to respond to the demand for talks on controversial subjects - against the wishes of the government and its supporters. The series 'Everyman and the Crisis' proved to be very popular with the audience. The BBC even appointed its own foreign correspondents to collect news and information from abroad to keep the audience in touch with the causes behind the rapidly deepening threat of war. [84]

Despite this late rally, the BBC failed to use the full potential of broadcast news and talks for the service of a more educated democracy. Great hopes were placed on the BBC: that broadcasting would break through the ignorance which prevailed in a class divided society and strengthen democracy to stand as a bulwark against fascism. [85] These aspirations were certainly ambitious if not impossible. The BBC failed to resist the powerful pressures of press and government which aimed to suppress freedom of discussion on the radio. It was a common criticism of the time that the BBC was only able to broadcast talks which would give pleasure to the most conservative suburbs of London. Many critics explained the timidity in the face of attempts at suppression in terms of the bourgeois class bias in staff recruitment. Others, including former employees such as Hilda Matheson, saw this problem further in terms of the deeply ingrained BBC programme values which preferred personal experience and choice to consultation and understanding of the needs of the audience. [86] Lacking this foundation, the BBC was ill-equipped to resist the forces of suppression or meet the wide ranging needs of listeners for political discussion.

The King Speaks!

The best examples of mass listening could be seen on the occasions when crowds gathered to listen to radio broadcasts made by the royal family. A particularly significant event was the first BBC broadcast by the King and the Prince of Wales at the Empire Exhibition held at Wembley on 23 April 1924. In many towns special provision was made for large crowds, often several thousand strong, to listen to the King and contemporary observers took the opportunity to wax

lyrical with their impressions of this new miracle. The
Oxford Times described the importance of the speech in suit-
ably glowing terms which, nonetheless, reflected the substantial impact which the association of radio and the monarchy
brought to the event:

> Many people have realised the wonders of wireless in
> their own home if they have taken the full opportunity
> made possible by broadcasting but it was not until some
> great national function took place like the State opening
> of the British Empire Exhibition at Wembley, and the
> Oxford Times and the Oxford Wireless Telephony
> Company arranged to give citizens the chance to hear
> the King's speech in St. Giles', that the full force of
> the miracle of science was realised. For the uniniti-
> ated to imagine that broadcasting gives them the oppor-
> tunity to hear spirited music and the spoken word is a
> very different thing to realising for the first time that
> it enables them to take part in some ceremony 60, 100,
> miles, or even greater distances away. It gave the
> sense of unity with a mighty people, the sense of parti-
> cipation in an unseen event. [87]

Similar arrangements applied to the High Street, where
the rival Oxford Chronicle and another retailer provided the
service. [88] The scene was typical of many others in the
country and the BBC estimated a national audience of ten
millions. [89]

It was widely recognised that this event was one of the
greatest early influences on sales of wireless sets of all
kinds. Clearly, this kind of broadcast to a mass audience
increased the desire to possess a set at home but, interestingly, it did not necessarily diminish the desire to listen to
such broadcasts in groups. During the Jubilee celebrations
of 1935, radio was often used as a highlight after a traditional
street party or fete. [90] The Coronation of 1937 also encouraged local celebrations which depended on good reception of
radio broadcasts. The day revolved around the radio set:
chapels and churches changed their ceremonies to suit broadcasting times. [91] Great emphasis was placed on the fact that
this was the first time that people had heard a King speak on
his Coronation Day. Some churches laid on the broadcast as
part of the service although instances of mass listening,
particularly in the open air, were much diminished - as one
observer noted: 'The broadcast kept thousands of people
indoors when they might have been expected to be abroad, and

Figure 7.2: Advertising and the Coronation

I**T is not too late to install one of our super sets to hear the ———**

First Coronation to be broadcast

To mark this occasion we are offering

£3 for **YOUR OLD SET**

In part exchange, no matter what age or condition.
Balance on Easiest Terms.

PHILCO,   FERRANTI,

MARCONI,   EKCO,

ULTRA,   GILBERT,

BRUNSWICK,   ETC.

GORDON SHORE
& CO.
16, Knifesmithgate, Chesterfield
Phone 3102.
and PARK ROAD, BASLOW.

Derbyshire Times, 7 May 1937, p. 18.

Reproduced by permission of the British Library.

it was this, rather than the weather, that gave the streets at times an almost deserted appearance. [92]

The Coronation celebrations underlined the evolution in the relationship of the royal family to the nation. First, the King had been brought into direct contact with his subjects by means of his broadcasts and, then, this contact had been translated from an act of communal veneration to a more intimate relationship between the sovereign and the family at home. The ties between the King and the nation were strengthened and subtly reformed during a reign in which public broadcasting was born and reached its maturity. In 1932, George V began what was to become a regular series of Christmas broadcasts and these were greatly appreciated by listeners. These listeners were part of a mass audience, but it was not the mass audience of the street crowd, rather a collection of millions of homes listening to what appeared to be a very personal message from the King. [93] The Brentford and Chiswick Times made this latter point strongly during the final illness of George V. Comparing the reaction of the public to the death of Edward VII, the paper noted the contribution of radio:

> ever since the first disquieting news of the King's illness was made known last week, practically every home in the kingdom has followed with keen anxiety every phase of the last hours of a loved monarch. This new fact in the life of the people has intensified the ties between the subject and the King, and in that measure the feeling of grief and the sense of loss are more poignant today. [94]

It should not be assumed that the benefits of broadcasting were confined entirely to the nation. With the development of the Empire service, beginning in 1932, the King also spoke to an immense audience throughout the world. By means of the Daventry transmitter, nations very distant from the British Isles could feel a greater sense of involvement in royal occasions. [95]

Chapter Eight

BROADCASTING AND LEISURE

Leisure

Changes in the pattern of leisure in Britain before 1939 were frequently attributed to the influence of broadcasting. This relationship needs to be examined carefully, to see if the taste for entertainments or the pursuit of pastimes such as sport owed anything to the presence of broadcasting.

First of all, the nature of inter-war leisure, the product of an advanced industrial society, needs to be clarified. Long working hours in the nineteenth century gave limited scope for free activity and it appeared to observers, such as Karl Marx, that any respite from work was filled by the necessities of eating, drinking and sleeping or by procreation. This was undoubtedly an accurate description of the lives of many industrial workers but, even at its worst, the factory system did not completely eliminate a British tradition of sports and pastimes and, as the length of the working week was progressively reduced for many industrial workers before 1918, this description of life away from the workplace was clearly less and less appropriate.[1] For most workers, there were clearly defined, regular periods of spare time providing ample opportunities for self-expression in numerous leisure activities. Leisure was now not only an escape from the tyranny of work but also from ordinary social or domestic necessities and obligations, so that leisure described any non-obligatory activity outside the workplace.[2] Obviously, the amount of free time and the use made of it for leisure pursuits was a function of variables, such as disposable income, but even the most disadvantaged were experiencing more leisure, if only in the cruellest way by enforced unemployment. Certainly, broadcasting arrived as the time available for non-obligatory activities was

increasing at a significant rate. In his New Survey of London
Life and Labour, Llewellyn Smith thought that the emergence
of the five and a half day week was one of the most significant
influences on social changes since Charles Booth's original
survey. [3]

Radio also arrived at the time when the consumer
society was gaining considerable strength. The use of more
household goods was reducing the number of obligatory
domestic activities, such as the drudgery of household work,
thus increasing the time available for other leisure activities.
This was particularly true in the case of electrical goods.
Clearly the rate at which households absorbed consumer
goods varied according to the economic group of the occupants, the rate of expansion of the national grid for electric
power and the rapid technological development of electrical
devices. Consequently the share which radio took from this
expanding leisure time was certain to vary tremendously -
by geographical situation, by socio-economic class and by
time. Social surveyors certainly lacked sufficient detailed
evidence to make many serious judgements on this point.
They were able to do little more than indicate the attractiveness of radio and the consequent likelihood that radio would
be employed increasingly as a leisure activity. BBC audience
research figures gave a more definite answer only for the
period when licence holding was the rule rather than the
exception and broadcasting was already a very considerable
leisure activity.

Inevitably, some particular social effects of broadcasting were expected from the beginning. It did not require
a tremendous imagination to foresee that an inherent part of
the medium was its capacity to concentrate attention on the
home. Even following the introduction of portable sets, this
prophecy was confirmed by the most casual social observation. It was also expected that a radio set would be a great
solace to the housebound, the aged, the sick and the handicapped. This, too, was confirmed and radio became another
positive means of aid for philanthropy. Campaigns to
purchase radios for the blind or particularly for those confined by sickness or age to public institutions became a new
part of charitable action and social concern. Rowntree went
further, arguing from his observations in York, that the
solace of radio ran much wider:

> Again and again, the idea is expressed, that the wire-
> less is a companionable thing. 'It is a good companion.'

It is used 'to keep the family company.' Wireless is a companion to anyone alone in a room with some hand occupation, e. g. knitting or sewing. [4]

The concomitant of this home-centred existence could be seen as a reduction of the extended family system, where radio helped to concentrate attention on the immediate occupants of the dwelling itself. [5] It could also be seen as the means for affecting a reduction of interest or participation in leisure activities which fell outside the home. The only flaw in this line of thought is that it implies a straight-forward correlation between the extension of licence holding and the tendency to remain in the home. In the first few years of broadcasting, the reverse was generally true. Communal listening was the rule rather than the exception and this might be expected to create an outward-looking tendency, away from the confines of the home. At some point, probably from 1927 onwards but with some regional variations, this aspect of broadcasting declined and the home-centred consequences of broadcasting were now satisfied. Yet there were still sufficient cases of listening outside the home - in pubs or in the course of celebrations such as the Coronation - to suggest that radio was not a wholly domesticating influence. Moreover, broadcasting did not necessarily lead to harmony at home. Collective listening within the family circle could easily be disrupted by divergent programme preferences and broadcasting might become 'one of the petty tyrannies of family life'[6] if parents and their children could not agree. Jennings and Gill found in their research that the dominant role in the choice of programmes was the father but in many cases collective decisions were taken. Evidently home-centred listening was rarely an individual experience and programmes were heard either by consensus or dominant parental decisions. [7]

It is not difficult to demonstrate that broadcasting eventually became an essentially home-centred pursuit. It is rather more difficult to decide whether broadcasting played a complementary or competitive role in the enjoyment of leisure pursuits. Rowntree implied that other tasks could be more readily carried on with radio and other contemporary social surveyors have something to offer in this context. They discovered quite quickly that listeners could be occupied with other activities whilst listening. Even obligatory tasks, such as housework, were carried on with the radio switched on. [8] Thus, it is perfectly reasonable to suppose that many other activities continued whilst the radio was on, even at peak listening times.

This complementary role is noticeable amongst house-bound listeners, particularly women. In the daytime the social composition of listeners was quite different to the largely homogeneous audience after 6 p.m. Apart from the lunch hour, the audience was restricted to women, children, the sick, handicapped and the elderly. Before 1939, the majority of women were still largely at home during the day. Social prejudice towards women at work produced a neglected education and a restriction of opportunity outside the home. Child bearing and routine domestic activities held women away from the labour market.[9] The BBC was presented with a good opportunity to educate or entertain an enormous, captive section of society. In fact, the BBC did not exploit the full potential because of limits on programme choice and the restricted hours of broadcasting during the morning. Nevertheless, women were exposed to broadcasting for a considerable part of the day. On weekdays during the late morning and early afternoon, the BBC provided a range of talks, plays and musical offerings which it was expected would appeal to women.[10] Listener research showed that these were appreciated - often as a background to routine domestic tasks. This complementary role does seem to have extended the range of interests and depth of knowledge of women as they went about their daily housework. The work of the Women's Institutes and Townwoman's Guilds[11] in using broadcasting for philanthropic and educational purposes show-ed their recognition of its importance, felt all the more strongly by women because it provided a limited substitute for their more restricted domestic lives and experience.

Jennings and Gill found that, apart from reading, there was little sign of hobbies being adversely affected by radio and they were often carried on simultaneously with listening.[12] Whilst noting the debilitating effect of broadcasting upon children's homework, Rowntree also observed the widespread tendency to use radio broadcasts as a background to many other activities: 'Most cases of the more indiscriminate use of wireless occur on Sundays when it is often customary to switch on to Luxembourg first thing in the morning and leave it on all day.' Or, as he argued more generally, 'it is also to a large extent customary to put on dance music, or other light music, at meal times.'[13] Thus, apart from activities away from the range of a set, portable or otherwise, or the influence of direct competitors where the full concentration of the participants was needed, such as reading, playing a

musical instrument or singing, many activities were supplemented rather than supplanted by radio.

Several of the social surveyors observed how broadcasting was beginning to gain ground as a pastime in its own
right, particularly for popular entertainment. As Llewellyn
Smith argued:

> It looks as if 'wireless', though an entirely post-war
> development, has already come to play a part in London
> working class life not less important than the cinema.
> As an agreeable means of passing leisure time in
> comfort, with no effort and little expense, 'listening-in'
> is difficult to beat, and at the same time broadcasting
> is an immensely powerful instrument for the diffusion
> of popular cultural entertainment. [14]

Despite the undoubted popularity of broadcasting, either
for its own sake, or in its context as a complement to other
leisure activities, it is imperative to keep a sense of proportion. For instance, in the questionnaire used in his survey
of Merseyside, Caradog Jones placed radio amongst twenty-
three alternative categories of potential leisure activities
during a given week. [15] Unfortunately, the size of sample he
used was so small that its reliability must be in doubt and, in
any case, it was less useful as a means of judging qualitative
effects. Rowntree also organised a sample which suffered
from similar weaknesses. [16] Jennings and Gill were quite
openly critical of the efficacy of their questionnaires where
the qualitative contribution of broadcasting was concerned:
'Mere statistics as to listeners and programmes listened to
are not sufficient in themselves to give a picture of qualitative
effects. '[17]

Music and Entertainment

To remedy this deficiency a further investigation is needed -
to assess the relationship of broadcasting to the most important areas of leisure activities. Music, entertainment,
reading and outdoor pursuits such as sport or even gardening
were all covered in one form or another by the BBC and were
influenced by the presence of radio.

In Broadcast over Britain, Reith unequivocally expressed his determination that the BBC should not yield to the
temptation of providing just entertainment.

Nonetheless, it requires no great degree of perception
to discover that the greatest and most persistent pressure

placed on broadcasters was for entertainment. This was the dominant concern, exemplified by the massive levels of listening to the commercial stations on Sundays whilst the BBC resolutely refused to concede to the pressure. [18] Contemporary social surveyors pointed out the importance of entertainment programmes to the audience. Furthermore, commercial lobbies and crude press surveys always showed this preference. Eventually, BBC audience research figures confirmed the high levels of listening to such programmes and the considerable satisfaction which they aroused. Hence, there is nothing remarkable in discovering that musical programmes, variety or comedy shows and, to a lesser extent, radio drama were the real attractions for listeners. Most social surveyors agreed that radio had stimulated an interest in music and certainly broadened the knowledge of music. [19] As with much of their research, the difficulty was finding a base to work from. It was difficult to establish the level of musical knowledge before radio arrived. If anything more than a guess could be made at this, then the new level had to be judged by more sophisticated means than regular visits to building sites to listen for labourers whistling Schubert's Unfinished Symphony as they carried their hods. It was left to BBC listener research to fill the gap. Silvey and his colleagues did a great deal to establish the actual position in the thirties in an area which continued to arouse much ill-informed speculation and controversy.

The national press poured scorn on leading figures in music, such as Sir Hamilton Harty and Sir Thomas Beecham, who criticised the value of broadcast music on the grounds that the sound was distorted and that the BBC had helped to put musicians out of work by discouraging live performances. Both individuals were soundly condemned for uttering such beliefs. [20] Most of the press preferred to believe that the lesser quality was more than compensated by the increased knowledge and interest in music held by an immeasureably wider audience, which might even be tempted to attend live performances on the strength of a broadcast.

In his survey of leisure in London, Llewellyn Smith agreed vaguely that musical knowledge was expanding because of the increased opportunities for hearing popular cultural entertainments but his real concern was speculative and lay elsewhere:

> A much more subtle and imminent danger is lest the
> systematic broadcasting of good music rendered by the

best artists may react unfavourably on the demand for the services of musicians of lower rank, and so on the prospects of a musical career as a profession, with the result that eventually the basis of selection of first rate executants, on whom the quality of BBC concerts depends, may be dangerously narrowed. [21]

On this question of intervention in the commercial market, the national press was virtually unanimous. The cause of lost jobs in the musical business was not confined to the encroachment of radio. The Spectator argued:

Many causes (not peculiar to this country alone) must have been at work: changes in the habits of the public, the modern multiplicity of possibilities of amusement, the coming of the gramophone and the sound-film, and so on - for which the BBC cannot be held responsible. While in so far as wireless has thrown musicians out of work it has done so purely and simply qua wireless. The same results would have followed if instead of the BBC we had the DEF or the XYZ. [22]

Furthermore, many critics felt that the purge of a labour force overcrowded with second rate musicians might actually have benefits for live audiences. Certainly there was praise for the standard set by the BBC Symphony Orchestra, partly because of the quality and extensive repertoire it was able to build up through its permanent status and partly because it prevented the old abuses of poor rehearsals and the 'substitution' of players by understudies. [23]

There was unanimity in the support for the BBC's take-over of the Queen's Hall and the related fate of the Promenade Concerts. Many newspapers approved of the necessary intervention by the BBC, even if it had in part been responsible for the economic crises which made such absorption virtually obligatory. 'The Proms' under BBC control were thereafter consistently praised. [24]

Despite the gratitude for the elimination of bad professional playing there was some faint residual sympathy for the amateur performer. The People hoped that once the novelty of radio had worn off, children would return to playing whilst the Spectator thought that the BBC should offer some incentive by organising more amateur broadcasts and competitions. [25]

The real debate amongst the critics came after the BBC had established itself. Most critics eventually accepted that

listening to broadcast music would not necessarily damage
musical taste and appreciation or threaten the quality of
performance of professional or amateur players but they
could not agree on the kind of music which should be broadcast.

Very broadly speaking, critics writing for the popular
Sunday or daily newspapers wanted the BBC to pay more
attention to listeners' tastes - as the critics saw them - and
arrange to broadcast more 'popular' music such as jazz,
dance band or cinema organ music, whereas the critics at
the more serious weekly or daily newspapers urged the BBC
to set their own standards and broadcast more classical
orchestral and operatic works. It was a debate which the
BBC could not hope to win. The slightest suggestion of concession to one side or the other brought forth streams of
criticism.

When more jazz or dance band music was broadcast,
accusations flew that the BBC was 'defeatist', conceding to
the enemies of culture who wanted to reduce the BBC to the
level of a mere public entertainer.[26] W. J. Turner put the
case:

> By having a 'defeatist mentality' I mean that the BBC
> is inclined to abandon - if it has not already abandoned -
> the ambition to lead, and its directors are now to be
> found in the familiar and pitiable posture of demago-
> gues, listening with their hands to their ears to catch
> any fleeting rumours of what the public wants.[27]

Writing in the New Statesman in 1933, Leonard Woolf denounced the 'timid authoritarianism' of the BBC. Where
musical and cultural considerations were concerned, he
charged, the greatest danger of a broadcast monopoly was
the imposition of a dictatorship of taste upon the long-suffer-
ing audience:

> A dictatorship of people who will only allow 'light'
> music to be broadcast and eliminate all 'serious'
> music (except religious of course) from the pro-
> grammes - a process which seems to indeed to have
> begun already.[28]

Critics in the serious press generally supported Reith's intention to raise public taste and oppose the popularising of
vulgarising of music which they saw in 'popular' music.
Altogether, more vitriol and prejudice was espoused for the
cause of broadcast music than for any other subject.

Criticisms were full of remarks denouncing 'lowbrow' music, and appealing for music to appeal to the more 'discriminating taste'. [29] Critics like W. J. Turner liked the expansion of the audience for music which broadcasting generated but adhered strictly to the theory that 'highbrow' or 'serious' music would only remain good if the BBC resisted the proliferation of 'lesser' material - or the threat of 'democratisation' as he termed it. [30]

The popular press, such as the People or the News of the World did not, of course, share these views of the BBC music service or the audience for broadcast music. Their view, backed up eventually by listener research, was that the public really wanted to hear dance bands led by Jack Payne or Henry Hall and listen to cinema organ music played by Reginald Foort. [31] Jazz relayed from the USA or broadcast from gramophone records was also particularly popular.

Even when the BBC did broadcast the sort of music which they demanded, neither the critics nor the listeners were always happy. Their most sustained criticism was devoted to two practices in particular. A large proportion of the letters sent to the popular press on broadcasting questions and to the BBC Programme Correspondence Section concerned these subjects. Throughout the thirties, the singing style 'crooning' was a common source of annoyance for listeners and often dominated letters of complaint to the BBC, as did 'plugging', where musicians constantly introduced and played their latest gramophone record release. [32]

Critics from all sides agreed on the most debilitating effect on broadcast music - Reith's strict control on the BBC output on Sundays. They were unanimous in pressing for a more palatable diet on the one day of the week when most working class men and women could listen regularly throughout the day.

Although it is evident that in later years there were serious differences of opinion amongst listeners about broadcast music - largely arising from widely divergent tastes - in the early years of broadcasting, the first broadcast performances of many pieces of music were very well received, especially tours de force in live opera and symphonic music. The appreciation of broadcast music, whether popular or classical, seemed to be almost limitless at that time. Indeed, music was often proposed as the earliest motive for paying any attention to broadcasting as a medium of communication. [33] Once the BBC began transmissions, it was inevitable that such performances should be eagerly sought throughout the country and local papers were profuse in their praise of these events whenever they were heard.

Soon performers became household names throughout the country, largely on the strength of their broadcasting appearances. Leading performers like Dame Nellie Melba were known to a much wider audience than would otherwise have been possible but many stars owed almost everything to radio. The fame of dance band leaders was particularly noticeable, indeed it was interesting that Jack Payne made his name at the BBC before moving out of the studio on to the more familiar road to success of the dance halls. [34] Apart from a select band of stars in the Music Halls, most performers could not have aspired to such renown so readily without the facility of radio.

In fact an increased interest in national broadcasting personalities was quite compatible with a similar devotion to more familiar local performers. Locally based artistes received considerable attention when they performed or became members of the BBC. Singers and musicians became local personalities after performing in just a single broadcast and a connection with radio, no matter how tenuous, was considered to be a great honour. The BBC announcer, Arthur Burrows was a local celebrity in Oxford simply because he had once lived there. [35] Whereas artistes with national reputations were restrained by their managers or feared for their reputations if they appeared on the radio, local artistes leaped at the chance. For instance, in Derbyshire, the Midland Regional Programme was the main source of these appearances. Musical activities were well favoured and local singers or, more particularly, brass bands received considerable attention. [36] The local press was certainly quick to denounce anyone who got in the way of a chance for national, or even regional, fame by making a broadcast. [37] Local papers were equally unimpressed by those who tried to block national celebrities in the entertainment world from performing on the air. [38] They realised that an interest in local personalities and parochial news did not make listeners any less eager to listen to such famous personalities. No local community could hope to offer such a rich cultural choice of high quality and certainly not at a comparable cost.

The economy of listening to radio entertainment undoubtedly made it an attractive and acceptable alternative to live performances outside the home. The Music Hall was already dying with the competition from the cinema; radio merely added to its serious problems. Yet if radio kept people at

home because it was cheap, it also introduced entertainments
to many of the really poor who could not afford any live entertainments. In this sense, radio was a great boon to all but a
small residuum of the poor before 1939.

Increased exposure to radio could kill some features of
musical performance or variety. In comedy, the life of a
joke was reduced tremendously. One exposure to a national
audience killed a 'gag' which would otherwise have done the
rounds of the country for a year or more. However, social
surveyors found little to suggest that radio was actually
sapping the will to play a musical instrument in the home -
either through the sheer enervation induced by listening to
broadcasts or through a fatalistic acceptance that a higher
standard could not be reached. Jennings and Gill felt that
the decline was marginal. When broadcasting began there
was a temporary decline, but then broadcasting began to act
as an incentive to amateur playing: the enormous variety of
musical performances was an inspiration to the performer.
Hymn singing was definitely reduced in the home but this
could have been due to the decline in religious observance.[39]
In York, Rowntree found little evidence to suggest a general
decline of musical performance in the home.[40] Like
Jennings and Gill he turned to musical instrument salesmen
and sheet music sellers for evidence. No decline was reported in either Bristol or York. There was, however, the
suggestion that the interest stimulated by music was reflected more and more in increased sales of gramophone records
rather than in the sheet music. As one correspondent remarked: 'You hear something you like on the wireless - then
you go out and buy a record of it, and you get the music and
play it. '[41] The increasing success of gramophone records
in the twenties and thirties was proof enough of that tendency.

In the case of drama the effect was less easy to dis-
cern. Audiences were smaller for radio plays even if the
books so dramatised were widely demanded from libraries.
A decline in theatre attendance could be attributed rather
more to the onslaught of the cinema. It seems that the main
beneficiaries were those, such as housewives, who were
exposed to drama for the first time through day-time broadcasts from the BBC. Many had previously had little contact
with theatres because of the cost of admission.[42] Inevitably
the effect of broadcast drama was limited mostly to middle
class listeners. Before the expansion of broadcasting,
working class listeners generally preferred the Music Hall
and variety to the theatre and the play. Broadcasting was

unlikely to challenge such preferences easily.

Talks

The real educational effect of broadcasting was almost completely informal and this factor attracted the attention of
social surveyors. Broadcast talks were sometimes very
effective in broadening the outlook of the casual listener.
Talks had wide audiences and where they were implicitly
rather than overtly didactic, they formed an important supplement to the purely educational programmes. Some of the
most favourably received talks were those which allowed men
and women to talk for themselves. The series 'Time to
Spare' was very popular because it allowed the unemployed
to express their feelings for themselves. At that time the
approach was an innovation but it was so well received that
it eventually became a standard broadcasting technique.
Gradually, more and more participants in talks were allowed
to put their views across for themselves. The only difficulty
was the strict terms with which this was done. Apparently
spontaneous comments were normally scripted and the
slightly stilted, unnatural speech of those interviewed frequently gave the game away. Careful scripting was the
product of live broadcasting and close programme control.
As the Ferrie case showed, there was also a continuous fear
of incurring Government disapproval if controversial subjects slipped out over the microphone. Occasionally the
critics acknowledged the pressures placed on the BBC. As
one commentator put it:

> Diehards have been indicting the BBC because some of
> its talks have exposed the evil conditions in which
> millions of our population dwell. They call it 'left
> propaganda'. It is merely truth. [43]

Good talks programmes on subjects of social concern
were the highlights of the BBC output aimed at educating the
listener. They were rightly acclaimed but the real work of
informing and enlightening the population was not confined to
news bulletins, commentaries or talks, it was imbued in the
entire BBC output. Reith was concerned to ensure that all
programmes conformed to his determination for higher
cultural standards - the 'cultural uplift' presented by the
metropolitan, social élite at the BBC.
Some critics such as Leonard Woolf approved of Reith's
intentions:

The staff of the BBC particularly those in charge of programmes, have obviously become aware of the dangerous dominance of these two psychological states of mind and have seen that they must choose between the Scylla of bad temper and the Charybdis of solemnity. They have quite rightly chosen the Charybdis - a slightly etherialised Charybdis, for the dominant note in the BBC, in its programmes, in the tone of its announcers' voices, in its music, and its talks, is cheerful uplift. [44]

Many critics agreed that broadcasts should be slightly above the popular standard. [45] Others were less sure. Robert Byron argued in the New Statesman against the axiom that,

the British public must be uplifted. At the same time it does not like being uplifted (who does?). Therefore it must be bribed. The bribery must be done with music and variety whose cultural standard is important only so far as it renders the bribe acceptable to the greatest number of listeners ... Then, the bribe having been accepted, uplift in the form of talks of an instructional or topical character, of debates, plays, readings, criticism and religious services, must be sandwiched in at intervals, in the pious hope that listeners will be too lazy to leave their chairs and switch their receivers on to something else. [46]

Reith's policy was difficult to challenge. Vague protestations that 'brighter programmes' were needed were also easy to ignore. There was no consensus on what this meant - did it mean more popular music, better speakers or a better balance of programmes? Certainly this confusion helped the BBC to deflect criticism, particularly from the press. The press ran an almost continuous campaign for more 'light' entertainment and, by implication, fewer talks or features and less classical music. The British Boredcasting Company, as one paper labelled the BBC, generally resisted the onslaught. Reith was certainly not prepared to end the policy of mixed programming which he believed was a vital part of the campaign for 'cultural uplift'. If programmes were separated into different channels, listeners would no longer be exposed to the full programme range. The introduction of the Forces Programme in 1940 was the first setback for this policy, followed by the creation of the Third Programme post-war and, finally, the creation of Radio One, Two, Three

and Four in 1967.[47] The separation of programmes which
this involved was the antithesis of Reithian philosophy.
Before 1939, however, there were only marginal concessions
to the critics. Reith was always able to point to the limited
wavelengths available and the BBC's efforts to provide a
choice between the National and Regional Programmes.
Generally the balance was tilted firmly towards the talk or
the chamber concert and away from popular light entertainment.

The range of interests covered by BBC talks was impressive. Broadcasts on subjects such as travel or gardening were manifestly popular, but the general picture was of
a wide range of minority programmes which cumulatively
attracted a large audience. Jennings and Gill bear this out:

> Nine-tenths of those questioned said that broadcasting
> had introduced fresh subjects to them, and of this
> number two-thirds had kept a lookout for further
> reference to the subject in the press or in general
> conversation.[48]

Further:

> Approximately 50% of the listeners who said that the
> wireless had introduced new interests to them also
> replied that they had taken some steps to follow up
> these interests. As a rule, such steps did not include
> more than reading a book or books on the subject of
> the talk.[49]

This was clear evidence that radio could stimulate interest,
stir people into action and almost certainly broaden their
knowledge of a wide range of topics. In York, Rowntree
analysed the returns of the local relay company, then serving
3,000 subscribers. He discovered a considerable minority
interest in talks and concurred that, 'the wireless is also
carrying on educational work of considerable importance.'[50]
This effect owed much to the BBC's determination to eschew
an image of the standard listener and appeal to an audience
with a whole series of overlapping minority interests.

As with music and entertainment, talks threw up all
kinds of personalities who were experts in their own fields
but who now acquired a national reputation. Many speakers
who were asked to speak were already well known, some,
like Kingsley Martin, the editor of the New Statesman, felt
that they were black-listed by the BBC, but others such as
Professor John Hilton, Vernon Bartlett and J. B. Priestley

added an extra dimension to their standing because of the quality of their broadcasts. [51] Great skill was needed to make a good talk and few speakers grasped the intimacy of the radio set in the home. They were usually overcome by the idea of the great unseen audience. One broadcast by an unknown speaker on a subject of minority interest, transmitted outside peak listening times, would reach more people than could normally be crowded into the largest lecture hall. [52]

Indoors

Jennings and Gill showed that radio could provide the incentive to read a book cited in a broadcast: there was evidence from libraries that novels dramatised for the radio were quickly put under heavy demand. Whilst it was true that reading suffered if it came into direct competition with radio, simply because it was difficult to read and listen at the same time, no diminution of reading was discerned by any of the social surveyors.

For information on this question it is necessary to look elsewhere and, fortunately, public libraries are an excellent source of evidence. The use of public libraries increased greatly in the period and it seems plausible to suggest that broadcasting stimulated the use of books. It is rather more difficult to prove the connection. First, the collection and preservation of data undertaken by many libraries was less than adequate. Many did not take care to regularly record the number of borrowers using the library and without this vital information it is impossible to prove categorically whether the expansion of borrowing was due to an increased intensity of borrowing by a similar number of borrowers or whether the expansion can be attributed to the addition of borrowers. Where good records are available it appears that a combination of the two possibilities was more likely. [53]

There are also many difficulties in establishing a causal relationship between broadcasting and library reading. In the rural shires, the expansion of book lending was predictable because the provision of a service only began in the middle to late twenties. In these cases the number of centres where books were lent increased enormously. In other libraries there was usually some expansion but on a more modest scale. Often, more public finance was available, grants from voluntary bodies such as the Carnegie Trust were provided and the adoption of better facilities for readers such as the 'Open Access' system helped to stimulate demand. The libraries themselves were not slow to point out these self-created explanations for increased lending. [54]

Without these complications there would still be other influences on lending. Unemployment was one. It is noticeable that the greatest increases in lending were from 1930 to 1933, when unemployment was at its height. [55] Furthermore, other media had some effect on reading. The Brentford and Chiswick library made this point:

> That the cinema has an influence on reading must be acknowledged, and in this connection it is interesting to note that when a popular film is based on an old romance or novel, the public demand for the work is increased. An example may be given such as the film 'Victoria the Great', the showing of which caused a surprising demand for books dealing with the Victorian era and biographies of the Queen and the Prince Consort and other books of the period .... So also with broadcasting. It was difficult to meet the great demand for Duma's 'The Count of Monte Cristo' when the play was being broadcast. The trinity consisting of the public library, the wireless and the cinema have together an influence which is incalculable. [56]

The statistics can, therefore, only provide a general guide: broadcasting probably increased the amount of lending, it may also have encouraged an increase in the use of non-fiction - an area which all librarians noted as a sign of increased literary and educational standards. The librarian for Oxfordshire was explicit in drawing this connection:

> The number of readers, especially in the rural districts is growing rapidly and the requisitions for special books are also increasing. There is a marked improvement in the choice of books, owing to the BBC Talks. [57]

Unfortunately even these generalised references were often complicated by the fact that a decline of fiction lending could have been caused by the growth of commercial lending libraries which blossomed briefly in the thirties and which succeeded for a time in reducing total lending from public libraries. [58] Nonetheless, the virtually uninterrupted growth in borrowing shows that, assuming the most negative effect on reading, broadcasting could only have diminished the rate of growth in lending and certainly did not reduce the level of reading to the extent which some critics had feared. [59] However, it is possible to argue that the increase in reading was attributable solely to the unemployed without sets, disguising a decline in borrowing from those with sets. This hypothesis serves to emphasise the difficulty in producing an accurate assessment of cultural effects. The only solution is to return to direct reference - to learn what librarians had to report on the subject. Fortunately, in the midst of some caution and contradiction, there was a broad consensus on the role of broadcasting.

Many librarians showed a positive response to the presence of broadcasting. A common example of cooperation was the book display related to BBC talks - either for general consumption or, more specifically, for group listening. Most of the displays began in 1929 and the public response for books connected with broadcasts was encouraging. [60] In Oxford there is a good description of the facilities for those interested in broadcast education in both a casual and formal sense:

> Listeners-in are well catered for at the Oxford City
> Library at the Town Hall, thanks to the enlightened
> policy of the Librarian, Mr. E. E. Skuce. Librettos
> of opera broadcast by the BBC can be obtained from
> the Library for twopence, thus saving the trouble of
> writing to Savoy Hill and the cost of postage. The
> Library also has copies of the excellent little hard
> books issued by the BBC from time to time in connec-
> tion with their quarterly programme of talks and
> lectures. These may be consulted in the Reference
> Department of the City Library. Those who would
> like to take up the subject of the lecture further, or
> who have formed themselves into study groups for
> that purpose, will find the Librarian and his staff
> ready to render assistance by suggesting helpful books
> on the subject and arranging for the same to be
> borrowed. [61]

The inference being that the effect of broadcasting on reading could often be measured by the specific volumes which were lent. This sort of connection was made confidently by many librarians. There was a general feeling that libraries were sensitive to most of the changes in public tastes which the BBC inspired. One exception was Derby. Initially, the Library seems to have adhered to the consensus, particularly that broadcasting contributed to the reading of more serious and non-fictional literature. [62] By 1931, there was much more doubt about the value of providing literary support for broadcasting. The Librarian would now only grudgingly concede that: 'Judging from the use made of our BBC books I should say that listeners are more interested in broadcast music than in adult education.'[63]

By 1933, the value of BBC Talks was compared very unfavourably with other educational methods:

> Our experience is that the BBC talks have little or no effect on the reading of our borrowers. We make a special display of books recommended for various talks (BBC) and also for the University Extension Lectures, WEA and other special courses. We find that all the various groups are well used with the exception of the BBC. On March 31st last we had 31,395 borrowers, and our issues for a year totalled 821,104 and with numbers such as these better results should have been visible from our efforts to provide books for BBC listeners.[64]

This statement needs to be examined with some care, because the Librarian had prejudice:

> My personal experience, as one who is keenly interested in many subjects, is that listening to wireless talks is the most ineffectual way of learning anything.[65]

On the question of broadcast adult education he had this to say:

> In some public libraries Wireless Discussion Groups have been organised in connection with the BBC; but lack of room and the necessary wireless equipment prevents this being done at Derby, and it is doubtful whether there are enough listeners interested in BBC talks to make the equipment worthwhile here. So far we have had only one request of this kind. The best way in which we can cooperate is to supply the books recommended in the printed handbooks, as at present.[66]

This alleged lack of interest was noted by many other libraries, which were similarly inactive.[67] The consensus amongst librarians was that group listening and other formal educational responses to broadcasting were not a success even when they were supported and any efforts in this direction were wasted.[68] Libraries felt that the groups were generally a good thing but had to accept that their ideal of broadcast education could not be achieved. The allocation of resources was best aimed at the more casual, informal educational consequences of radio programmes - despite the difficulty of meeting the surges of demand which each passing excitement created.

The strong temptation to stay indoors and listen to the radio set was quickly appreciated by those shrewd observers of the social scene - the publicans. When radio sets were scarce, the set was purely an attraction for the curious but later it was a real competitor with the persuasive comforts of the fireside.[69] George Orwell described listening to the wartime news in the pub and concluded from the apparent indifference of the clientele that the installation simply served to provide background music.[70] In Derby the practice began in 1922 and evidence of its use remains in the proceedings of the Licensing Bench. In March 1923 action was taken to regulate the growing number of installations and, following the debate in court, the Chairman of the Bench ruled in favour of granting a licence - but with this interesting reservation:

> Listening-in is in its infancy, and they did not know what the developments might be. It was possible that they might be undesirable, the experiment would be carefully watched, and if it were found necessary the licences would not be renewed.[71]

The bench also decided to limit the licence to six days per week because of the successful objection to listening on Sundays raised by the Temperance Society, which evidently had no doubts about the drawing power of radio. The licensed victuallers had argued rather disingeniously that broadcasts were of great educational value and the magistrates' clerk stated with unwitting humour that, 'in view of my experience that sermons have been heard on Sundays, it would appear to be a desirable thing. It may be that people will hear sermons who have never heard one before.' This was not upheld and almost everywhere religious authorities objected to this form of listening, whether in pubs or not, because of the deleterious effect on church attendances.

The commercial acumen of public houses was clearly demonstrated by the speed with which they seized on radio as a means of attracting custom. In Oxford several pubs had fitted sets very soon after broadcasting commenced. One pub, the 'Welsh Pony' was a particularly interesting case because it was situated near the Gloucester Green cattle market and as the Oxford Chronicle observed: 'Many country people have gone to the house for the special purpose of "listening-in".'[72]

Thus, pubs were another means of spreading the example of radio amongst those who might not otherwise have come into contact with it at such an early stage.

Outdoors

In the case of outdoor pursuits, there is little evidence to suggest that broadcasting discouraged spectating or participation. Again, despite radio's powerful attraction as an indoor leisure activity in its own right, the impression is one of broadcasting complementing, and frequently expanding the interest in outdoor leisure pursuits such as gardening and travel and, above all, sport. The success of Mrs. Cran and later Mr. Middleton in gardening talks was indisputable from the moment the broadcasts began in 1924.[73] Similarly, travel programmes met the growing desire to take longer and more adventurous holidays. Listener research demonstrated the growing interest in features and talks which actively encouraged listeners to take up pursuits outside the confines of the home. However, it was in sport that broadcasting really expanded public interest in a wide variety of games. Once again listener research showed the popularity of sporting news, particularly on Saturday when the early evening bulletin filled the void before the sports editions of the local press emerged.[74]

Radio emphasised the national character of sport. Jennings and Gill suggested that the Boat Race grew in importance because of the intervention of broadcasting: quoting one of their informants in Bristol, 'Look how that's come to the fore. We never used to hear anything about that, and now there's many wouldn't miss it.'[75] In fact, more typical examples would seem to be boxing and Association Football. Boxing at national and international level had been a big radio attraction since the days before the formation of the BBC. The Lewis-Carpentier fight relayed from the USA in 1922 was one of the great radio triumphs for the wireless amateurs in many localities, attracting as much interest as the Marconi broadcast of Dame Nellie Melba in 1920.[76]

The formation of the Corporation on 1 January 1927 permitted running commentaries for the first time. Rugby and Association Football commentaries followed within the first month and were an instant success. Running commentaries on horse racing, golf, tennis, cricket and the Boat Race soon followed.[77] Commentators such as Howard Marshall and John Snagge soon became as familiar and popu-

lar as the leading figures in broadcast entertainment. The
running commentary was, of course, a completely new
technique and BBC staff strived to improve it, particularly
trying to compensate for the lack of a visual image. One
approach was tried and found wanting. The pitch was marked
out in a grid printed in the Radio Times and a second commentator read out the grid position of the ball during the
course of the game. Eventually, the BBC began complete
afternoon broadcasts of sport. These magazine programmes
covered several sports during the afternoon, including many
sports new to broadcasting such as rifle and clay pigeon
shooting, motor racing, power-boat racing, air racing
(especially the Schneider Trophy), hockey, speedway, gliding,
darts, pigeon racing, fencing and table tennis. [78]

In general, the chance to have outside broadcast coverage was well received by sports organisers and listeners
alike. By means of the microphone, lesser known sports
were introduced to new audiences. Even in the case of well
supported sports, such as soccer, listeners were delighted
to have the opportunity to hear internationals or games of
national importance. This was characterised by the widespread annoyance at the activities of the Football Association
which prevented the BBC from giving a running commentary
on the 1929 F. A. Cup Final. [79] Scorn was poured on the
authorities and the BBC's contingency plan involving the
broadcast of regular eye-witness accounts from a relay of
reporters was warmly received. [80] When running commentaries finally became commonplace their popularity was not
in doubt. Cricket and horse racing were well provided for in
addition to soccer, considerably enhancing their fortunes.
Higher admission charges for these sports had kept many
working class men away from cricket grounds and race
courses (even with the lure of betting) and radio provided a
new means of contact for them. [81] This increase in interest
does not seem to have had an adverse effect on actual attendance at any sport, indeed, it is possible to see some growth
in support for all of the major national sports. [82] Of course,
increased leisure time and greater affluence may have explained this effect but it does appear that many national
sporting occasions increased in popularity because of broadcasting's power to extend the sense of immediacy and eventually a feeling of participation to the whole listening population. [83]

In the seventeen years after the beginning of regular
public service, radio rose from the status of an occasional

novelty to become a major influence on the leisure activities
of the British public. Where it did not directly occupy the
evening hours of the listener by the fireside, radio was at
work introducing new interests and stimulating active participation in other pastimes. Although portable sets were available, they were still cumbersome and broadcasting put the
emphasis on home-centred activities - either listening in
direct competition with other pastimes or as a background to
other activities.

The obvious audience preference for more light entertainment and sport were confirmed by the BBC listener
research. It was also clear that the BBC made some concessions to this point of view and allotted more resources to
such programmes. At the same time, the policy of mixed
programming was broadly sustained and evidently expanded
the range of interests held by listeners. Listeners also
showed a preference for direct involvement in programmes
but received relatively few opportunities, largely in talks
and outside broadcasts. The real beneficiaries in this sense
were the select group of stars in light entertainment and
broadcasters attached to the BBC itself.

In the twenties, some people did not take radio serious-
ly, as one critic remarked:

> A good many rather 'superior' people - of whom I am
> one - have hitherto been inclined to regard broadcast-
> ing for domestic consumption as at best a rather vulgar
> and stupid business, and at worst an intolerable
> nuisance. [84]

Most people gradually appreciated that radio was more than
an occasional means of hearing exceptional events like the
Boat Race or the F.A. Cup Final. It was capable of serving
many different needs, satisfying many new interests and
filling an expanding leisure time. Almost without realising
it, the British public had turned the radio set into one of the
centrepieces of the home. [85] Although by contemporary
standards the valve set was a fairly sophisticated piece of
technology, it was very rapidly accepted. Indeed, radio led
the way in the almost irresistible advance of electrical
appliances which came to dominate British domestic life. A
radio set or radiogramophone was often the first electrical
appliance to arrive in the home and it was closely followed by
the vacuum cleaner, washing machine, refrigerator and
cooker. Most of these appliances were designed to remove
domestic drudgery and leave more time for leisure: radio

Broadcasting and Leisure

was uniquely well equipped to provide for it.

Chapter Nine

ASSESSMENT

On 5 August 1914, British citizens probably discovered that
war had been declared by reading a newspaper. On 3 September
1939, they almost certainly heard the news of the outbreak of hostilities from the Prime Minister himself. Such
was the impact of broadcasting. In 1914, citizens normally
had to gather news of events, usually some time after they
had occurred, from a local or national newspaper. By 1939,
it was much easier to sit by the fireside, turn a switch on
the wireless set and hear the news almost as soon as it was
made - often from the lips of the very people who were
making it. As a means of spreading news and information,
the spoken word regained its ascendancy over the written
word.

The technological revolution of radio effected numerous
changes in the social behaviour of the nation in the era
between two terrible and traumatic conflicts. Several important themes have emerged. Broadcasting made a significant contribution to the creation of a more cohesive sense
of British national identity. Broadcasting broadened the
knowledge and interests of listeners, it changed the pattern
of family life and introduced a completely new phase of
leisure activity.

The contribution of broadcasting to a greater sense of
national identity must be placed in its context. A country
which had needed the mobilisation of human resources to
work and fight in the Great War already had a sense of
cohesion. Furthermore, radio was adopted in a country
which possessed a well-developed national communications
system of roads, railways, postal services, telephones and
national newspapers. [1] Trade and migration had already
increased the exchange of culture and customs. In entertain-

ment, music hall artistes had well-established tours of the country and, at the cinema, the newsreels were introduced to create a visual, albeit retrospective, image of national events. [2] In sport, there were national structures for cricket with the County Championship and for soccer with the Football League. [3] Radio had the flexibility to build upon these established trends - it could give immediacy, intimacy and engender a great sense of participation in the spirit and emotion of national events. It far exceeded any other medium of communication in its penetrative power, with the potential to reach the homes of the most isolated or disadvantaged.

Although the rise of radio technology was extremely rapid, it was not without certain problems. Technical limitations on the number of wavelengths available and the high cost of extending the number of transmitters placed some restrictions on the service. Consequently, it was some way short of universal availability. Similarly, on the listening side the technical deficiencies and high cost of wireless sets restricted the number of regular listeners. In the poorest communities, broadcasting was never omnipresent in domestic life before 1939. Generally, public and official opinion lagged well behind the rate of technological change. Usually, some time elapsed before the potential influence of the changes could be grasped. This was probably one explanation for the lack of a sustained and organised protest against the assumptions behind the BBC's Regional Scheme policy and the rather negative official approach towards the idea of cable or relay installations.

There were problems but there were also many obvious benefits. The power of immediacy meant that the public was better informed about events in Britain and overseas. Listeners were well served by the BBC news bulletins, even though their frequency was artificially restricted by the national press. The General Strike gave the BBC a chance to show the value of an unrestricted news service. The BBC suppressed the spread of rumour with its authoritative presentation and helped the Government to keep control of the situation by broadcasting official statements. Despite this clear advantage, restrictions on the news service were only slowly relaxed before the outbreak of war.

Radio waves are no respecters of national borders and listeners ranged far and wide over the European stations, often in search of music programmes but sometimes for news. The BBC's motto, 'Nation shall speak Peace unto

Nation', was eventually given greater substance in an Empire Service with a potential audience of hundreds of millions. [4] In the thirties, listeners' knowledge of international affairs was noticeably increased, exemplified by the interest in listening to broadcasts by William Joyce from Radio Hamburg. [5]

The changing relationship between the British public and the royal family was an obvious example of the power and influence of broadcasting. The emotion of the Coronation of George VI was sharpened by radio coverage, the abdication of Edward VIII was given extra poignancy by his final broadcast, but the most important change was the closer contact between George V and listeners in Britain and the Empire due in some small part to his Christmas broadcasts. [6]

The tendency of broadcasting to give greater publicity to national events was often at the expense of local activities. In politics, the focus moved inexorably towards the broadcast speeches of national leaders, anxious to contact a newly enfranchised mass electorate. Local candidates soon found that their speeches were addressed to dwindling audiences. The national coverage of major occasions was a valuable contribution to national life and, in the case of sport, appeared to do little harm, but, for music and entertainment, there were dangers of damage to local culture. At first, the risk of causing irreversible damage to local identities and culture was overlooked in the euphoria of a nationally available service. Introduced in 1925, the national service was intended to supplement the rather restricted, locally based, BBC service. The later provision of a regional alternative throughout the country did not prevent nationally generated material from continuing to take precedence over programmes of predominantly local interest. This definitely damaged locally produced entertainment and had an adverse affect on the careers of local artistes. Radio, in common with the cinema and the gramophone, made great inroads into the audiences for local theatres and music halls. [7] Hence, in the long term, broadcasting was definitely tending to substitute home-based, etherial contacts, shared with an unseen national community, for more traditional local activities.

Against this, it must be said that radio was actually used as a means of stimulating dying communities in isolated rural areas, where the need for more contact with the rest of the country was badly felt. Moreover, the enjoyment of national events was compatible with the preservation of many local communal activities. In 1939, it was obvious that most communities had been very resilient, retaining their own dialects and resisting many of the more insidious influences of broadcasting on their local customs and pastimes.

Indeed, the social changes which occurred were often much less marked than expected. At the BBC, broadcasters were confident of the superior quality of their productions. They were determined to use only the best actors and musicians and move towards greater uniformity in the spoken language. This metropolitan based outlook was considered to be positively beneficial by most BBC staff and also by most contemporary commentators on British social and political life.

This centrally controlled attempt at social engineering was characteristic of the BBC's approach. The Director-General, Sir John Reith, was determined to use 'the brute force of monopoly' to raise the cultural and educational standards of listeners. [8] This policy of 'cultural uplift' was not popular with the majority of listeners and there was great pressure for fewer educational talks, feature and classical music and more light music or variety programmes. BBC programmes on Sundays were particularly unpopular and there was a massive defection to the commercial stations, Luxembourg and Normandie. Critics in the popular press led the attacks, and they achieved limited successes, but they were never supported by any concerted mass campaigns for more consultation in programme policy. Before the outbreak of war, the BBC steadfastly held to its policy of mixed programming and refused to do anything as vulgar as create a separate network for popular music and variety. It took the adversity of war to break down this attitude. [9]

The BBC's overtly educational approach clearly failed. Although there were isolated successes when listening groups were formed, the adult education programme was dropped. The early enthusiasm for an assault on low educational standards was frustrated by poor presentation, the lack of a separate wavelength and the clear lack of public support. The real success was, instead, purely informal. Just as listeners were kept in touch with daily events, so they were exposed to a much broader diet of interests. Nothing could then compete with radio for introducing such a vast array of activities in such a readily understandable and attractive form with such regularity. The BBC had more success in schools broadcasting but, even here, the real benefits came from the 'Children's Hour' which amused, entertained and educated parents and children alike. [10]

Whatever the complaints about the BBC, it was clear that radio programmes were contributing to numerous changes in family life and leisure. Radio did not dictate the rapid increase in leisure which took place, but it ensured that much of it was taken up in the home, with broadcasting as a pastime in its own right or as a complement to innumerable other home-based pursuits. For a short period, when wireless sets were relatively uncommon, listening in a crowd had been a normal activity but the pattern of home listening was firmly established before 1927. Leisure activities with strong physical, emotional or visual qualities, especially mass spectator sports, survived almost untouched by radio. In fact, running commentaries and the results service, far from inducing domestic lethargy, often stimulated interest in a wider variety of sports. Broadcasting was more likely to reduce the desire to go out to the more passive concert, speech or entertainment. Indoors, radio was a strong competitor for singing or music making and they clearly suffered adversely. Normally, however, the effect on participation in rival activities was selective and not necessarily regressive. Access to a wider range of excellent performances could encourage greater achievement in some cases. The growth of public libraries showed that broadcast readings, criticism and dramatisation did not necessarily reduce the demand for books.

The influence of broadcasting on leisure depended greatly on the circumstances of listeners. The old, very young, sick and disabled were more readily lured indoors, whilst the physically active were stimulated to take up new activities outside the home. Although the BBC deplored 'tap listening', broadcasting was most frequently used as a background to games, hobbies and even meals or as a comfort to ease the drudgery of routine domestic tasks. [11] The radio set was often the first electrically powered consumer good in the home and led the way as the most powerful of a huge array of products which emerged to exploit the introduction of mains electricity supply and provide the domestic basis for the consumer society.

The importance of broadcasting to the life and leisure of listeners was not matched by any significant influence by them in the control of the BBC. Although listeners had played a crucial role in pressing for the introduction of a regular broadcasting service in 1922, technical and economic considerations helped to concentrate power over the Broadcasting Company into very few hands. This position was not markedly improved in practice by the creation of the Corporation in 1927. The BBC staunchly defended its independence from political scrutiny or control so that, apart from the debates on the Charter, there was little scope for Parliament or ordinary listeners to influence programmes and programme policy. Broadcasters did reach a closer understanding with listeners before 1939 but, in spite of this, editorial control of the output was held firmly in the hands of BBC staff. [12] The BBC did eventually concede that the opinions of listeners were worth more active consideration than a casual perusal of correspondence and wider consultation through an improved advisory committee structure in association with a belated programme of listener research supplemented the decidedly selective impression which BBC employees had hitherto held. For instance, researchers and broadcasters alike were amazed to discover that the tastes and habits of listeners were determined less by sex or locality, which had been assumed to be dominant,and rather more by age and social class.

By 1939, the BBC had successfully reached an enormously wide variety of groups in British society by exploiting the great power of broadcasting. However, this very success also exposed the weaknesses in its relationship with this audience. The BBC effectively represented the tremendous social void which existed between political authority and most of the British working class. Despite the politically independent, public service status which it resolutely defended, the social composition of its employees and speakers meant that the BBC nearly always represented the voice of a ruling élite when it transmitted to the audience. [13] The BBC eschewed the image of the 'standard listener' and always insisted on the varied composition of the audience, pointing to the greater efforts which it had made to discover the views and behaviour of listeners. Moreover, the audience had been composed predominantly of middle class listeners in the early stages of public broadcasting and the failure of the BBC to widen its social contact and understanding had been of less consequence. The rapid expansion of licence holding soon brought most of the population into the audience and the need to build a greater understanding of other social, non-metropolitan cultures was imperative. This was not simply a matter of concession to majority opinion by producing a greater proportion of popular music or variety programmes - although they were undoubtedly important considerations - but of showing more sympathy and understanding of the rich variety of working class life throughout the country. Neither of these qualities were properly reflected in the programmes produced before war was declared in September 1939.

NOTES

Introduction

1. A. Briggs, History of Broadcasting in the United Kingdom, Vol. II. The Golden Age of Wireless, 1965, p. 235; BBC Written Archives Centre (WAC), File 123.3, 1924-6, Wireless Receiving Licences, 'Table Shewing Development of BBC Services', 16 July 1926.
2. Examples include: D. C. Thomson, Radio is Changing Us, 1937; B. S. Maine, The BBC and Its Audience, 1939; M. Cole, (ed), Beatrice Webb, Diaries 1924-32, 1952; G. Orwell, Collected Essays, Journalism and Letters, 1968, Vol. I, An Age Like This, 1920-40; Vol. II, My Country, Right or Left, 1940-43.
3. Briggs, Vol. I, The Birth of Broadcasting, 1961, pp. 6-7. Others have been more pessimistic, J. H. Goldthorpe, review in Economic History Review, 1962-3, p. 566.
4. The following have been the most useful: A. Smith, The Shadow in the Cave, 1976, 2nd Edition, pp. 1-50; E. Katz, Social Research on Broadcasting: Proposals for Further Development, 1977; J. D. Halloran, The Effects of Mass Communication, Television Research Committee, Working Paper No. 1, Leicester, 1970; J. T. Klapper, The Effects of Mass Communication, 1960; J. M. Trenaman and D. McQuail, Television and the Political Image, 1961. For a more unorthodox view, M. McLuhan, Understanding Media, Chapters 1, 2 and 30.
5. H. Lasswell, 'The Structure and Function of Communication in Society,' in B. Lyman (ed), The Communication of Ideas, New York, 1948, p. 37.
6. J. G. Blumler, 'British Television: The Outlines of a Research Strategy', British Journal of Sociology, Vol. XV, No. 3, 1964, pp. 223-33; J. Tunstall (ed), Media Sociology, 1970, p. 23.
7. Wireless Telegraphy Act, 15 Aug 1904, in force 1 Jan 1905; for preferred BBC usage of other words on broadcasting see Briggs, Vol. I, p. 242.
8. The data is insufficiently detailed for an innovation diffusion analysis - see, for instance, T. Hägerstränd, Innovation Diffusion as a Spatial Process, 1967, pp. 12, 163-4.
9. BBC (WAC), Listener Research File, LR/75, 26 June 1939; Briggs, Vol. II, pp. 519-622 for an excellent account.

Notes

Chapter One

LISTENING PATTERNS

1. Later corrected: BBC Handbook, 1937, p. 59 and BBC
    Handbook, 1938, p. 73.
2. Persons per Private Family derived from:
        1921-1925 1921 Census   P. P. P. F. : 4. 14
        1926-1931 Estimate   P. P. P. F. : 4. 00
        1931-1935 1931 Census   P. P. P. F. : 3. 77
        1936-1939 BBC Estimate   P. P. P. F. : 3. 82
    Population Figures derived from: Statistical Abstract
    for the United Kingdom, Vol. 79, Mar 1936, pp. 4-5,
    Table 5. Estimated population of the UK at the middle
    point of each year, 1921-1935. Except 1921 and 1931,
    derived from the respective censuses. Annual Abstract
    of Statistics, Vol. 88, 1952, 1938-1950. Population of
    UK, p. 7, Table 6.
3. Also, Wireless and Gramophone Trader, Supplement,
    17 Mar 1934.
4. A contrary opinion is expressed in Filson Young, Shall I
    Listen? 1933, p. 184.
5. BBC Yearbook, 1931, pp. 32-3, BBC Annual, 1936,
    pp. 72-4. BBC Handbook, 1939, pp. 156-8. Some
    figures are adjusted by regions for the purposes of
    comparison.
6. See The Times, 7 Nov 1977, p. 4; The first station was
    Leicester, opened on 8 Nov 1967.
7. Asa Briggs, 'Local and Regional in Northern Sound
    Broadcasting', Northern History, Vol. X. 1975, pp. 165-
    187.
8. E. L. E. Pawley, BBC Engineering 1922-1972, 1972, p. 57.
9. For a glossary of technical terms and their uses see:
    BBC Handbook, 1928, pp. 265-282; RSGB, Radio Com-
    munication Handbook, 4th Edition, 1969; ARRL, The
    Radio Amateur's Handbook, 1974.
10. For terms of the agreement see Cmd 1822, Wireless
    Receiving Licence, 1923.
11. BBC WAC, P. P. Eckersley, 'The Distribution of the
    Service', 6 Nov 1925, p. 2.
12. Pawley, BBC Engineering, pp. 50-1; Also BBC Hand-
    book, 1928, p. 234.
13. Pawley, BBC Engineering, pp. 21-36.
14. BBC WAC, 'Table Shewing Development of BBC Services,'
    16 July 1926.

15. Wireless Constructor, July 1927, p. 147 and Feb 1927, p. 350.
16. Pawley, BBC Engineering, pp. 21-3.
17. K. Geddes, Guglielmo Marconi 1874-1937, 1974,for account of the international character of early broadcasting.
18. Wireless World, 1 Oct 1921, pp. 415-7, supported by British listeners long before other commercial stations.
19. BBC Listener Research Report, LR/74, The British Audience for German Broadcasts in English, 16 May 1939, 29% had heard the German broadcasts in English from Hamburg, 7% admitted regular listening - probably much below the actual figure.
20. Pawley, BBC Engineering, p. 67.
21. Ibid., p. 69.
22. Ibid., p. 30.
23. Briggs, Vol. II, pp. 342-4.
24. P. P. Eckersley, The Power Behind the Microphone, 1941, p. 116.
25. BBC WAC, BBC Board Minute, 17 Nov 1926.
26. BBC WAC, Conference at the GPO, 19 July 1927.
27. BBC WAC, Postmaster-General - Director-General, 22 July 1927.
28. Briggs, Vol. II, pp. 300-1.
29. Ibid.
30. BBC WAC, P. P. Eckersley, 'Report on Proposed Regional Scheme for BBC by Chief Engineer,' 1929.
31. Pawley, BBC Engineering, p. 27.
32. Chairman's speech to AGM of BBC on 19 June 1924.
33. For an account of the struggle over the licence, see Chapter Four.
34. Licence and Agreement, 1 Jan 1927, Appendix C, p. 69; Cmd. 5091, The Report of the Broadcasting Committee 1935, Feb 1936.
35. Briggs, Vol. II, p. 380.
36. Pawley, BBC Engineering, p. 85.
37. Eckersley, 'Distribution of the Service', pp. 1-2.
38. The Spectator, 22 Nov 1930, p. 765, 'Broadcasting and a Better World.'
39. Briggs, 'Local and Regional in Northern Sound Broadcasting', p. 176.
40. J. C. W. Reith, Broadcast over Britain, 1924, pp. 119-124.
41. Briggs, Vol. II, p. 167.
42. T. W. Freeman, Geography and Regional Administration, 1830-1968, 1968, pp. 58-81.

43. W. A. Robson (ed), Public Enterprise, 1937, Especially Chapter IV, pp. 73-104.
44. BBC WAC, R. H. Eckersley - Reith, 20 Oct 1927.
45. Eckersley, 'Distribution of the Service', p. 3.
46. Eckersley, 'Report on the Proposed Regional Scheme for BBC', p. 27 and p. 66.
47. Eckersley, Power behind the Microphone, p. 12.
48. BBC WAC, Crystal Sets and the Brookmans Park Transmitter, 1929.
49. BBC Handbook, 1929, pp. 342-8; Also, Modern Wireless, Oct 1929.
50. Eckersley, Power behind the Microphone, p. 118.
51. Pawley, BBC Engineering, p. 97.
52. Birmingham Evening Dispatch, 6 Sept 1934.
53. BBC Yearbook, 1931, pp. 387-393.
54. Evening Standard, 7 Mar 1930.
55. Daily Mail, 1 Feb 1930.
56. BBC Handbook, 1929, pp. 342-8.
57. Manchester Evening Chronicle, 8 Mar 1931, also complained at the loss of the Northern Wireless Orchestra.
58. Leeds Mercury, 8 Aug 1930, 'Big Wipe-out Area'; Manchester Guardian, 9 June 1931.
59. Yorkshire Post, 11 Oct 1930, 1 Apr 1931; Yorkshire Observer, 4 Oct 1930; Yorkshire Herald, 24 Mar 1931; Yorkshire Evening News, 22 Jan 1931.
60. Yorkshire Evening News, 1 Apr 1931.
61. Daily Herald, 26 Mar 1931.
62. 25 May 1931.
63. Northern Mail, 5 Aug 1931; Evening World, 17 Aug 1931.
64. South Wales Echo and Evening Express, 23 May 1931.
65. Devon Daily Herald, 7 Apr 1931.
66. Aberdeen Press and Journal, 9 May 1934; Inverness Courier, 28 Feb 1933.
67. BBC WAC, C. A. Siepmann, 'Report on the Regions', 1936, pp. 2, 3, 5 and 11.
68. Eckersley, Power behind the Microphone, p. 127.
69. Siepmann, 'Report on the Regions', p. 3.
70. BBC WAC, Control Board Minutes, 16 July 1936.
71. Siepmann, 'Report on the Regions', p. 9.
72. BBC Handbook, 1939, pp. 60-3; Also Listener Research Report LR/74, 16 May 1939, by N. R. P. R. O.
73. Penmon opened Feb 1937; Start Point opened June 1939; during 1939 North Staffordshire and North Nottinghamshire were reallocated to other Regions and the Channel Islands were reallocated from South to West Region.

74. Ariel, June 1938, p. 25; Oxford Mail, 14 May 1929, p. 1.

Chapter Two

THE MEANS OF LISTENING

1. Wireless Weekly, 11 Apr 1923, a typical example.
2. See below, pp. 45-7.
3. Wireless Weekly, 11 Apr 1923, p. 25 and p. 27.
4. Wireless Constructor, Nov 1924, p. 7.
5. BBC Handbook, 1929, pp. 342-8, reasons for a wave-trap and the method of building one.
6. Manchester Guardian, 30 Sept 1929.
7. Modern Wireless, 1923-1933; Wireless Constructor, 1924-1934; But also see News of the World, 27 Dec 1925, p. 10, 'The Fireside Two'.
8. Pawley, BBC Engineering, p. 9.
9. Eckersley, Power behind the Microphone, p. 122, the BBC gave crystal set demonstrations to prove their point.
10. BBC Yearbook, 1932, p. 30, notes that headphone sets had almost disappeared from Radiolympia.
11. Ibid., 25 Mar 1933, p. 320.
12. Wireless World, 1 May 1936, pp. 433-45, excellent summary of changes.
13. Oxford English Dictionary definition of to heterodyne: 'Production of a lower frequency from the combination of two high frequencies.'
14. The Spectator, 11 July 1925, p. 65.
15. Pawley, BBC Engineering, p. 27.
16. Wireless and Gramophone Trader, 25 Mar 1933, p. 320.
17. Ibid., pp. 28-9.
18. BBC Yearbook, 1933, pp. 421-6, in the year ending 30 June 1932, there were 4,738 such complaints to the BBC.
19. Pawley, BBC Engineering, pp. 27-8.
20. BBC Handbook, 1929, p. 349.
21. Ibid., pp. 349-52, details of the oscillation pamphlet and the action taken by the BBC.
22. Derby Daily Express, 14 May 1929, p. 6.
23. Notes to BBC WAC, File 123.3. 'Wireless Receiving Licences 1922-1923.'
24. BBC Handbook, 1929, p. 350 and p. 352.
25. Conference of the GPO and BBC, Minutes 11 Jan 1923.
26. Evening Standard, 10 Mar 1923.

27. Note by GPO, 19 Apr 1923; Also Cmd. 1951, Broadcasting Committee Report, Aug 1923.
28. Briggs, Vol. I, pp. 183-97.
29. Speech by the Chairman (Lord Gainford) at AGM of the BBC, 19 June 1924.
30. BBC WAC, Reith - R. A. Dalzell, 26 May 1926.
31. Daily Herald, 2 Oct 1931, p. 2, estimated 400,000 evaders, or approximately 10%. Compare with a 1977 estimate, in The Times, 1 Dec 1977, p. 4, 750,000 evaders - with 18,000,000 licences issued - or an evasion rate of 4.7%. Likely average for 1922-1939 is 5-7%.
32. On evasion, BBC WAC, Reith - Postmaster-General, 4 Dec 1924; on instalment scheme, F. J. Brown - Reith, 17 July 1924 and BBC - Sir Evelyn Murray, 18 Sept 1925.
33. BBC WAC, BBC - Dalzell, 25 Feb 1925.
34. BBC WAC, Reith - F. J. Brown, 4 Nov 1924; People, 2 Nov 1924, p. 5, for an impassioned defence of Mr. Ford on the grounds of invasion of privacy.
35. BBC WAC, Reith - BBC Station Directors, 24 Nov 1924.
36. Briggs, Vol. I, p. 19.
37. Oxford Chronicle, 19 Jan 1923, p. 4.
38. Oxford Times, 24 Oct 1924, p. 19.
39. Derby Daily Telegraph, 31 Oct 1924, p. 4.
40. Oxford Chronicle, 12 Jan 1923, p. 10.
41. G. Bussey, Vintage Crystal Sets 1922-1927, 1976, an excellent guide with full list of manufacturers, prices, trademarks and an explanation of crystal set construction and operation.
42. BBC WAC, GPO Document, 15 Apr 1924.
43. 509,000 + 5% x 4.14 = 2,212,623.
44. Wireless World was the first wireless magazine. Issued as Marconigraph in 1911.
45. Wireless Constructor, Nov 1924, p. 19-37. A three valve receiver.
46. Briggs, Vol. I, p. 219.
47. Wireless Constructor, Nov 1925, p. 38.
48. Wireless, 1st Issue, 19 Sept 1925.
49. Willing's Press Guide and Mitchell's Newspaper Directory, 1918-1939.
50. Wireless Constructor, Mar 1925, p. 491.
51. Ibid.
52. Ibid., Feb 1925, p. 383; The Listener, 2 Nov 1972, p. 572.
53. Wireless Constructor, May 1925, p. 607.

54. Ibid., Nov 1924, pp. 4-7.
55. Prices derived from advertisements in Wireless World during 1924.
56. Derbyshire Times, 29 Aug 1931, pp. 1, 5 and 7.
57. Oxford Times, 1 Nov 1935, pp. 8 and 13.
58. The deficiencies in the available data can be seen in: R. Stone and D. A. Rowe, The Measurement of Consumers' Expenditure and Behaviour in the United Kingdom 1920-1938, Vol. II, Cambridge 1966, pp. 17 and 112, Figure 10; the Fourth Census of Production, 1930, or Fifth Census of Production, 1935. Some clues to prices in Wireless and Gramophone Trader, 28 March 1931, p. 346, 'Cheaper Radio.'
59. A. L. Chapman and R. Knight, Wages and Salaries in the United Kingdom 1920-1938, Cambridge, 1953, p. 27.
60. Stone and Rowe, Measurement of Consumers' Expenditure, p. 114; 22nd Annual Abstract of Statistics, 1937, pp. 122-3; and B. R. Mitchell and P. Deane, Abstract of British Historical Statistics, Cambridge, 1962, p. 345; Ministry of Labour Indices of Retail Prices 1914-38, Annual Abstract of Labour Statistics 1914-1938; Chapman and Knight, Wages and Salaries, p. 30.
61. Ministry of Labour Gazette, 1918-1939; Also in Mitchell and Deane, Abstract, p. 66; for percentage of insured workforce unemployed, see A. H. Halsey (ed), Trends in British Society since 1900, 1972, p. 119.
62. T. Cauter and J. S. Downham, The Communication of Ideas, 1954, p. 150.
63. Hire Purchase Act, Royal Assent 2 August 1938, Commenced 1 Jan 1939; an example of the practice in News of the World, 15 Mar 1931, p. 11.
64. BBC Handbook, 1940, p. 79, 'The Listening Public' by R. J. E. Silvey.
65. Cmd. 5091, Report of the Broadcasting Committee 1935, Feb 1936, Para 141, p. 42.
66. S. G. Sturmey, The Economic Development of Radio, 1958, p. 147.
67. Ibid., Chapters VIII and IX, pp. 137-189.
68. Cmd. 1822, Wireless Broadcasting Licence, 1923.
69. Cmd. 1976, Wireless Broadcasting Licence, 1923.
70. Bussey, Vintage Crystal Sets, p. 71.
71. Briggs, Vol. I, pp. 401-3, for account of manufacturers' views.
72. BBC Handbook, 1928, p. 377; Sturmey, Economic Development of Radio, p. 161.

73. Wireless Trader, 29 Feb 1936, pp. 126-7, review of RMA in 1935.
74. Everyman, 17 Dec 1932.
75. Bussey, Vintage Crystal Sets, pp. 43-69, list of companies 1922-1927.
76. Wireless and Gramophone Trader, 25 Mar 1933, p. 324. 500,000 home constructed sets were estimated to be in use in 1932. 50,000 new ones were built in that year - many from kits.
77. Bussey, Vintage Crystal Sets, p. 12.
78. Labour Research Department, Monthly Circular, Dec 1932, pp. 272-3.
79. BBC Yearbook, 1933, p.79; Wireless and Gramophone Trader, for 1930, 28 Mar 1931, p. 349; for 1931 and 1932, 25 Mar 1933, p. 320; for 1933, 17 Mar 1934, p. 263.
80. Oxford Chronicle, 8 June 1923, p. 4, Oxford Wireless Telephony Company Limited.
81. News of the World, 15 Mar 1931, p. 11.
82. Derby Daily Telegraph, 17 Sept 1931, p. 4.
83. Oxford Times, 21 May 1926, p. 16; The Spectator, 15 Dec 1928, p. i; Derby Daily Express, 28 May 1929, p. 6 and Oxford Times, 7 May 1937, p. 15.
84. There are many other examples in J. Hill, The Cat's Whisker: Fifty Years of Wireless Design, 1978; for the design work behind the AD65 see also S. Cantacuzino, Wells Coates A Monograph, 1978, pp. 24-7 and 32-6.
85. The Grafton China Set was manufactured by A. B. Jones and Son Limited, Longton, Staffs, probably in 1922, the 'Listener' Set was manufactured by Kenmac Radio Limited, Hammersmith, London, and is on display in the Science Museum, Kensington, London.
86. More illustrations of sets and advertisements can be seen in: Philips Post, 'V & A Supplement', Oct 1977; Sunday Times, Colour Magazine, 16 Oct 1977, pp. 28-9. Permanent exhibitions of sets can be seen in the Science Museum, Kensington, London and the National Wireless Museum, Arreton Manor, Newport, I. O. W.
87. N. Pevsner, An Enquiry into Industrial Art in England, 1937, p. 105.
88. Victoria and Albert Museum. The Wireless Show: p. 5, Pamphlet prepared for an exhibition of sets held Oct-Dec 1977.
89. Wireless World, 1 Sept 1926, Special Show Number pp. 337-56. The first National Wireless Exhibition was held at the Royal Horticultural Hall in 1922. See News

of the World, 1 Oct 1922, p. 3, for description of
events.
90. BBC Yearbook, 1934, p. 29, attendance figures were as
follows:

Year	Days of Duration	Stand Area (sq. ft.)	Demonstration Room Area (sq. ft.)	Attendance
1924	10	11,700	-	46,000
1925	10	15,000	-	54,500
1926	13	34,053	-	116,570
1927	7	34,642	-	99,315
1928	7	40,445	-	123,593
1929	10	42,177	7,006	140,627
1930	8	54,464	8,769	161,128
1931	8	70,993	15,129	198,070
1932	8	74,154	19,368	180,750

Also from Wireless and Electrical Trader, 29 Jan 1938,
p. 153 and 14 Jan 1939, p. 46, Radiolympia attendances:
1935 - 192,202: 1936 - 202,517: 1937 - 174,818:
1938 - 144,363.
91. New Statesman, 5 Oct 1929, p. 773; and News of the
World, 13 Sept 1925, p. 9, + Cartoon.
92. Eckersley, Power Behind the Microphone, pp. 211-2.
93. BBC WAC, File 133. 3, Ullswater Committee, Paper
49, Memorandum on Wireless Broadcasting by Lt. Col.
A. G. Lee, Engineer-in-Chief, GPO, 29 May 1935, p. 2;
Wireless and Gramophone Trader, 25 Mar 1933, p. 324.
In 1932, 4,433,000 out of 12,300,000 homes had a
mains electricity supply.
94. Eckersley, Power Behind the Microphone, p. 212.
95. R. H. Coase, British Broadcasting: A Study in Monopoly, 1950, pp. 70, 76, 90 and 93.
96. Ullswater Committee, Paper 49.
97. Ibid. , and Paper 68, Supplementary Memorandum
(Wireless Exchanges.) Submitted to the Broadcasting
Committee, 1935 by the BBC (undated). The BBC was
certainly in little doubt about the general lack of competitiveness. It disputed the claim of economy made to
Ullswater by the R SA G B: 'The plea of serving the
poor man is, it is submitted, largely 'political'''.
98. Ullswater Committee, Paper 69, evidence by the Relay
Services Association of Great Britain, 31 May 1935.
99. Rowntree, Poverty and Progress, pp. 409-10.
100. BBC WAC, Listener Research File 172. 2, File 2, filed
11 Dec 1935.

101. Ibid., Filed 20 Mar 1936, Nottingham Evening News, 15 Apr 1935, for Derbyshire & Nottinghamshire Radio Relay Company.
102. Already well described and analysed in Briggs, Vol. II, pp. 356-60; and Coase, British Broadcasting, pp. 69-101.
103. Ullswater Committee, Paper 69, pp. 1-4.
104. Briggs, Vol. II, p. 359.
105. Eckersley, Power Behind the Microphone, p. 213: 'This rediffusion business, convenient as it is a method of reception, does not give programmes any different character, nor does it represent any increased facility for the programme builder.'
106. Ullswater Committee, Paper 38, Postmaster-General's Committee of Inquiry. Memorandum presented by the Relay Services Association of Great Britain; Paper 42, Supplementary Memorandum presented by the R SA GB, Folio E(b), Broadcasting Committee Minutes of Evidence, 6th Meeting, 22nd May 1935.
107. Ullswater Committee, Paper 33, British Insulated Cables Limited 'Electric Mains' Rediffusion. Memorandum for submission to BBC Advisory Committee /sic!/ May 1935.
108. Ullswater Committee, Paper 68, Folio Q(b), Broadcasting Committee Minutes of Evidence, 17th Meeting, 4th July 1935, pp. 791-3; Report of the Broadcasting Committee, 1935, p. 40 para. 134.
109. Cmd 5027, Memorandum by the Postmaster-General on The Report of the Broadcasting Committee, 1935, June 1936.
110. Coase, British Broadcasting, p. 69, pp. 72-3 and pp. 77-8; also BBC Yearbook, 1933, pp. 71-2, for details of the licence and a BBC critique.
111. Coase, British Broadcasting, pp. 90-1.
112. Eckersley, Power Behind the Microphone, p. 213.
113. Coase, British Broadcasting, pp. 79-80.
114. Eckersley, Power Behind the Microphone, p. 212 and pp. 231-4.
115. The Times, 30 Apr 1936, p. 15, 'The Middlemen'.

Chapter Three

WIRELESS ORGANISATIONS

1. See for instance the debate at the First Annual Conference of Amateur Wireless Societies, Wireless World,

3 Apr 1920, pp. 16-22.
2. Wireless World, 18 Nov 1922, pp. 219-20.
3. See for instance: The Sunday Times, 15 Jan 1978, p. 2, 'Hancock's ghost stalks fans at Marconi jubilee.'
4. Daily Express, 12 Mar 1925, p. 1.
5. Wireless World, Aug 1913, p. 340.
6. English Mechanic, 6 June 1913, p. 430, letter by R.H. Klein.
7. The Derby Wireless Club. See Derby and District Amateur Radio Society, A Brief History of Fifty Years of Progress made by the Amateur Radio Enthusiasts in Derby, published privately, 1961, p. 10.
8. J. Clarricoats, World at their Fingertips, 1967, p. 35.
9. Ibid., p. 40.
10. Wireless World, Nov 1919, p. 480, letter from former member of RNVR, on 'The Amateur Position'.
11. Ibid., May 1919, p. 89.
12. Ibid., Dec 1919, p. 521; Mar 1920, p. 711; 3 Apr 1920, p. 16 and p. 21.
13. Ibid., 3 Apr 1920, p. 22 and 16 Apr 1921, p. 52.
14. Ibid., Mar 1919, pp. 667-71, appeal by Marconi, Dr. J.A. Fleming and Professor W.H. Eccles for the relaxation of wartime controls.
15. Clarricoats, World at their Fingertips, pp. 40-3; for a good summary of the position.
16. Wireless World, May 1919, p. 89; Nov 1919, supplement.
17. Wireless World, 16 Apr 1921, p. 51.
18. Ibid., 6 Aug 1921, p. 292.
19. Ibid., 5 Mar 1921, pp. 823-6; Jan 1920, pp. 607-8; 2 Apr 1921, p. vi.
20. For instance, News of the World, 1 Oct 1922, p. 8, 'Wireless Wonders.'
21. Begun Apr 1913, p. xxxiv.
22. Wireless World, 20 Aug 1921, pp. 325-31.
23. Ibid., 16 Apr 1921, pp. 42-52.
24. Briggs, Vol. I, pp. 45-6.
25. Wireless World, 11 July 1920, pp. 268-9.
26. Daily Mail, 16 June 1920, p. 7. The paper sponsored the broadcast.
27. Hansard, 23 Nov 1920, Vol. 135, Col. 204.
28. Wireless World, 1 Oct 1921, pp. 415-7.
29. Ibid., 29 Apr 1922, pp. 143-4, for a more favourable view.
30. Ibid., 16 Apr 1921, p. 51.

31. Clarricoats, World at their Fingertips, pp. 57-60 and pp. 295-6; Wireless World, 21 Jan 1922, pp. 649 and pp. 665-6.

32. Wireless World, 4 Mar 1922, pp. 750, 754-5; 22 Apr 1922, pp. 129-31.

33. Ibid., 13 Feb 1922, p. 772; 21 Apr 1923, pp. 89-90.

34. H. G. Wells, The Sleeper Awakes, 1910, Revised Edition.

35. Wireless World, 13 May 1922, pp. 204-5, Kellaway's speech to House of Commons on 4 May 1922. Also, ibid, 5 Aug 1922, p. 594, Kellaway's speech to House of Commons on 27 July 1922.

36. Wireless World, 4 Mar 1922, p. 756.

37. Ibid., 22 July 1922, p. xxx.

38. Ibid., 19 May 1922, p. 204.

39. The Ordinary General Meeting of the WSL, 27 Sept 1922, discussed the question. See Wireless World, 14 Oct 1922, p. 61-2.

40. Ibid., p. 220.

41. Ibid., 25 Dec 1922, pp. 394-5.

42. Ibid., 28 Oct 1922, p. 117; 25 Nov 1922, p. 257; 8 Aug 1923, p. 616 and pp. 640-1.

43. Hansard, 19 Apr 1923, Vol. 162, Cols. 2440-6; the terms of reference were extremely broad.

44. BBC WAC, File 128.04, The Broadcasting Committee, 7 June 1923, précis of evidence, paras. 4-11.

45. Wireless Weekly, 30 May 1923, pp. 503-4.

46. Cmd 1951, The Broadcasting Committee Report, Aug 1923.

47. BBC WAC, File 123.3, Joynson-Hicks to BBC Board 13 Apr 1923.

48. Cmd 2599, The Report of the Broadcasting Committee, 1925, p. 22, gave details of the surge in licence holding. Sir Capel Holden gave this RSGB membership figure in his evidence to the Sykes Committee on 11 Jan 1926, BBC WAC, File 129.03.

49. Clarricoats, World at their Fingertips, pp. 84-9; a Transmitter and Relay Society was created. This was absorbed as the T & R Section of the RSGB.

50. Wireless World, 8 Aug 1923, p. 616.

51. Cmd 2599.

52. Captain Ian Fraser was the only representative of the RSGB on the Committee. He was also a member of the Wireless League and a former member of the RTS which merged with the RSGB to form the T & R Section.

53. BBC WAC, File 129 01, Minutes of the Broadcasting

Committee 1925, 6th Meeting, pp. 8 and 10.

54. BBC WAC, File 129.03, Memorandum of the RSGB to the Crawford Committee, 11 Jan 1926, p. 3 para. 9.

55. Briggs, Vol. I, pp. 327-38.

56. Cmd 5091, Report of the Broadcasting Committee 1935, Feb 1936, Appendix A, pp. 54-5.

57. Derby Daily Telegraph, 26 Nov 1923, p. 2 and 27 Nov 1923, p. 2.

58. Wireless Weekly, 30 May 1923, p. 463, a list of the main European stations.

59. Wireless World, 27 Dec 1923, pp. 412-3.

60. The RSGB moved into the international arena by organising the International Amateur Radio Union (IARU) which held its first conference on 14 Apr 1925 and also created the British Empire Radio Union (BERU).

61. Clarricoats, World at their Fingertips, pp. 130-2.

62. Briggs, Vol. II, pp. 369-77, 380-1.

63. August 1922 was claimed as the date of foundation by Lt. Cmdr. J.M. Kenworthy, GPO File M15796/1926, Minutes of evidence to the Crawford Committee, 7th Meeting, 21 Jan 1926. For an account of activities see Popular Wireless, 5 Dec 1925, p. 823.

64. BBC, File 129.01, Broadcasting Committee 1925, Minutes of the 3rd Meeting, 4 Dec 1925, p. 2: 'The need for some such body is the more pressing by the very nature of Broadcasting. There is no effective method of communication by which the listener can express his approval or disapproval, except by means of a letter addressed to the BBC, which is a much too cumbersome process to be useful.'

65. BBC WAC, File 129.03, Memorandum of the Radio Association to the Crawford Committee on Broadcasting, Jan 1926, pp. 2-4.

66. BBC WAC, File 129.03, Evidence before the Select Committee on the Future of Broadcasting, 7th Meeting, 21 Jan 1926, p. 14; GPO File M11253/1924.

67. Radio Association Handbook, 1925, in GPO File M15796/1926.

68. For the general tone of the Wireless League objections see the Wireless League Prospectus, in GPO File M11253/1924.

69. BBC WAC, File 129.01, Minutes of the 3rd Meeting, Evidence given by the Wireless League, 4 Dec 1925, p. 4.

70. 40,000 paid only 1s., subscription compared with the 2s., charged after the initial membership drive. See

Daily Express, 20 Mar 1925, p. 1.

71. Financial News, 23 Jan 1926, p. 6; The GPO rejected applications on the grounds that the organisation had been founded too recently, GPO file M11253/1924.

72. Minutes of the 3rd Meeting, 4 Dec 1925, p. 3.

73. Authorised dealers displayed the emblems of the respective societies, see Radio Association Handbook, 1925.

74. The Wireless League also used this opportunity to draft collective letters to the BBC, Minutes of the 3rd Meeting, 4 Dec 1925, p. 14.

75. Minutes of the 3rd Meeting, 4 Dec 1925, pp. 11-4.

76. Wireless World, 24 Mar 1926 to 6 June 1928, Supplement entitled 'The Listener'.

77. GPO File M15796/1926, Crawford Committee.

78. BBC Handbook, 1928, pp. 347-8 and BBC Yearbook, 1933, pp. 73-6.

79. Daily Dispatch, 29 Oct 1936, p. 8.

80. BBC WAC, File 129.01, Gladstone Murray to Stanley 4 Jan 1927; see also File 129-03, Assistant Director of Publicity to Reith (undated but probably Dec 1925).

81. GPO File M14019/1923, Broadcasting Board. Includes a complete set of membership, minutes and correspondence.

82. Ibid., Postmaster-General (Mitchell Thomson) to Sykes 15 Nov 1926.

83. Ibid., Director General's report to the Board of Governors 9 Feb 1927. Meeting held 31 Jan 1927, p. 3.

84. Ibid., 9 Mar 1927, pp. 9-10, Wireless Organisations Advisory Committee Meeting held 28 Feb 1927.

85. Evening Standard, 23 Nov 1933.

86. Minutes of the 3rd Meeting, 4 Dec 1925, pp. 5-6.

87. Minutes of the 3rd Meeting, 4 Dec 1925, pp. 10-2.

88. BBC WAC, File 129.03, Radio Association Evidence, 21 Jan 1926, p. 1.

89. BBC WAC, File 129.03, Wireless Associations of Great Britain, 'Memorandum of Information' - on the scope and conduct of the Broadcasting Service submitted as evidence to the Broadcasting Committee 1925.

90. A. T. Fleming, General Secretary of the Wireless League to Ullswater, 5 June 1935, BBC WAC File 133.3, Ullswater Committee, Paper 79. A copy of the new BBC Charter is attached to the Report of the Broadcasting Committee 1935. Appendix A.

91. Wireless and Electrical Trader, 7 Jan 1939, pp. 6-7.

92. GPO File M804/1939, Listeners' League Report on

Relays, June 1938; Tallents to H. G. G. Welch, 3 May 1938; GPO Memorandum, 25 May 1938.

93. BBC WAC, File Acc., No. 7235, GAC Preliminary Correspondence 1934.

94. Minutes of the 7th Meeting, 21 Jan 1926, p. 20.

95. Wireless and Electrical Trader, 7 Jan 1939, p. 7, quoting M. E. Cavendish, General Secretary of the Wireless Retailers' Association.

Chapter Four

THE BROADCASTERS

1. New Statesman, 11 Nov 1933, pp. 581-2; see Figure 4.1, a cartoon by Low.
2. Reith, Broadcast over Britain, p. 57.
3. Ibid., p. 17.
4. Ibid., p. 34.
5. Ibid., p. 35.
6. Ibid., p. 32.
7. Detailed in BBC WAC, File 441, Adult Education, Papers and Reports 1924-1940.
8. Briggs, Vol. I, pp. 247-8.
9. New Statesman, 15 June 1935, p. 893, 'Conduit Street' controversy.
10. Reith, Broadcast over Britain, p. 19.
11. Ibid., p. 205.
12. Ibid., p. 119.
13. BBC WAC, File 172. 2, Audience Research Policy, File 1, 1937, 14 Oct 1937, Draft of a Talk on Listener Research.
14. Reith, Broadcast over Britain, p. 119.
15. Ibid., p. 120.
16. F. Young, Shall I Listen?, 1933, p. 206.
17. Ibid., p. 205 - an example of his cordial relationship.
18. J. C. W. Reith, Into the Wind, 1949, p. 99.
19. Interview with Silvey, 24 Mar 1976.
20. Seven Talks, broadcast 17 Feb to 7 Apr 1932.
21. BBC WAC, Programme Board Minute 11, 9 May 1930.
22. BBC WAC, Gielgud to R. H. Eckersley (Director of Programmes), 12 May 1930.
23. Ibid.
24. For example, London Press Exchange, The Home Market and Reader Interest Survey, in 1936.
25. R. J. E. Silvey, Who's Listening? 1974, pp. 51-2.

26. BBC WAC, B. Nicholls to C. Carpendale, Listener Survey, 14 Aug 1935.
27. BBC WAC, Memorandum by Cecil Graves, 17 July 1930.
28. BBC WAC, Board Meeting Minute 2, 14 Jan 1931.
29. Yearbook, 1932, p. 161.
30. BBC WAC, 'Memorandum on Survey of Listening Public.'
31. Educational Broadcasting: Report of a Special Investigation in the County of Kent during the Year 1927, Dunfermline, 1928, Carnegie UK Trustees.
32. BBC, File 441.4, Carnegie Experiment Reports, 1930-32.
33. BBC WAC, Memorandum by C.A. Siepmann, 26 May 1930.
34. BBC WAC, V. Gielgud to R.H. Eckersley, 18 Nov 1933.
35. Ibid.
36. BBC WAC, Memorandum by R.E.L. Wellington, 21 Nov 1934.
37. BBC WAC, Gorham to Murray, 15 Nov 1934.
38. BBC WAC, Memorandum by C.F. Atkinson, 2 Aug 1935.
39. Reith, Into the Wind, p. 89.
40. Briggs, Vol. II, pp. 152-60.
41. Gorham was Art Editor from 1926-33 and editor from 1933-41.
42. Circulation figures are available in the BBC Handbooks; or Briggs, Vol. II, p. 281.
43. BBC WAC, File 183.2. Originally the adult education role was more pronounced, but as the fortunes of this activity faded, a less precise role was decided on.
44. New Statesman, 22 Dec 1928, p. 346.
45. Good accounts of the Radio Times can be found in: D. Driver, The Art of the Radio Times, 1981. S. Briggs, Those Radio Times, 1981.
46. See also Reith, Broadcast over Britain, p. 205.
47. Daily Herlad, 1 Mar 1927, p. 9; Daily Mail, 1 Feb 1927, p. 9; Yorkshire Observer, Feb 1936; Birmingham Gazette, Jan 1936.
48. Interview with Silvey, 24 Mar 1976.
49. BBC WAC, A.P. Ryan to M. Farquharson, 16 Mar 1936.
50. Institute of Incorporated Practitioners in Advertising, Radio Research, Mar 1936.
51. Wireless Constructor, May 1927, pp. 53-4, for critique of these results and a table of the replies.
52. BBC WAC, Radio Manufacturers Association, Memorandum, Nov 1935.
53. BBC WAC, Atkinson to Carpendale et al, 19 Jan 1931; Noel Ashbridge to Murray, 11 Sept 1930.
54. BBC WAC, Maurice Gorham, Note on a conversation

with Pear, 20 Aug 1934.
55. BBC WAC, Director-General to Graves, 12 June 1930.
56. BBC WAC, Tallents to Carpendale, 6 Mar 1936.
57. BBC WAC, Control Board Minute 155, 10 Mar 1936.
58. Press Release 14 Sept 1936; Silvey began work on
    1 Oct 1936.
59. Remark often attributed to Frank Muir.
60. BBC WAC, Memorandum by Siepmann, 29 May 1930.
61. L. Fielden, The Natural Bent, 1960, p. 109.
62. BBC WAC, Director-General to Tallents, 8 July 1937.
63. Exemplified by his work with Mark Abrams, The Home
    Market, 1936
64. BBC WAC, Farquharson, Paper for Discussion, 25 Mar
    1936.
65. BBC WAC, File 172.201, undated Paper by Silvey,
    probably for first meeting of the committee, 15 Oct 1936.
66. Interview with Silvey, 24 Mar 1976.

Chapter Five

LISTENER RESEARCH

1. BBC WAC, Listener Research Report, LR/56, Drama
   Reports Scheme, General Summary, 25 June 1937. All
   Listener Research Reports in the 'LR' series are
   retained in the BBC Written Archives Centre. A complete index for 1937-39 can be found in M. W. Pegg,
   'British Radio Broadcasting and its Audience 1918-1939',
   (unpublished D. Phil thesis, Oxford, 1980) pp. 339-40.
2. Listener Research Committee, Minute 69, 19 Apr 1937,
   quoting Gielgud.
3. LR/29, Drama Reports Scheme, 16 Apr 1937, Second
   General Questionnaire.
4. LR/56.
5. LR/43, Drama Reports Scheme, 24 May 1937.
6. LR/28, Drama Reports Scheme, 13 Apr 1937.
7. LR/56.
8. LR/61, The Microphone at Large Series - Opinions, 13
   Dec 1937; LR/63, Clear Thinking Talks Panel, 26 Apr
   1938.
9. LR/60, Cinema Talks - Opinions, 18 Nov 1937.
10. LR/70, Autumn Talks, 1938, Mar 1939.
11. LR/62, Roster of Critics, 14 Mar 1938.
12. Listener Research Committee, Minutes, 23 May 1938.
13. LR/69, Children's Hour Searchlight, 9 Jan 1939.
14. LR/56.

15. LR/58, Proposals for a Variety Listening Barometer, 24 Aug 1937.
16. Ibid.
17. Silvey, Who's Listening? p. 81, for details of the control group.
18. LR/65, Variety Listening Barometer, 29 Nov 1938.
19. Ibid.
20. LR/65, Interim Report 4, 8 Feb 1938.
21. LR/65, Interim Reports 3(a) to 3(e), Jan to Feb 1938.
22. LR/65, Interim Report 3(d), 2 Feb 1938.
23. LR/65, Interim Report 3(e), 2 Feb 1938.
24. LR/65, Variety Listening Barometer, 29 Nov 1938.
25. LR/65, Interim Report 4, 8 Feb 1938.
26. LR/65, Interim Report 3(a), 4 Jan 1938.
27. LR/65, Interim Report 12, 31 Mar 1938.
28. LR/65, Interim Report 9, 22 Feb 1938.
29. LR/65, Interim Report 6, 9 Mar 1938.
30. Silvey, Who's Listening? p. 84.
31. LR/79, General Listening Barometer, Religious Broadcasts, 20 July 1939.
32. LR/77, General Listening Barometer, 5 July 1939; LR/81, General Listening Barometer, Home Service, 11 Oct 1939; LR/86 BIPO, Wartime, 22 Dec 1939.
33. LR/74, General Listening Barometer, German Bulletins, 16 May 1939.
34. LR/77, Interim Report 1(b), 8 Feb 1939.
35. LR/77, Interim Report 9, 17 Mar 1939.
36. LR/77, Interim Report 16, 28 Apr 1939.
37. Interview with Silvey, 24 Mar 1976.
38. Silvey, Who's Listening? p. 89.
39. LR/67, First Random Sample, 1 Sept 1938, Appendix I.
40. Ibid.
41. LR/67, Table IV; LR/71, Second Random Sample, 15 Feb 1939, Table II.
42. LR/71, Table I.
43. LR/67, Table V(a.); LR/71, Table III(a).
44. LR/67, Tables V(b) and V(c); LR/71, Tables III(b) and III(c).
45. See also LR/68, The Time of Meals, 21 Oct 1938.
46. LR/67.
47. Silvey, Who's Listening? p. 70.
48. LR/71, Table I.
49. Silvey, Who's Listening? p. 70.
50. Crossley Incorporated, Radio Listening Habits, Feb 1939; Social Surveys Ltd., (Gallup), The Radio Luxembourg

Audience, Reports 1-10.
51. Silvey, Who's Listening? pp. 75-6.
52. BBC Archives, File 133.4, Ullswater, Broadcasting Committee 1935, Minutes of Evidence, Folio M, 13th Meeting, 20 June 1935.
53. M. Baron, Independent Radio: The Story of Commercial Radio in the United Kingdom, Lavenham, Suffolk, 1975.
54. Crossley Incorporated, Radio Listening Habits, pp. 13, 17, 20.
55. Radio Times, Vol. I, No. I, 28 Sept 1923, p. 15, and subsequent issues passim.
56. International Broadcasting Company, Unknown Date.
57. Sir William Crawford with H. Broadley, The People's Food, 1939, pp. 36-8.
58. Ibid., pp. 60-1.
59. Ibid., p. 59.
60. LR/68, The Time of Meals, 21 Oct 1938.
61. Radio Times, 16 Dec 1938, p. 6, 'The BBC Taps the Barometer.'
62. Audience Research Policy, File 172.2, 1938-44, paper for the General Advisory Council, GAC 92, 8 Mar 1938.
63. Birmingham Daily Mail, 2 Mar 1938; Observer, 31 Oct 1937.
64. M. Gorham, Sound and Fury, 1948, p. 166.

Chapter Six

BROADCASTING AND SOCIETY

1. Derby Daily Telegraph, 24 Oct 1924, p. 4.
2. H. Jennings and W. Gill, Broadcasting in Everyday Life: A Study of the Social Effects of the Coming of Broadcasting, 1939, p. 6. Ogilvie, the new Director-General, commented on this tendency in the introduction to the book.
3. The licence returns for 1922-27 have been destroyed. For figures of other years, see Chapter Two. There was no census question on set ownership and no household survey.
4. BBC WAC, Listener Research Committee Meetings, 22 Feb and 23 May 1938; see Chapter Five for abortive examples of BBC sponsored research.
5. See for instance, Mass Observation, May the Twelfth, 1937.
6. W. Beveridge, Changes in Family Life, 1932, pp. 11, 13, 138; Audience reaction - People, 10 Apr 1932, p. 10.
7. Jennings and Gill, Broadcasting in Everyday life, pp. 7, 40.

8. Ibid., p. 15.
9. Briggs, Vol. I, pp. 263-4.
10. Spectator, 15 Sept 1939, p. 376.
11. For instance, Derby Daily Telegraph, 14 Aug 1923, p. 2.
12. Oxford Chronicle, 15 July 1923, p. 5; Derby Daily Express, 2 Apr 1929, p. 7, 'Radio Wrinkles'.
13. Derby Mercury, 14 Sept 1923, p. 7; 31 Oct 1924, p. 12.
14. Oxford Chronicle, 8 June 1923, p. 4.
15. Rowntree, Poverty and Progress, pp. 411-2.
16. Spectator, 15 Sept 1939, p. 376.
17. New Statesman, 18 Aug 1934, p. 202.
18. Oxford Chronicle, 30 Mar 1923, p. 15; 6 Apr 1923, pp. 17, 23.
19. Manchester Guardian, 11 Jan 1930, p. 9.
20. BBC WAC, File 129. 01, Crawford Committee, 1925, 11th Meeting, 29 Jan 1926.
21. Oxford Chronicle, 6 Apr 1923, p. 4; it is worth adding here that not all rural communities were agricultural - Durham or South Wales pit villages were good examples of small, isolated industrial communities, frequently suffering from poor reception.
22. Derby Mercury 28 Sept 1923, p. 11.
23. Ibid., 26 Oct 1922, p. 11.
24. Oxford Chronicle 12 Sept 1924, p. 20.
25. Derby Daily Telegraph 12 May 1937, pp. 5-6.
26. This is difficult to prove directly. Licences were collected by Head Post Office areas but the populations in these areas did not coincide with administrative areas. These statistics are not available - estimates have to be made. If these are at all accurate, then listening levels were higher in urban areas than the surrounding rural areas. Apart from inaccurate estimates more error could be caused by registration of licences by rural inhabitants at urban post offices.
27. See Table 1. 2.
28. S. P. B. Mais, Britain Calling, 1938.
29. Chiswick UDC, Minutes, Apr 1924-Apr 1925, General Purposes Committee Meeting, 28 Jan 1925.
30. Oxford City Council, Minutes 1928, pp. 134, 136, General Purposes Committee Meeting, 13 Feb 1928.
31. Brentford and Chiswick UDC, Minutes, Works and Highways Committee, 14 Oct 1931, p. 281, Minute 23, (Sub-Committee Meeting, 17 Dec 1930); General Purposes Committee, 17 July 1939, p. 435, Minute 10.
32. Report of the Broadcasting Committee, 1935, p. 42,

Notes

para. 142.
33. City of Oxford, Byelaws, Wireless Loudspeakers and Gramophones, 2 Oct 1933. Revised 1938.
34. Jennings and Gill, Broadcasting in Everyday Life, p. 19.
35. T. Harrisson, Britain Revisted, 1961, p. 32.
36. Briggs, Vol. I, p. 242.
37. A. Lloyd James, The Broadcast Word, 1935, pp. 3-5.
38. Briggs, Vol. I, p. 243; Lloyd James, Broadcast Word, pp. 56-7.
39. S. Briggs, Those Radio Times, pp. 134-5.
40. Lloyd James, Broadcast Word, p. 41.
41. Ibid., p. 26.
42. Ibid., p. 27.
43. People, 14 Dec 1924, p. 3.
44. Spectator, 3 Aug 1929, pp. 151-2.
45. New Statesman, 19 Jan 1929, p. 464.
46. Spectator, 24 Mar 1933, p. 444.
47. People, 17 Sept 1933, p. 11; 5 Dec 1937, p. 19; 4 June 1939, p. 20.
48. Rowntree, Poverty and Progress, pp. 408, 471-2.
49. Jennings and Gill, Broadcasting in Everyday Life, p. 33.
50. People, 27 Dec 1925, p. 9.
51. Ibid., 26 Sept 1926, p. 6; Brentford and Chiswick Times, 1 Nov 1935, p. 6.
52. Oxford Times, 7 May 1937, p. 20.
53. R. Postgate, What to do with the BBC, 1935, p. 52; New Statesman, 27 June 1931, pp. 8-9.
54. New Statesman, 20 Feb 1932, p. 223.
55. Ibid., 6 Feb 1932, p. 158.
56. People, 25 Jan 1931, p. 11.
57. Ibid., 29 May 1932, p. 2; 26 Apr 1936, p. 11.
58. Oxford Times, 14 May 1926, p. 14; 4 June 1926, p. 7.
59. Derby Daily Express, 15 Nov 1926, p. 9; 16 Nov 1926, p. 5.
60. Derby Mercury, 12 Mar 1926, p. 14, a photograph of elderly women listening to a set in an almshouse.
61. Spectator, 17 Dec 1937, p. 1099; 14 Jan 1937, p. 99.
62. Wireless Trader, 7 Jan 1933, p. 6.
63. President of the RSGB, 1928; Committee member of the Wireless League, 1926; see also Wireless World, 21 Oct 1922, p. 100; 11 Nov 1922, p. 206; his autobiography, Whereas I Was Blind, 1942, pp. 156-61.
64. Hansard, 10 Nov 1926, Col. 1088.
65. BBC Yearbook, 1932, p. 469; the BBC also produced the Braille Radio Times, the details are in the BBC Hand-

book, 1928, pp. 362-3.

66. BBC WAC, File 441.1, CCBAE, 1928-9; File 440, Educational Broadcasting, Reports, 1924-8. Latter includes the BBC report which recommended the creation of the CCBAE in 1928: New Ventures in Broadcasting. A Study in Adult Education, 1928. Sir Henry Hadow was the chairman of the Committee.

67. Llewellyn Smith, London Life and Labour, Vol. IX, p. 50.

68. BBC WAC, File 441.4, Carnegie Experiments Reports, Sept 1930 - Mar 1932.

69. Ibid., Yorkshire Area Council for Broadcast Adult Education, 'Report of the Carnegie Experiment in Yorkshire'. 1930-32, Appendix.

70. Ibid., 'Report of the Scottish Committee on the Carnegie Experiment in Scotland, Sept 1930 - Mar 1932.'

71. Ibid., 'Report of the Carnegie Experiment in Yorkshire'.

72. Ibid., Appendix.

73. Ibid., 'Report on the Carnegie Experiment in the West Midlands', 1 Jan 1930 - 30 Apr 1931.

74. BBC WAC, File 441, Press Release, 14 Dec 1934.

75. Yorkshire Telegraph and Star, 1 Apr 1932, p. 8.

76. Derbyshire Education Committee, County Library Service, 11th Report, 1934-5; 14th Report, 1937-8.

77. Oxford Times, 25 Nov 1927, p. 5.

78. Plebs, Sept 1927.

79. Burton Chronicle, 1 Oct 1931, p. 7.

80. Oxford Chronicle, 5 Oct 1923, p. 4.

81. From the Glasgow Station, Call sign 5SC.

82. Chiswick UDC, Education Committee, Hogarth Senior School, Head's Notes, 4 Apr 1924.

83. Brentford UDC, Education Committee, Rothschild School for Boys, School Log Book, 16 May 1924, p. 198.

84. Ibid., 13 Oct 1924; 22 Oct 1924.

85. Chiswick UDC, Education Committee Minutes, 11 Nov 1924, p. 234, Minute 16; Brentford and Chiswick Borough Education Committee, Elementary Education Sub-Committee, 24 Mar 1931, Minute 5.

86. Wireless World, June 1913, p. 209.

87. Derby Evening Telegraph, 24 Feb 1939, p. 6.

88. Oxford Chronicle, 16 Mar 1923, p. 4; 13 Apr 1923, p. 11, an excellent photograph of boys listening to the set at Cowley Boy's School.

89. Derby Education Committee, Minutes, Elementary Education Sub-Committee, 28 Jan 1925, Minute 389; 7 Sept 1925, Minute 1063; 8 Apr 1929, Minute 620; 5 Jan 1931,

Minute 291; 3 Dec 1934, Minute 154; 2 Sept 1935, Minute 1027; some local authorities eventually relented, City of Oxford, Council Reports, Education Committee Meeting, Minutes 15 July 1936, p. 836, '£226.10s., to Edison Swan for Wireless Education.'

Chapter Seven

MASS LISTENING

1. Chiswick Times, 19 Jan 1923, p. 2.
2. Derby Daily Express, 28 May 1929, p. 13; Derby Evening Telegraph, 7 May 1937, p. 9; see also Figures 7.1 and 7.2.
3. Oxford Chronicle, 25 May 1923, pp. 11, 13.
4. Ibid., 23 Feb 1923, p. 4.
5. Ibid., 2 Mar 1923, p. 22.
6. Ibid., 27 Oct 1922, p. 24.
7. Chiswick Times, 8 Dec 1922, p. 2; Wireless Trader, 7 Jan 1933, p. 5; Oxford Chronicle, 24 Nov 1922, p. 7.
8. Oxford Chronicle, 9 Jan 1923, p. 4; 16 Mar 1923, p. 4; 11 Apr 1924, pp. 11, 13; Oxford Mail, 24 May 1937, p. 8.
9. Oxford Chronicle, 9 Jan 1923, p. 4.
10. Baldwin spoke specially for the radio whilst MacDonald, misunderstanding the greater intimacy of the medium, simply used a speech prepared for a public meeting.
11. For good accounts see, J. Symons, The General Strike, 1957, pp. 177-82; Briggs, Vol.I, pp. 360-84.
12. C. Stuart (ed), The Reith Diaries, 1975, diary entry for 7 May 1926.
13. Ibid., 10 May 1926; G.A. Phillips, The General Strike, 1926, p. 185; R. Page Arnot, The General Strike, May 1926, Its Origin and History, 1926, p. 190.
14. BBC WAC, Reith to Senior Staff, 15 May 1926.
15. M. Morris, The General Strike, 1976, p. 244.
16. Page Arnot, General Strike, pp. 193-4, 211; Briggs, Vol.I, p. 373.
17. S. Mews, 'The Churches', in Morris, General Strike, pp. 254, 328, 330-4; British Worker, 8 May 1926, p. 1; 11 May 1926, p. 2.
18. Oxford Chronicle, 7 May 1926, p. 6.
19. Reith, Into the Wind, p. 106; BBC WAC, File 811 and Memo 811/1.
20. Briggs, Vol.I, pp. 380-3.
21. Reith Diaries, 6 May 1926.

22. Morris, General Strike, p. 252.
23. Briggs, Vol. I, pp. 370-1.
24. BBC WAC, R. Wade to Gladstone Murray, 14 June 1926.
25. The BBC's 10 o'clock bulletin on the 4 May laid great stress on the BBC's intention to produce 'plain objective news' and 'maintain our tradition of fairness'. News Bulletin, 4 May 1926.
26. Page Arnot, General Strike, pp. 194-6.
27. Briggs, Vol. I, p. 371.
28. M. Cole (ed), Beatrice Webb, Diaries, 1924-31, 1956, 11 May 1926.
29. Oxford Chronicle, 21 May 1926, p. 10, the paper also observed that even the poorest districts in Oxford, such as St. Aldates and Jericho, were displaying tell-tale wireless aerials in large numbers during the strike.
30. Oxford Times, 10 May 1926, p. 2.
31. Oxford Chronicle, 6 Apr 1923, p. 4, 'Apart from a great over-supply of the British Gazette. '
32. BBC WAC, Correspondence, 8 May 1926.
33. Chiswick Times, 14 May 1926, p. 3.
34. New Statesman, 8 May 1926, p. 103.
35. See Table 1. 1.
36. BBC WAC, Memorandum by C. F. Atkinson, May 1926.
37. E. Wilkinson, A Workers' History of the General Strike, 1927; her protest in Radio Times, 28 May 1926.
38. H. Fyfe, Behind the Scenes of the General Strike, 1926, p. 26; Phillips, General Strike, p. 169; A. Mason, The General Strike in the North East, Hull, 1970, pp. 38-40.
39. Phillips, General Strike, pp. 167-170, 172-7; S. Bhaumik, 'Glasgow', in Morris, General Strike, p. 405; TUC Local Collection Box No. 9; Symons, General Strike, pp. 171-7.
40. Mason, General Strike, p. 41.
41. Symons, General Strike, p. 174; Mason, General Strike, p. 42.
42. Mason, General Strike, pp. 29, 33-4.
43. The British Worker's circulation is laid out in Phillips, General Strike, p. 177; the British Gazette, for comparison, p. 179.
44. Mason, General Strike, p. 43.
45. E. Burns, The General Strike, May 1926. Trades Councils in Action, 1926, pp. 121-2; Labour Research Department, Monthly Circular, July 1926, p. 161; Plebs, Aug 1926, p. 288. According to the price and the income received, only 22, 290 copies would appear to

have been sold, perhaps some were distributed free but estimates of 50,000 appear excessive.

46. Burns, Trades Councils in Action, p. 43.
47. British Worker, 8 May 1926, p. 1.
48. Briggs, Vol. I, opposite p. 376.
49. Symons, General Strike, p. 174.
50. Minutes of the TUC Publicity Committee.
51. Oxford Chronicle, 14 May 1926, p. 4, Morris Motors workers stayed at work during the strike.
52. Burns, Trades Councils in Action, pp. 156-7.
53. Briggs, Vol. I, p. 375; Page Arnot, General Strike, pp. 214-5.
54. Chiswick Times, 14 May 1926, p. 3.
55. R. Page Arnot, The Miners, Years of Struggle, 1953, p. 445.
56. E. W. Edwards, 'The Pontypridd Area', in Morris, General Strike, pp. 423-4.
57. Jennings and Gill, Broadcasting in Everyday Life, pp. 15, 19.
58. Derby Daily Telegraph, 7 Dec 1923, p. 2.
59. Oxford Times, 18 Apr 1924, p. 6; but a change of heart is clear in the issue of 24 May 1929, p. 11.
60. Frequent warnings by the BBC against copyright infringements were printed in the local press. The BBC was apparently concerned about unauthorised use, see Derby Daily Express, 28 May 1929, p. 1.
61. Brentford and Chiswick Times, 30 Oct 1931, p. 7.
62. Oxford Times, 2 Nov 1923, p. 8 and Derby Daily Telegraph, 30 Nov 1923, p. 5.
63. Oxford Mail, 12 Apr 1929, p. 6.
64. Derby Daily Telegraph, 26 Aug 1931, p. 4; 5 Sept 1931, p. 4; 22 Sept 1931, p. 4.
65. Brentford and Chiswick Times, 7 June 1929, p. 4; Derbyshire Times, 1 June 1929, p. 8.
66. Derby Daily Express, 5 April 1929, p. 4.
67. Oxford Times, 24 May 1929, p. 11.
68. Chiswick Times, 17 Nov 1922, p. 5.
69. Derby Daily Telegraph, 28 Oct 1931, p. 4.
70. Brentford and Chiswick Times, 15 Nov 1935, p. 7; Derbyshire Times, 15 Nov 1935, p. 12.
71. Reith, Broadcast over Britain, passim.
72. The Talks Department was gradually dismantled by Reith in 1934-5. For an analysis of the motives, see P. Scannell and D. Cardiff, 'Serving the Nation: Public Service Broadcasting Before the War', in B. Waites,

A. Bennett and G. Martin, (eds), Popular Culture: Past and Present, 1982; Briggs, Vol. II, pp. 141-9.

73. New Statesman, 4 Apr 1931, p. 209.
74. Ibid., 19 Nov 1932, p. 615.
75. Spectator, 21 Nov 1931, p. 670.
76. Quoted by Forster in New Statesman, 4 Apr 1931, p. 210.
77. People, 11 Mar 1934, p. 12.
78. New Statesman, 15 Aug 1931, p. 187; 3 Feb 1934, p. 154.
79. Ibid., 14 July 1934, p. 69, King-Hall was prominent in the peace movement, founding his own organisation.
80. Briggs, Vol. I, p. 267; the BBC's proposal was supported by the press, Spectator, 22 June 1934, p. 956; People, 1 Dec 1935, p. 12.
81. A. Briggs, Governing the BBC, 1979, pp. 198-201.
82. See full account and references in B. Harworth, 'The BBC, Nazi Germany and the Foreign Office, 1933-1936' in Historical Journal of Film, Radio and Television, Vol. I, No. I, 1981.
83. Scannell and Cardiff, 'Serving the Nation', pp. 177-8.
84. J. Dimbleby, Richard Dimbleby, 1975, pp. 82-9.
85. See an example of optimistic thinking in Spectator, 10 Jan 1931, p. 36.
86. New Statesman, 17 Mar 1934, pp. 398-9; 24 Mar 1934, p. 466; 31 Mar 1934, p. 476.
87. Oxford Times, 25 Apr 1924, p. 5.
88. Oxford Chronicle, 11 Apr 1924, p. 5, advertisement.
89. Briggs, Vol. I, p. 290-1.
90. Oxford Times, 10 May 1935, p. 16.
91. Derby Daily Telegraph, 12 May 1937, p. 5.
92. Ibid., 13 May 1937, p. 6; Oxford Times, 14 May 1937, p. 16.
93. People, 23 Dec 1934, p. 1.
94. Brentford and Chiswick Times, 24 Jan 1936, p. 1.
95. People, 11 Sept 1927, p. 11.

Chapter Eight

BROADCASTING AND LEISURE

1. A. Clayre, Work and Play, 1974; R. W. Malcolmson, Popular Recreations in English Society 1700-1850, Cambridge, 1973.
2. K. Roberts, Leisure, 1970; J. Durmazedier, Towards a Society of Leisure, New York, 1967, p. 14.
3. Llewellyn Smith, London Life and Labour, Vol. I, p. 297.

Notes

4. Rowntree, Poverty and Progress, p. 411.
5. A disputed point. M. Young and P. Willmott in their Family and Kinship in East London, 1957, show how other factors could resist home- centredness.
6. Jennings and Gill, Broadcasting in Everyday Life, p. 23.
7. Ibid.
8. N. Dennis, F. Henriques and C. Slaughter, Coal is our Life, 1956, pp. 168-70; Rowntree, Poverty and Progress, pp. 411-2.
9. Women went out to work in increasing numbers throughout the inter-war period, see, A. H. Halsey, Trends in British Society Since 1900, 1972, pp. 114-5.
10. BBC WAC, LR/77, General Listening Barometer, Interim Reports 10-13, 28 Mar 1939; apart from a few examples, such as the BBC 'Aunts' in Children's Hour and Hilda Matheson in the Talks Department, very few women were actively involved in programme making or planning.
11. Townswoman, Feb 1935, p. 210; June 1937, p. 61 and Nov 1937, p. 183.
12. Jennings and Gill, Broadcasting in Everyday Life, pp. 24-8; 67% engaged in other activities when listening to the wireless.
13. Rowntree, Poverty and Progress, pp. 407-8.
14. Llewellyn Smith, London Life and Labour, Vol. IX, Life and Leisure, p. 8.
15. Caradog Jones, Survey of Merseyside, Vol. III, p. 275, Table V.
16. Rowntree, Poverty and Progress, pp. 406-12, 530.
17. Jennings and Gill, Broadcasting in Everyday Life, p. 8.
18. Rowntree, Poverty and Progress, p. 409; the most popular programme in the relay company's service was the Littlewood's Pools Programme, broadcast on Luxembourg at 1.30 p.m. each Sunday. It had a 100% load.
19. Jennings and Gill, Broadcasting in Everyday Life, pp. 34-7.
20. People, 7 Nov 1926, p. 10; Spectator, 6 Sept 1930, pp. 301-2.
21. Llewellyn Smith, Vol. IX, p. 11.
22. Spectator, 5 July 1935, p. 8.
23. New Statesman, 13 Sept 1930, p. 705.
24. Spectator, 12 Mar 1927, pp. 413-4.
25. People, 3 Mar 1929, p. 5; Spectator, 20 Apr 1929, p. 616.
26. New Statesman, 16 Nov 1935, p. 733.

27. Ibid., 19 Sept 1936, pp. 390-1.
28. Ibid., 22 July 1933, p. 100.
29. Spectator, 5 Apr 1924, p. 539, 'Music for the Masses', by Cecil Hann.
30. New Statesman, 8 Nov 1930, p. 145; W. J. Turner, Facing the Music, 1933.
31. Briggs, Vol. II, pp. 86-9, 105.
32. People, 10 Mar 1929, p. 11; 28 Mar 1937, p. 16; Briggs, Vol. II, pp. 85-6, 109-10, 116-7.
33. Spectator, 10 Feb 1923, p. 242.
34. Briggs, Vol. II, pp. 75-119; J. Snagge and M. Barsley, Those Vintage Years of Radio, 1972, for more details of the personalities.
35. Derby Daily Express, 24 May 1929, p. 11; Oxford Mail, 14 May 1929, p. 1; Oxford Times, 5 Dec 1924, p. 16.
36. Derby Daily Telegraph, 14 Sept 1931, p. 4.
37. Ibid., 16 Sept 1931, p. 4.
38. Oxford Chronicle, 18 May 1923, p. 5; Derby Daily Telegraph, 16 Aug 1923, p. 3.
39. Jennings and Gill, Broadcasting in Everyday Life, pp. 33-7.
40. Rowntree, Poverty and Progress, pp. 410-1.
41. Jennings and Gill, Broadcasting in Everyday Life, p. 37.
42. Rowntree, Poverty and Progress, p. 410.
43. People, 31 Jan 1937, p. 14.
44. New Statesman, 22 July 1933, p. 99.
45. Spectator, 18 June 1932, p. 856; People, 30 Sept 1934, p. 12.
46. New Statesman, 6 May 1933, p. 564.
47. The debate on generic broadcasting is laid out in the BBC publication, Broadcasting in the Seventies, 1969; Ariel, 1 Dec 1969; ABS Bulletin, Aug/Sept, 1969. The new channels were proposed as Radio 1 - popular music, Radio 2 - light music, Radio 3 - classical music, Radio 4 - news and information, accompanied by a Radio 5 - local radio and possibly a Radio 6 - education.
48. Jennings and Gill, Broadcasting in Everyday Life, p. 13.
49. Ibid., pp. 17-8.
50. Rowntree, Poverty and Progress, pp. 409-10, 472, 530.
51. Martin complained of his black-listing, see C. H. Rolph, Kingsley: The Life, Letters and Diaries of Kingsley Martin, 1973, p. 275.
52. The Reith lectures, beginning in 1948, are a good example of this.
53. Derby Public Free Library, 60th Annual Report, 1931.

54. Manchester Guardian, 7 Apr 1931, p. 10.
55. Contrast with Derby Public Free Library, 63rd Annual Report, 1934.
56. Borough of Brentford and Chiswick, Report of the Libraries and Museums Committee, 1937-8, p. 3.
57. Oxfordshire Education Committee, Report of the County Librarian, 1930.
58. Derby Public Free Library, Annual Reports, 1934-7.
59. City of Oxford, Library Committee, Minute Book, 1913-37, Report for 1925, p. 304.
60. Derbyshire County Library, 5th Annual Report, Apr 1928 - Mar 1929.
61. Oxford City Library, 1854-1954, Centenary File, undated, uncited press cutting, probably of 1927.
62. Manchester Guardian, 7 Apr 1931, p. 10.
63. Everyman, 14 Jan 1933, p. 45.
64. Ibid.
65. This was not accepted by everyone concerned with the library, see Derby Borough Council, Free Public Library Committee, Minute Book, 1915-1930; General Committee Meeting, 9 June 1932.
66. Derby Public Free Library, 61st Annual Report, Mar 1932.
67. The BBC did its best to arouse interest. Apart from pamphlets and posters, a lecture series was organised. There was a BBC lecturer, J. H. A. Whitehouse, who toured the country in 1927. There is an account of a well attended lecture in May 1927 in Chiswick Public Library and Museum, Annual Report, 1926-7.
68. City of Oxford Library Committee, Minute Book, 1927-40, Proceedings of Library Committee, 22 Sept 1936, pp. 236, 239.
69. R. Roberts, The Classic Slum, Manchester, 1971.
70. G. Orwell, Collected Essays, Journalism and Letters, Vol. 2, My Country Right or Left, 1940 - 1943, 1968.
71. Derbyshire Advertiser, 9 Mar 1923, p. 9.
72. Oxford Chronicle, 23 Feb 1923, p. 4.
73. Briggs, Vol. I, p. 285.
74. Halsey, Trends in British Society, pp. 538-73, shows the limited information on the level of participation and attendances at sports and entertainments at this time. Listener research could only show the growing popularity of the sports results.
75. Jennings and Gill, Broadcasting in Everyday Life, p. 33.
76. Derby Daily Express, 12 May 1922, p. 5; 16 June 1920.

77. Briggs, Vol. II, p. 80.
78. Ibid., pp. 119-20.
79. Wireless World, 20 May 1922, p. 23; the Football
    League also banned running commentaries on occasions.
    In this case, the Football Association wanted the BBC to
    pay £50 to a charity for the privilege of broadcasting the
    match. The BBC refused on principle, BBC, WAC,
    Memorandum by G. Cock, 9 Apr 1929.
80. Derby Daily Express, 1 Apr 1929, p. 13, 17 Apr 1929,
    p. 1; Oxford Mail, 1 Apr 1929, p. 7.
81. Jennings and Gill, Broadcasting in Everyday Life, p. 38.
82. Ibid; Briggs, Vol. II, p. 121.
83. Rowntree, Poverty and Progress, p. 409.
84. New Statesman, 27 Aug 1927, p. 593.
85. Spectator, 24 May 1930, p. 856.

Chapter Nine

ASSESSMENT

1. W. Ashworth, An Economic History of England 1870-1939,
   1960, pp. 116-8, p. 340; for instance, 50,000 telephone
   call boxes were installed in the 1920s.
2. A. J. P. Taylor, English History 1914-1945, 1970,
   pp. 392-6; R. Busby, The British Music Hall, 1976;
   D. Howard, London Theatres and Music Halls 1850-1950,
   1970.
3. A. Mason, Association Football and English Society,
   1863-1915, 1979.
4. The motto on the coat of arms was created in 1927.
5. Joyce, or Lord Haw Haw as he was more commonly
   known, began his broadcasts in the autumn of 1939 but
   broadcasts from Hamburg and Köln began much earlier,
   BBC WAC, File LR/74, The British audience for German
   broadcasts in English, 16 May 1939.
6. Christmas broadcasts by George V began in 1932.
7. Halsey, Trends in British Society, pp. 558-9, for some
   very limited information on attendances. A better indicator is the number of theatre or music hall closures in the
   period. A glance at the advertisements in any local
   newspaper shows the changing pattern of local entertainment.
8. Reith, Broadcast over Britain, passim; Into the Wind,
   passim.
9. Briggs, Vol. III, pp. 125-40. In 1940 a wavelength was
   allocated to variety and popular music, ostensibly to

provide a service for the Armed Forces but of course everyone could listen.

10. The 'uncles' and 'aunts' who presented these programmes were some of the most popular broadcasters. Derek McCulloch (Uncle Mac) was particularly well known. In the early days of the BBC even senior staff broadcast on 'Children's Hour' - for instance, Cecil Lewis who was 'Uncle Caractacus'.

11. Silent intervals between programmes were intended to discourage non-selective listening.

12. Editorial control by broadcasting institutions is not inevitable. Cmnd 6753, The Committee on Broadcasting, 1978, chaired by Lord Annan, advocated a fourth television channel with the control of a publisher rather than an editor; in 1936, some critics wanted a Minister for Broadcasting but this course was rejected by the Ullswater Committee.

13. H. Nicolson, Diaries and Letters 1939-1945, 1967, p. 99, 'Attlee is worried about the BBC retaining its class voice and personnel and would like to see a far greater infiltration of working-class speakers,' Entry for 3 July 1940; Wilfred Pickles was the first radio personality to be allowed to really exploit his natural accent for broadcasting purposes.

SELECT BIBLIOGRAPHY

Manuscript Sources

BBC Written Archives Centre, Caversham Park, Reading

Sound 1-3 General Enquiries, 1937-8
Sound 5 Audience Research Reports, General Interim Reports,
    Jan-May 1939
Audience Research Special Reports, 1-4 Sound and General,
    1937-May 1941
Sound 40-2 Drama Reports Scheme, Jan-June 1937
Sound 94 Audience Research Reports, Talks, Oct-Dec 1938
Sound 110 Experimental and Pioneer Broadcasting
Sound 117 Audience Research Reports, Variety, Oct-Dec 1937
121, 121.01 Broadcasting Committee, 1922
123.32 Wireless Receiving Licences for the Blind
128.02, 128.04, 128.2 The Broadcasting Committee, 1923
    (Sykes)
129.01 The Crawford Committee, 1925
133.3, 133.4, 133.61, 133.62, 133.7 Ullswater Committee
172.2 Audience Research and Audience Research Policy,
    1930-44
172.201 Audience Research, Listener Research Committee
    Minutes, 1936-38
172.21 Audience Research Finance File, July 1937-Dec 1939
172.22 Audience Research, Early Experiments and Projects
172.3 Publicity, Programme Correspondence Section
172.64 Wireless Receiving Licences
183.2 The Listener
441 Adult Education, Papers and Reports, 1924-40
441.1 Central Council for Broadcast Adult Education, 1928-9
441.4 Carnegie Experiment Reports
460 Report of the Director for Regional Relations, Jan-Sept
    1936
700 Regions and the Regional Service, 1925-27
GAC Preliminary Correspondence, 1934

Post Office Records, St. Martin's-le-Grand, London

M10984/1922 Wireless Broadcasting Scheme, Formation of
    BBC Licence and Agreement
M14019/1923 Broadcasting Board 1923
M3942/1924 Crawford Committee
M39/1925 Revision of Licences 1925
M1695/1926 Crawford Committee
M15796/1926 Minutes of Evidence to the Crawford Committee

Select Bibliography

M8708/1927 BBC Licences
M7993/1929 Unlicenced Reception 1925-38
M10436/1929 Wireless Interference caused by Tramcars and
    Trolley buses

Official Papers

Cmd 1822, Wireless Broadcasting Licence, 1923
Cmd 1976, Wireless Broadcasting Licence, 1923
Cmd 1951, Broadcasting Committee Report, 1923
Cmd 2599, Report of the Broadcasting Committee, 1925
Cmd 5091, Report of the Broadcasting Committee 1935, 1936

Printed Sources

BBC, Crystal Sets and the Brookmans Park Transmitter, 1929
___ New Ventures in Broadcasting, 1927, (Hadow Report)
___ Handbook, 1928-30, 1938-39
___ Yearbook, 1930-34
___ Annual, 1935-37
___ British Broadcasting: A Bibliography, 1957
Baron, M. Independent Radio: The Story of Commercial
    Radio in the UK, Cavenham, Suffolk, 1975
Beveridge, W. H. Changes in Family Life, 1932
Blumler, J. G. 'British Television. The Outlines of a
    Research Strategy' in British Journal of Sociology, Sept
    1964
Briggs, A. The History of Broadcasting in the United
    Kingdom.
    Vol. I, The Birth of Broadcasting, Oxford, 1961
    Vol. II, The Golden Age of Wireless, Oxford, 1965
    Vol. III, The War of Words, Oxford, 1970
    Vol. IV, Sound and Vision, Oxford, 1979
    ___ 'Local and Regional in Northern Sound Broadcasting'
    in Northern History, Vol. X, 1975
    ___ Governing the BBC, 1979
Briggs, S. Those Radio Times, 1981
Burns, T. The BBC: Public Institution and Private World,
    1977
Bussey, G. Vintage Crystal Sets, 1922-27, 1976
Caradog Jones, D. et al, (eds) Survey of Merseyside, Vol. III
    1934
Clarricoats, J. World at Their Fingertips, 1967
Cauter, T. and Downham, J. S. The Communication of Ideas.
    A study of contemporary life, 1954
Coase, R. H. British Broadcasting: A Study in Monopoly, 1950

Crawford, Sir William and Broadley, H. The People's Food,
    1938
Driver, D. The Art of the Radio Times, 1981
Eckersley, P. P. The Power behind the Microphone, 1941
Geddes, K. Guglielmo Marconi 1874-1937, 1974
___ Broadcasting in Britain, 1922-72, 1972
Gorham, M. Sound and Fury, 1948
Haworth, B. 'The BBC, Nazi Germany and the Foreign
    Office, 1933-1936' in Historical Journal of Film, Radio
    and TV, Vol. I, No. 1, 1981
Hill, J. The Cat's Whisker: Fifty Years of Wireless Design,
    1978
Jennings, H. and Gill, W. Broadcasting in Everyday Life:
    a study of the social effects of the coming of broadcasting,
    July 1939
Katz, E. Social Research on Broadcasting: Proposals for
    further development, 1977
Llewllyn Smith, Sir Hubert. New Survey of London Life and
    Labour, 9 Volumes, 1930-35
Lloyd James, A. The Broadcast Word, 1935
Matheson, H. Broadcasting, 1933
___ 'Listener Research in Broadcasting' in Sociological
    Review, Vol. 27, 1935
Pawley, E. L. E. BBC Engineering 1922-1972, 1972
Reith, J. C. W. Broadcast over Britain, 1924.
___ Diaries, Stuart, C. (ed.), 1975
___ Into the Wind, 1949
Rowntree, B. S. Poverty and Progress, 1941
Silvey, R. J. E. Who's Listening? 1974
___ 'Methods of Listener Research Employed by the BBC' in
    Journal of the Royal Statistical Society, 1944
Smith, A. The Shadow in the Cave, 1973
___ (ed.) British Broadcasting, 1974
Sturmey, S. G. The Economic Development of Radio, 1958
Waites, B. , Bennett, A. and Martin, G. (eds.) Popular
    Culture: Past and Present, 1982
Williams, R. Communications, Second Edition, 1966
Young, F. Shall I Listen? 1933

INDEX

Index

DATE DUE

AG 23 '83			
DE 16 '87			
DEC 14			
FEB 2 8 1998			
		WITHDRAWN	